ORIGINAL
RANGE ROVER
CARBURETTOR MODELS

Other titles available in the *Original* series are:

Original AC Ace & Cobra
by Rinsey Mills
Original Aston Martin DB4/5/6
by Robert Edwards
Original Austin Seven
by Rinsey Mills
Original Austin-Healey (100 & 3000)
by Anders Ditlev Clausager
Original Citroën DS
by John Reynolds with Jan de Lange
Original Corvette 1953-1962
by Tom Falconer
Original Corvette 1963-1967
by Tom Falconer
Original Ferrari V8
by Keith Bluemel
Original Ferrari V12 1965-1973
by Keith Bluemel
Original Honda CB750
by John Wyatt
Original Jaguar E-Type
by Philip Porter
Original Jaguar Mark I/II
by Nigel Thorley
Original Jaguar XJ
by Nigel Thorley
Original Jaguar XK
by Philip Porter
Original Kawasaki Z1, Z900 & KZ900
by Dave Marsden
Original Land-Rover Series I
by James Taylor
Original Mercedes SL
by Laurence Meredith

Original MG T Series
by Anders Ditlev Clausager
Original MGA
by Anders Ditlev Clausager
Original MGB
by Anders Ditlev Clausager
Original Mini Cooper and Cooper S
by John Parnell
Original Morgan
by John Worrall and Liz Turner
Original Morris Minor
by Ray Newell
Original Porsche 356
by Laurence Meredith
Original Porsche 911
by Peter Morgan
Original Porsche 924/944/968
by Peter Morgan
Original Rolls-Royce & Bentley 1946-65
by James Taylor
Original Sprite & Midget
by Terry Horler
Original Triumph TR2/3/3A
by Bill Piggott
Original Triumph TR4/4A/5/6
by Bill Piggott
Original Triumph Stag
by James Taylor
Original Vincent
by J. P. Bickerstaff
Original VW Beetle
by Laurence Meredith
Original VW Bus
by Laurence Meredith

ORIGINAL
RANGE ROVER
CARBURETTOR MODELS

by James Taylor

Photography by Nick Dimbleby
Edited by Mark Hughes

BAY
VIEW
BOOKS
FROM
MBI Publishing
Company

First published in 1999 by MBI Publishing Company, 729 Prospect Avenue, PO Box 1, Osceola, WI 54020-0001 USA

MBI Publishing Company books are also available at discounts in bulk quantity for industrial or sales-promotional use. For details write to Special Sales Manager at Motorbooks International Wholesalers & Distributors, 729 Prospect Avenue, PO Box 1, Osceola, WI 54020-0001 USA.

Library of Congress Cataloging-in-Publication Data Available
ISBN 0 7603 0777 6

The photographs on the jacket and preliminary pages show the very first production Range Rover dating from 1970 (front cover), a 1985 four-door (half-title page), a 1983 In Vogue four-door special edition (title page), a 1973 model (contents page) and a six-wheeled Carmichael fire tender (back cover).

Printed in China

Contents

Introduction

The Range Rover caused something of a sensation when it was announced in 1970, and over the next few years it went on to exceed its manufacturer's expectations by a big margin. No matter that the 1970s were blighted by two major oil crises, by the collapse of British Leyland, and by the subsequent inability of the Range Rover's makers to fund major improvements to the vehicle. The Range Rover was so popular that it just went on selling.

However, when investment did finally become available, and the Range Rover was redeveloped as a luxury-class vehicle, many early examples fell on hard times. Owners wanted all the latest equipment on their Range Rovers, so many presentable examples were updated with later features. Other early models fell into disrepair and were butchered

Where the Range Rover story began. This Engineering prototype, numbered 100/6, is the earliest surviving vehicle.

The Featured Vehicles

Registration	Year	Colour	Model	Owner
AOY 289H	1970	Red	Pre-production	Mark Lockley
YVB 151H	1970	Green	Chassis no 1	Peter Garside
YVB 155H	1970	White	Two-door	Chris Elliott
AMW 669L	1973	Green	Two-door	Mark Clark
VUG 24R	1977	Yellow	Two-door	Tony Megginson
HOD 420V	1979	White	Two-door	Ken Knight
B967 YDV	1985	Red	Four-door	Mike Page
VPD 126X	1980	White	Monteverdi	Peter Kenworthy
TVC 383W	1980	Blue	In Vogue two-door	Elaine Cannon
A934 SRH	1983	Blue	In Vogue four-door	Tony Megginson
URX 372Y	1982	Green	Wood & Pickett	Heritage Motor Centre
TJA 972X	1981	White	Police	Manchester Police
YVB 158H	1970	White	Ambulance	Chris Elliott
SYC 124L	1973	Red	Carmichael fire	Somerset Fire Brigade
–	1980	–	Rolling chassis	Heritage Motor Centre

Terminology

It is important at this stage to explain how vehicles are identified in this book. Major variations in the mechanical specification of Range Rovers built before September 1979 were indicated by suffix letters. These letters did not correspond to model-year changes, and ran from A to G. Thus, these early vehicles are referred to as 'Suffix A' types, 'Suffix B' types, and so on. The introduction dates of each suffix are given in Chapter 14.

In September 1979, new Vehicle Identification Number (VIN) codes were introduced, and the chassis numbering system changed. The VIN prefix code identified the vehicle type, and the penultimate letter of this prefix was used to indicate major specification changes. From June 1984, these coincided with model-year changes. The final letter, always an A to indicate that the vehicle was built at Solihull, is always used with the model change identifier in Land Rover Service literature, and the same practice is followed here. Thus, there are AA-series vehicles, BA-series vehicles, and so on, through to the final carburettor models in the EA-series for the 1988 model year.

In the mid-1980s, the BA-series Range Rovers were sometimes referred to as 'Phase II' models, a description which was eagerly taken up by the second-hand motor trade. 'Phase III' models would, in theory, have been the CA-series vehicles, and the description 'Phase IV' was sometimes used of DA-series Range Rovers by the motor trade. As these descriptions are not in general use, they are not repeated in this book.

Standard coachbuilder's terminology is also used when referring to the construction of the body. Thus, the windscreen pillar is an A-pillar, the central pillar of a four-door body is a B/C-pillar (B for the pillar against which the front door closes, and C for the hinge pillar of the rear door), and the pillar on which the rear door closes is a D-pillar. The rearmost pillar of an estate car body like that of the Range Rover is called an E-pillar. On two-door bodies, the central pillar is a B-pillar, and the rearmost pillar once again an E-pillar.

Two abbreviations used throughout are RHD (right-hand drive) and LHD (left-hand drive).

by owners who used them as the basis of off-road trials machines. As a result, there are surprisingly few really good original examples of the early Range Rover still in running order today.

Fortunately, that situation is changing. The early Range Rover has now attained classic staus within the enthusiast movement, and the trend is increasingly towards preservation and restoration. This book is intended to help owners of early Range Rovers to determine exactly how their vehicles would have looked when new.

Trying to establish the correct original specification for every carburettor Range Rover has been much harder than it should have been. One result of the chaos within British Leyland during the 1970s was that records were often poorly kept. Even the Service literature issued to dealers was often annoyingly imprecise and sometimes even contradictory. For those reasons, it has not been possible to establish the exact points for some changes in the Range Rover's specification. It may never be possible to do so.

It would not surprise me, therefore, to find that there are some inaccuracies in this book, but I hope I have minimised them. In that task, I have been helped by dozens of Range Rover enthusiasts over the years, and in particular by those who made their vehicles available for my colleague and friend Nick Dimbleby to photograph. Their names are given in the accompanying panel.

Thanks also go to the archives staff of the British Motor Industry Heritage Trust, who dug out a number of very helpful documents for me, and to Peter Hobson (of Hobson Industries), who lent me some early service bulletins from his collection. I must record a special vote of thanks to the original Range Rover project engineer, Geof Miller. What Geof cannot remember about the specification of early Range Rovers is probably not worth knowing, so a very big 'thank you' goes to him for reading and correcting the draft chapters. Nevertheless, even Geof would accept that some mistakes or omissions may still be lurking undetected, and I would be delighted to hear from any readers who do find inaccuracies or can add to my information. If this book goes to a second edition, I will be more than pleased to make appropriate corrections and additions.

Lastly, this book does not cover all the Range Rovers built between 1970 and 1996, but only the carburettor models built up to 1988. There were far too many changes of specification to do justice to all of them between these covers, so I had to draw the line somewhere. I sincerely hope I shall have the opportunity to look at the diesel and fuel-injected models in a later volume.

James Taylor
Oxfordshire, June 1999

Chapter 1

Range Rover Past & Present

The name Range Rover today is synonymous with the concept of luxury car, to which the Solihull product adds the special attributes of all-terrain ability. Yet the original Range Rover, introduced in 1970, was a very different vehicle. Conceived as a sort of superior Land Rover, it was intended as a multi-purpose machine with the emphasis on practicality. Although it was undoubtedly expensive (it cost about the same as the top-model Rover luxury saloon of the time), it had an interior which could be hosed out after a hard day's work in a muddy farmyard. The way promotional literature saw it, the Range Rover could then serve its owner as acceptably refined transport to the theatre in the evening.

The concept of the Range Rover, in fact, went much further back. Arguably, its ancestry could be traced to the Road-Rover of the early 1950s. This started out as a cross between Rover saloon and Land Rover, and was very much intended as a rugged but 'roadable' estate car. Nevertheless, there was no direct link between the Road-Rover project, abandoned in 1959, and the Range Rover. The ideas for the vehicle that was to become the Range Rover started to come together in the middle of the following decade.

Rover's existing 4x4, the Land Rover, had been designed purely as a light utility vehicle with the ability to be driven in terrain that would defeat an ordinary road vehicle. The Land Rover engineers swore by its rugged leaf-spring suspension, which was ideal for off-road work but gave a poor ride on the road. Experiments to design a more comfortable suspension led Spen King, then in charge of the New Vehicle Projects team at Rover's Solihull home, to a new idea. He proposed

Numerically the first production Range Rover, YVB 151H has been restored to original condition by owner Peter Garside.

Practicality and versatility were essential to the Range Rover design. This is a 1973 Suffix A model, owned by Mark Clark.

trying long-travel coil springs in a dual-purpose 4x4 which would ride as well on the road as it did off it, and yet still retain the Land Rover's formidable rough-terrain ability.

So in the early months of 1966, King and his layout designer, Gordon Bashford, sketched out the schemes for such a vehicle on paper. While they were still planning, a report reached them from Graham Bannock, a market researcher then employed by Rover who had recently been looking at the North American market to find sales opportunities for Rover products. Bannock noted that there was an increasing demand in the USA – as indeed elsewhere – for a new breed of 4x4 that was designed not purely for utility or commercial work but for recreational use, such as towing caravans or small boats. The trend had been started by the 1961 International Scout, had continued with the 1963 Jeep Wagoneer, and most immediately had been given a strong boost by the Ford Bronco. Rover, reasoned Bannock, had the experience to develop a new product to suit that market.

King asked Bannock to take a look at what he and Bashford had been working on, and Bannock was astonished to find that their paper plans for a Land Rover 100-inch Station Wagon were a perfect fit for the type of vehicle he had in mind.

It was going to have exceptional road performance because the plans incorporated the 3.5-litre V8 engine, whose manufacture and further development had been licensed to Rover by General Motors' Buick division in 1964.

Despite scepticism from the Land Rover engineers, who felt that only they knew enough about cross-country vehicles to design a new one, Chief Engineer Peter Wilks authorised New Vehicle Projects to start work on their new machine. A project team was formed under the leadership of Land Rover engineer Geof Miller, and formal design work began in August 1966. Some 11 months later, the first running prototype of the 100-inch Station Wagon was completed. Initial flaws in the design were dealt with during 1968, and the original appearance was tidied up by the Styling Department under David Bache. One of Bache's stylists, Tony Poole, came up with the Range Rover name towards the end of that year, and in 1969 the design was finalised. Production began at the end of the year, building up to a launch in June 1970.

Perhaps the most important elements of the Range Rover's design lay in its drivetrain. The V8 engine gave road performance like no other 4x4 then available, all-round disc brakes with power assistance gave reassuring stopping ability, and

Design stagnated during the 1970s, and this 1977 model (above) belonging to Tony Megginson shows few significant differences over the earlier models.

A four-door body was introduced in 1981 (below), and quickly became more popular than the original two-door type. This is a 1985 example, belonging to Mike Page.

Land Rover explored the market for luxury Range Rovers through a series of specially-equipped limited editions in the early 1980s. This is a 1983 In Vogue model, owned by Tony Megginson.

The Range Rover quickly became popular as a Police motorway patrol car. This vehicle belongs to the Greater Manchester Police.

permanent four-wheel drive proved a boon in rough terrain as well as improving wet-road traction and towing performance. King had chosen this in preference to selectable four-wheel drive, which was then the norm for 4x4 vehicles, mainly because it enabled the massive torque of the V8 engine to be split between two relatively light axles. A rear axle capable of taking all the V8's torque would have been much tougher and heavier, and would therefore have increased the unsprung weight to the detriment of ride comfort.

Ride comfort, road performance, towing ability, practicality and rough-terrain ability equal to that of a Land Rover were in themselves a heady cocktail. To that, however, was added the appeal of a high seating position which enabled the driver to see over traffic ahead and to seize overtaking opportunities which were denied to

those in conventional cars. This factor – Land Rover would come to call it the Command Driving Position in the 1990s – was very important in selling the Range Rover.

In the beginning, the Rover Sales Department struggled with creating an image for the new vehicle. It did not fit into any existing market niches, and the sales people were dubious about the appeal of its two-door configuration – drawn up partly because most American recreational 4x4s had just two doors, and partly because a four-door body would have taken longer and cost more to develop. So early promotional material majored on the Range Rover's versatility, and the buyers soon decided what they wanted from it. They wanted it to be a prestigious yet practical vehicle, and they soon began to ask for improvements to the basic design.

Ambulance conversions were available from very early on, usually on a stretched 110-inch wheelbase chassis. This one was the prototype, bodied by Wadham Stringer, and is owned by Chris Elliott.

A third axle was added to an extended chassis for the Carmichael Commando fire tender. This 1973 example was delivered to Somerset Fire Brigade and now belongs to the Brigade's museum.

Aftermarket luxury conversions exploited the potential of the Range Rover long before its manufacturers were able to. Among the leading converters were Wood & Pickett of London. This early 1980s four-door was built for sale through Harrods, the famous London department store. It now belongs to the Heritage Motor Centre at Gaydon.

It was unfortunate that, just as demand began to build up for a slicker transmission, a more luxurious interior, and a four-door body, Rover's owners at British Leyland were sinking fast. All the profits earned by the new Range Rover went into a common pool that had to support poor sales of cars like the Morris Marina and Austin Allegro, and there was very little left over to plough back into Range Rover development. Late in 1974, British Leyland reached crisis point, and appealed for government help. So in 1975 the company was nationalised, and over the next few years costs were watched very carefully indeed. As the Range Rover was still selling well, despite its faults, no substantial sums of money were devoted to its further development.

All that changed in 1978, when Land Rover Ltd was established as a separate operating division within British Leyland. Large sums of capital were made available for investment in the future of the Solihull 4x4s, and the Range Rover entered a new phase of its existence. A facelift for the 1980 season was the first indication that things were changing, and increased production at the same time began to tackle the long waiting lists that had built up during the 1970s.

Nevertheless, Land Rover proceeded with caution. Before committing huge sums of money to major changes, the company tested the water with limited edition models which incorporated planned new features. Thus, in 1980, Land Rover commissioned conversion specialists Schuler Presses (known as Overfinch since 1985) to build 25 Range Rovers with automatic transmission. That same year, an expensive four-door luxury conversion by Monteverdi in Switzerland was marketed through Land Rover dealers. And in 1981, Land Rover collaborated with the established London conversion firm of Wood & Pickett to build a limited-edition luxury two-door called the In Vogue.

These vehicles established the way forward. A new assembly hall for Range Rovers was opened at Solihull in early 1981, and from June that year a factory-built four-door model became available. So successful was this that it quickly started to outsell the established two-door. Over the next few years, mechanical refinement was improved by the introduction in 1981 of a lower-revving, high-compression engine coupled to taller gearing, optional automatic transmission in 1982, and an overdrive five-speed manual gearbox instead of the agricultural four-speed of the earlier vehicles in 1983. Interior appointments were upgraded, and luxury features such as electric window lifts and central locking made their appearance.

Meanwhile, yet another influence was brought to bear on the Range Rover. Land Rover's traditional Third World markets collapsed suddenly in the early 1980s, for a variety of political, economic and trade reasons. The company's management swiftly decided that the best way to ensure survival was not to attempt (at this stage) to win back those lost markets, but to focus instead on developed countries. With the Range Rover, it was ideally placed to do this, and the twin targets of continental Europe and North America were chosen. Ironically, the Range Rover had never been sold in North America, even though it had been designed with that country's requirements firmly in mind. The reason was that poor sales of other models had forced Rover to pull out of the USA altogether in the early 1970s.

The implications of selling the Range Rover in Europe were straightforward enough – a diesel engine option was needed. A plan to 'dieselise' the 3.5-litre V8 had foundered in 1983, and so several bought-in units were tried before Land Rover settled on the VM 2.4-litre turbocharged four-cylinder, which was introduced in April 1986. The intention to sell Range Rovers in America, however, demanded much more consideration. American customers were notoriously demanding in terms of product performance, options and – perhaps above all – build quality. So a programme of enhancements was set in train to prepare the Range Rover for a US introduction in March 1987. These enhancements included smarter interiors, an all-welded bodyshell (to remove some of the dimensional variations inherent in the original bolted-together design) and a fuel-injected version of the V8 engine (to meet emissions control legislation).

The turbodiesel and fuel-injected derivatives took the Range Rover into a new phase of its career, which would not end until production stopped in February 1996 – some 15 months after the original model had been replaced in most markets by a new vehicle carrying the Range Rover name. These engines and this later period are beyond the scope of this book, but the carburettor models did remain available for some markets until 1988, picking up many of the modifications designed for the more numerous four-doors. However, their availability was restricted: there were no carburettor-engined four-door models after the end of 1986, by which time the two-doors were in any case in the minority.

Right from the beginning, the Land Rover engineers recognised that the Range Rover had enormous potential as the basis of an emergency services vehicle. Even before production started, plans were drawn up to equip the Range Rover as

a Police motorway patrol car, and Police Range Rovers soon became a familiar sight in Britain – and in other countries too – during the 1970s.

Ambulance and fire tender conversions were also on the agenda from the beginning, but it quickly became obvious that the standard vehicle was too small for either purpose. For ambulance conversions, therefore, the chassis was stretched by Spencer Abbott in Birmingham to give a wheelbase of 110in, and later on there were 135in wheelbase ambulances as well. For fire tenders, a third undriven axle was added and the chassis was extended by Carmichael of Worcester. In 6x4 guise, with bodies by Carmichael, Gloster Saro, HCB-Angus and others, the Range Rover became a firm favourite in many countries as a first-response airport crash tender.

The other principal variant – in this case actually built at Solihull – was the van. Based on the two-door model, with the rear seat deleted and the rear side windows panelled over, this first became available in the mid-1970s. Few were sold on the home market, but vans were popular in certain overseas countries where tax regulations were favourable. Range Rover vans were sold in Denmark (where they had fixed side windows), France (where they were known as 'utilitaires'), Greece and Portugal – and possibly other countries as well. The very last two-door Range Rover of all, built on 11 January 1994, was a van version destined for Portugal.

Finally, customised Range Rovers became enormously popular in the oil-rich countries of the Middle East during the 1970s. Mostly converted to four-door configuration, and often sitting on extended chassis, these hugely expensive vehicles were hand-built to individual order. Companies like Wood & Pickett, A.E. Smith, Glenfrome and FLM Panelcraft made a comfortable living from these conversions, which are so varied as to deserve a book of their own.

Just two special parade vehicles were built by Ogle for the Pope's visit to Britain in the early 1980s.

Chapter 2
Prototypes, YVBs & NXCs

The very first prototype was built in the Jig Shop at Solihull in the first half of 1967, and was road-registered in August or September of that year. At this stage, the vehicle was still known as a Land Rover 100-inch Station Wagon. A second, improved, prototype followed in the early spring of 1968, but by the time of the third – around a year later – the definitive body styling was in evidence and the name of Range Rover had been chosen. There were four subsequent prototypes, until the seventh – built at the end of 1969 – was virtually to production standard. All these proto-

types had special chassis numbers issued by the Rover Engineering Department.

The Rover Company took care to disguise the identity of these prototypes when they went out on public roads. A notional Velar car company was established, with headquarters in London, and the vehicles were registered and badged as Velars. The Velar name also appeared on their road tax discs, and a series of London registration numbers prevented the connection with Solihull from being made too easily. The first prototype had a specially-made badge which resembled the

This is the oldest surviving Range Rover and the only Engineering prototype still to exist. Numbered 100/6, it has been rebodied but retains many prototype features.

Production chassis number 1 has been owned for many years by Peter Garside and has been superbly restored. It was painted experimentally in a shade of green which was not used on other production vehicles.

Volvo symbol, but thereafter the Velar badges were made up out of the individual letters of the Rover badge on the boot lid of the company's P6 saloon: the L was an E with two bars cut away, and the A was an inverted V with an additional bar.

The second and third Range Rover prototypes had the 'small' (pre-1970) Rover P6 saloon digits attached directly to bonnet and tailgate. Numbers four, five and six had these initially and were then fitted with plate badges carrying the larger (1970-style) Rover P6 digits.

Only two of these seven vehicles are known to survive. The full list is given in the table.

YVBs: *pre-production models*

The first pre-production Range Rover was completed in December 1969, some six months before the model was announced to the world's media at the Blue Hills Mine, near St Agnes in Cornwall. The first vehicle to be despatched, however, was not chassis number 1 but rather chassis number 3 (355-00003A). The Rover Publicity Department had been allocated a white vehicle (chassis number 6), but wanted a blue vehicle for the first

PROTOTYPE RANGE ROVERS

Chassis no	Registration	Registration date	Steering	Remarks
100/1	SYE 157F	Aug/Sep 1967	RHD	–
100/2	ULH 696F	Apr/May 1968	LHD	–
100/3	AGN 316G	Apr/Jul 1969	LHD	First with production styling
100/4	AMV 287H	Aug 1969	RHD	–
100/5	WYK 315H	Oct 1969	LHD	–
100/6	AOY 289H	Sep 1969	RHD	Rebodied, survives
100/7	YVB 150H	Dec 1969/Jan 1970	LHD	Survives

Recreated by Geof Miller, who led the Range Rover development team, this is the Velar badge used to disguise prototypes. The letters are made from those used on the boot lid of Rover saloons.

publicity photographs. As number 3 was the first blue one, it was rolled off the assembly line in a partially-finished condition and handed to the Engineering Department for completion ahead of

The first Range Rover to be completed was chassis number 3, which is now owned by the Heritage Collection.

In as-found condition, NXC 231H represents the NXC-registered press vehicles.

the others. This vehicle, registered YVB 153H, survives in the Heritage Motor Centre at Gaydon.

Over the next few months, a further 26 chassis were built, bringing the total of pre-production Range Rovers to 27. Two chassis were built with LHD. One RHD chassis was not turned into a complete vehicle but was designated as a drive-able demonstration chassis and received no identification other than the Engineering Fleet number 100.12. This, too, survives, although it was modified during its time with the Rover Service School at Solihull. The body originally destined for it was set up in Solihull's Electrical Development department and used for component durability work.

All of the pre-production Range Rovers except for the demonstration chassis and one other RHD example were registered with numbers running from YVB 151H to YVB 177H. These London numbers were once again chosen to blur the connection with Solihull, and the pre-production models were registered as Velars. The odd man out was chassis number 6, the white vehicle originally destined for the Publicity Department. As that department was content to retain its blue vehicle, chassis number 3, the white one was used as a 'hack' at Solihull and not brought up to complete specification until it was registered as UXC 159J in May 1971. By this time, the Range Rover was available in the showrooms, so the vehicle

was registered as a Range Rover and given a Solihull number.

There were many detail differences between these pre-production Range Rovers and the full production-standard vehicles which followed. Some of them had bonnets made of aluminium alloy, but the alloy proved too difficult to draw and so steel was substituted before many had been made. They had different door seals and seal retaining lips on the body, and those finished in Lincoln Green, Masai Red and Sahara Dust had their wheels enamelled in Sahara Dust rather than the silver used with other colours and eventually adopted for production. The pre-production facia panels also had a smooth finish, instead of grained. They were made on production tooling and were used to check dimensional accuracy; once the dimensions had been signed-off, the grained finish was added to the tooling.

Three vehicles were used as prototypes for the extended-wheelbase emergency vehicles which

Like other Engineering prototypes, 100/6 had the SU carburettors used on Rover saloon versions of the V8 engine. Strombergs were later adopted for production.

This piece of trim (above) from 100/6 has a hand-made alloy backing panel, as the production tooling did not exist when the vehicle was being built.

YVB 151H also has a style of window winder not used on production vehicles.

PRE-PRODUCTION RANGE ROVERS (YVBs)

Chassis no	Registration	Rover Fleet no	Remarks
355-00001A	YVB 151H	100.9	–
355-00002A	YVB 152H	100.10	6x4 fire tender
355-00003A	YVB 153H	100.11	Heritage Museum
355-00004A	YVB 154H	100.13	–
355-00005A	YVB 155H	Quality Dept	–
355-00006A	UXC 169J	Publicity Dept	–
355-00007A	YVB 177H	Service Dept	–
355-00008A	YVB 160H	Publicity Dept	–
355-00009A	YVB 157H	100.15	–
355-00010A	YVB 158H	100.16	Ambulance
355-00011A	YVB 156H	100.14	–
355-00012A	YVB 159H	100.17	–
355-00013A	YVB 169H	Quality Dept	Not traced
355-00014A	YVB 161H	100.18	–
355-00015A	YVB 162H	100.19	–
355-00016A	YVB 171H	MA 1	–
355-00017A	YVB 163H	100.20	–
355-00018A	YVB 164H	100.21	–
355-00019A	YVB 170H	Service Dept	Not traced
355-00020A	YVB 172H	MA 2	–
355-00021A	YVB 173H	MA 3	–
355-00022A	YVB 165H	100.22	–
355-00023A	YVB 166H	100.23	–
355-00024A	YVB 167H	100.24	–
355-00025A	YVB 168H	100.25	Ambulance
Not allocated	Not registered	100.12	Driveable chassis
358-00001A	YVB 174H	100.26	Not traced
358-00002A	YVB 175H	100.27	–

Fleet numbers MA 1 to MA 3 were Management Assessment vehicles.

The original press launch pack from June 1970 contained black and white pictures of the YVB-registered vehicles.

Many pre-production vehicles had 'smooth' facia tops, as seen here on YVB 158H. No front finisher panel appears ever to have been fitted to the passenger's side parcels shelf.

This picture of a pre-production model shows a style of lettering in the wheel centre which was tried experimentally but not adopted for production. The vehicle is probably YVB 160H (chassis number 8).

PRESS LAUNCH RANGE ROVERS (NXCs)

Chassis no	Registration	Remarks
355-00026A	NXC 231H	–
355-00027A	NXC 232H	–
355-00028A	NXC 233H	Not traced
355-00029A	NXC 234H	–
355-00030A	NXC 235H	–
355-00031A	NXC 236H	–
355-00032A	NXC 237H	–
355-00033A	NXC 238H	–
355-00034A	NXC 239H	–
355-00035A	NXC 240H	–
355-00036A	NXC 241H	Not traced
355-00037A	NXC 242H	Not traced
355-00038A	NXC 243H	–
355-00039A	NXC 244H	Not traced
355-00040A	NXC 245H	–
355-00041A	NXC 246H	–
355-00042A	NXC 247H	Not traced
355-00043A	NXC 248H	Not traced
355-00044A	NXC 249H	Not traced
355-00045A	NXC 250H	–

later became commonplace on the Range Rover chassis. The second chassis became the prototype Carmichael 6x4 fire tender, while the tenth became the prototype Wadham Stringer ambulance. The 25th vehicle was also converted to an ambulance by Spencer Abbott, but this design did not go into production.

All but three of these vehicles are known to survive today. Their whereabouts have been enthusiastically recorded by former Range Rover Project Engineer Geof Miller, on whose research the accompanying list is based.

NXCs: *press launch vehicles*

Immediately following the pre-production batch, 20 RHD Range Rovers were built for the press launch in June 1970. All were registered in sequence from NXC 231H to NXC 250H. Despite the Solihull registration numbers and their Range Rover badges, they were all initially registered as Velars. These vehicles were close to production standard, with the grained facia panels but some pre-production details. Seven of the 20 remain untraced at the time of writing.

Chapter 3

Body

The first Range Rovers had two-door bodies with horizontally-split tailgates. A four-door version of this body was investigated as early as 1972, but British Leyland (as it was then) could not afford to put it into production. As a result, a number of four-door conversions were developed by outside companies during the 1970s, but the cost of these ensured that most were sold to wealthy clients in the Middle East. An exception was the Swiss Monteverdi company's neat conversion, which was announced in 1980 as a factory-approved luxury model. This short-lived version of the Range Rover is covered in Chapter 10.

Major investment in the newly-created Land Rover Ltd after 1978 allowed the new North Works assembly plant to be built at Solihull. This in turn created the space and flexibility needed for Land Rover to build its own four-door model. The first 'factory' four-door Range Rovers went on sale in July 1981, and in most markets the four-door quickly became the more popular model. No four-door carburettor models were built after the end of the 1986 model year, and the present section does not therefore cover the 1987 and 1988 four-door bodies. Two-door carburettor models continued to be available until the end of the 1988 model year, however, and their bodies are therefore discussed here.

Both two-door and four-door Range Rover bodies consist of unstressed skin panels bolted to a stressed steel skeleton frame which is in turn bolted to the chassis frame. This type of construction was inspired by the 'base-unit' structure of the 'chassis-less' Rover P6 (2000/2200/3500) saloon car of the 1960s and 1970s. The body is bolted to the chassis at ten points, each one using shock-absorbing mounting rubbers. Most of the outer body panels are made of Birmabright aluminium alloy; the exceptions are the bonnet and lower rear quarter panels (or tail lamp surrounds), which are made of steel.

Body frame

On all Range Rovers built up to the end of the BA-series in 1985, the skeleton frame consists of a number of sub-assemblies which are bolted

together. This suited the flat-packing necessary when vehicles were exported in CKD form for overseas assembly, but it could cause quite marked dimensional variations in the completed body, leading to wide panel gaps, leaks, and so on. Dust ingress was a major problem in some territories, and a series of modifications was recommended in a Service Bulletin for December 1973; these modifications were later standardised for all territories in June 1974.

When Land Rover decided to move the Range Rover firmly into the luxury car market, these dimensional variations and leak problems had to be eliminated. So during 1985, a jig-assembled, all-welded body frame replaced the original bolt-together type. These later frames have a number of important differences from the earlier types. The changeover point has been generally assumed to be the start of the CA-series, but in fact the all-welded frames were introduced at BA 160680. Approximately 2500 BA-series vehicles therefore had these later frames.

In the beginning, the body frames were painted in the same colour as the outer panels. However, four-door bodies always had satin black body frames, and from September 1982 the two-door frames were also finished in black. This is important when establishing the correct finish for some of the exposed parts of the vehicle. The windscreen pillars are part of the body frame, and are therefore painted in the body colour on all two-doors before September 1982, but in black on all subsequent two-doors and on all four-doors; they are also in body colour on the Monteverdi conversion, which was always based on pre-September 1982 two-door models. On two-door models before September 1982, the door shuts on

Coloured stripes along the lower body sides were introduced on carburettor Vogue versions of the Range Rover for the 1985 model year.

both A-pillars and B/C-pillars should be in body colour, as should the exposed upper faces of the rear wheelarches and the sides of the load floor. On all four-door models and later two-doors, the door shuts, rear wheelarches and load floor sides should be black.

Central to the body frame is the dash (front bulkhead) assembly. The same dash is used on both LHD and RHD vehicles, with unused holes for steering column, pedals and so on being closed off by blanking plates. Automatic models have a special additional blanking plate to close off the aperture for the clutch pedal. From the start of the BA-series in June 1984, a different blanking plate was fitted over the redundant steering column aperture. The later blanking plate carries a bracket to suit the new washer bottle.

The front bulkhead assembly on all-welded bodyshells is quite different from the earlier type, with much shallower side sections. It cannot be used to replace an early bulkhead without a great deal of modification. Worth noting is that the early bulkhead – which is prone to rusting in the footwells – has been unavailable new for some time. Footwell repair panels, however, are available from after-market sources.

Bolted or welded (as appropriate) to the dash assembly are the body-side assemblies, which include the outer edges of the floor, rear wheelarches and sills. These assemblies come with either a single door aperture for the two-door models, or with two door apertures for the four-door models. From July 1983, the B/C-post on four-door body sides is reinforced and fitted with a sliding plate to take the pillar-mounted safety belt top mountings introduced on 1984 models. The upper D-post was redesigned when the all-welded body frames were introduced during 1985 (at BA 160680), in order to conceal the black mastic sealant used in the area. It is worth noting that the lower D-posts were incorrectly formed on some early all-welded frames, and caused damage to the rear door seals as a result. The problem was corrected at monocoque body frame number M46 25085 in November 1985. On the EA-series vehicles, the A-pillar on each body side is pierced to take a drainage tube for the optional sunroof.

The body-side assemblies incorporate the end of the heelboard. On the early two-door models, this is vertical and is some distance in front of the wheelarch. The heelboard was redesigned for the four-door body to improve legroom in the rear, and on all four-door body sides the heelboard end is angled back towards the rear wheelarch. Two-door body sides were redesigned to incorporate the same angled heelboard end from September 1982, as part of a cost-saving commonisation programme which affected the rear seating area. From this date, two-door and four-door Range Rovers could share a common heelboard panel joining the two body sides.

Special body sides with detail differences were used on the French-market 'utilitaire' (van) models in the early 1980s.

The body sides are joined over the windscreen by a header panel, and at the rear by a rear end frame. This frame was modified in April 1975 with the introduction of Suffix D models, losing the central bulge at the top which had earlier helped to retain the headlining. The frame has brackets for the top tailgate struts bolted to it up to May 1984, but with the introduction of the BA-series the strut fixings are welded to it.

Working forwards, there is a load area floor panel, of which three different types were used. The first type is found on all two-door Range Rovers up to August 1982, and has longitudinal ribs or corrugations. The second was introduced on four-door models in July 1981 and then used on two-doors as well from September 1982. The third was unique to the French-market 'utilitaire' (van) two-door Range Rover of the early 1980s.

Ahead of the rear floor panel is the heelboard panel, which differs between body frames with angled heelboards and those with the vertical type. A modified type was introduced with the BA-series in June 1984. The rest of the floor is then made up by the tunnel cover plate assembly, which includes a substantial cross-member at its rear edge. Three different tunnel cover plates are used: the earliest suits the four-speed gearbox, a second suits both five-speed and automatic models built up to the end of the AA-series, and a third is found on BA-series and later models. A top structure bolted to the tunnel cover plate carries the gearchange levers on AA-series automatic models, and a second type carries the levers on AA-series five-speed models. From June 1984 (the start of the BA-series), a common structure is used for manual and automatic models.

Ahead of the dash assembly are the left-hand and right-hand inner wing assemblies, bolted in place on early shells and welded on CA-series and later. These include the inner wheelarch panels and the headlamp support panels. The battery support platform on the right-hand inner wing assembly is mirrored on the left-hand assembly. On Range Rovers with alloy grilles (up to the end of the CA-series), there are welded bosses on the front of each assembly, below the headlamp support panel, to take spire nuts for the grille and headlamp panel mounting screws. The top surfaces of the wings also have apertures for spire nuts to take the screws securing the top of the grille and lamp surrounds. On DA-series and later vehicles, the lower mounting bosses are absent, and there are metal loops on the top surface to accept the clip fixings of the later plastic grille.

The inner wing assemblies are joined at their lower ends by a cross-member. This has a channel-section black polythene closing panel, which also ducts water towards the sides of the vehicle. At the top, the inner wing assemblies are joined by the bonnet lock platform panel. The bonnet lock itself is a spring-loaded sliding type, the same as that used on Rover P5 and P5B cars, and is released by a sheathed cable from the footwell. This cable is held to the inner wing by four white plastic brake-pipe clips. Diagonal cross-braces, which are handed, are bolted between the underside of the bonnet lock platform and the lower cross-member.

The vertical surfaces of the inner wings alongside the bonnet lock platform carry various plates and decals. On early models, the right-hand surface (ie, on the left of the bonnet lock platform when looking into the engine) has a red printed metal plate warning that the vehicle has a negative-earth electrical system; this is pop-riveted into position. From approximately 1973, the corresponding opposite surface carries black decals with white print detailing various European standard compliance numbers. Early vehicles have just one decal, while later examples have three long, narrow ones covering 'Steering' (E11-12R-0032), 'Door Locks' (E11-11R-0032) and 'Suppression' (E11-10R-180).

To the bonnet lock platform itself is pop-riveted the chassis number or VIN (Vehicle Identification Number) plate. On all vehicles up to the introduction of VINs, this plate is made of alloy and is printed black with the lettering showing through in the silver colour of the alloy. The later VIN plates are slightly larger. and have black printing on an alloy background.

Sills

Plastic sill finishers are attached to the body sides under the side doors. The two-door and four-door types are visually similar when fitted, but have some differences. Both are attached to the body sides by a single nut and bolt at each end; the two-door type has five push-fit plastic fasteners and the four-door type has six fasteners.

Bonnet

The Range Rover's bonnet, a steel pressing with a steel reinforcing frame, is attached to the front bulkhead by two hinges with large set-screws. On all models to the end of the CA-series, the hinges protrude above the line of the bonnet and scuttle panel, and the rear edge of the bonnet has cut-outs to accommodate them. With the DA-series, concealed hinges were introduced and the bonnet panel was modified to suit; a concealed torsion bar

was also added to make the panel easier to lift.

Hinge stiffeners were added to the bonnet panel at Suffix C for the 1974 model year. Just before the end of the CA-series, at CA 264660, the rivets were removed from the rear of the bonnet to tidy up its appearance.

On all Range Rovers up to the end of the CA-series sold in Germany, the protruding hinges were shielded by black plastic protectors to meet safety regulations. These protectors are handed, and have two pegs on their undersides which push into sleeved holes drilled in the bonnet panel.

Range Rovers built before the end of the 1977 model year always had mirrors mounted on the bonnet. These were handed, had alloy bodies and were painted black. They were normally bolted through the bonnet a few inches back from the

The bonnet catch and the early type of bonnet prop, seen on Range Rover number 1.

Range Rovers for Germany had special plastic shields for the exposed bonnet hinges.

Pre-1979 vehicles had plastic lettering on bonnet and tailgate.

top of the castellation feature. For the 1978 model year (from October 1977), door-mounted mirrors replaced the bonnet-mounted type.

Three types of bonnet badge were used over the years. Early models had separate plastic letters giving the Range Rover name; these had pegs on the backs and were held to the bonnet by plastic friction bushes inserted into drilled holes. The letters are identical to those used on the tailgate.

The mounting holes in the bonnet and tailgate for these letters allowed water to get in and cause rust, and the letters themselves also tended to fall out. So a switch was made in summer 1979 to tape decal badges. It is generally assumed that these badges were introduced at the start of 1980-model production, at AA 100783; in fact, they arrived rather earlier, at 356-59271G. The tape badges normally have letters in black with a white outline, although it appears that a silver-grey outline was used on white vehicles. Bonnet and tailgate decals differ, that for the bonnet having a slight curve to suit the profile of the panel.

Badging changed again with the introduction of the BA-series in June 1984. New tape decals were introduced, their letters having no contrasting background and coming in Brown, Green or Silver to suit the paintwork of the vehicle, as detailed in the table at the end of this chapter. Once again, the bonnet tape decal is not the same as the one used on the tailgate.

There is an insulation pad which fits to the centre of the bonnet's underside, between the strengthening ribs. It consists of a glass-fibre pad, which has a sprayed-on black neoprene covering on all models up to some point in the CA-series.

Decal badges used from 1979 normally came in black and white (below), although black and silver (right) seems to have been used on white vehicles.

From that point on, a black cotton covering replaced the neoprene, the cotton being retained on the glass-fibre by a compressed edge. The pad was also shortened at the hinge end to prevent fouling with the bonnet stiffener. Sources conflict on whether the cloth-covered pad arrived at CA 261902 or at CA 263818. The early insulation pad is attached by adhesive whereas later types have a diagonal retaining rod at each front corner, held to the bonnet by a spring clip at each end.

The bonnet prop rod pivots from a bracket on the front lip and when not in use is secured to the underside of the bonnet by a clip which is pop-riveted to the left-hand strengthening rib; it is thus angled towards the left-hand side of the vehicle (right-hand side when looking from the front). Very early prop rods were a push-fit into the pivot bracket on the underside of the bonnet panel, but from December 1972 approximately there was a more secure fixing using a split pin and washer. On Suffix C models for the 1974 model year, the retention of the prop rod was improved again by the addition of a safety hook.

All bonnets have an adjustable buffer stop on each side of the front lip. The screwed section passes into a nut welded to the reverse side of the lip and is adjusted by means of a locknut. From CA 158570, stronger brackets were used, to prevent the distortion encountered on some earlier examples. The bolt heads of these buffer stops are capped by push-fit black rubber buffers.

The bonnets on Suffix A and Suffix B Range Rovers have a catch directly in front of the spring striker in the centre of the front lip. The striker is held on by two set bolts which pass through the catch retaining plate, and a third bolt further secures the catch plate. The catch is pulled to release it. On Suffix C and later vehicles, the striker is attached by three set bolts, and the catch is relocated on the left-hand side of the front lip (right-hand side when looking at the bonnet from the front). The catch itself is also a different type. From BA 161700, the bonnet safety catch is relocated, and the stop bracket on the lock platform is relocated to suit; this later catch has to be pushed to be released.

Twin under-bonnet lamps were fitted from July 1981, when the four-door models were introduced. These have a metal body and a clear plastic dome over the bulb.

Details of the windscreen washer jets mounted on the bonnet panel will be found in Chapter 9.

Grille area

The grille panel on Range Rovers up to the end of the CA-series is made of alloy painted matt black. It has vertical slats and is held by drive screws to spire nuts in the bonnet platform and in bosses on the lower rim below the headlamp panels in the front inner wing assemblies. It is flanked by headlamp finisher panels, also alloy and painted to match, which are secured by drive screws and spire nuts. Special finisher panels were used on vehicles for Finland and Sweden with the headlamp wash-wipe system.

DA-series and later models have a one-piece black plastic grille with horizontal slats which incorporates the headlamp surrounds. This grille has short extensions at the top which fit under metal loops on the bonnet lock platform to hold it in place. The upper face of the grille's lower flange is painted to match the colour of the body.

Below the grille, a front finisher panel is bolted to the lower body cross-member. It has cut-outs for the starting handle on pre-1983 models and further cut-outs for the dumb irons to which the front bumper is bolted.

Scuttle area

The scuttle or front decker panel is an alloy pressing with reinforcing plates at its front corners. It is bolted to the dash (bulkhead) assembly and to the tops of the front wings. The panel is often a poor fit on early vehicles, as the result of wide manufacturing tolerances. On Range Rovers with exposed bonnet hinges, the scuttle panel is shaped to fit around the hinges; on DA-series and later models, it has a plain leading edge.

Different scuttle panels are used for LHD and RHD, to suit the different positions of the wiper wheelboxes. Both early and late panels have three apertures in the raised centre section for the heater air intake. The air intake should have three push-fit black plastic grille panels, with matching black plastic filler panels between them and triangular end finishers. Each of the three grilles should be backed by a filter pad. At DA 296142, washers were added behind the plastic inserts and there were changes to the holes in the support bracket to improve fit and retention of the inserts.

The scuttle panel normally carries the radio aerial when a radio is fitted to pre-DA-series Range Rovers. The aerial is fitted to the driver's side, and is a chrome and stainless steel fixed-mast type on models built before the start of four-door production in mid-1981. A manually retractable type was pioneered on the In Vogue limited edition in February 1981, and manually retractable types were fitted to all models with a radio from summer that year. However, the standard-fit type has a flat base rather than the adjustable angled type fitted to the In Vogue model. It also has a small bullet-shaped section at the top which can be grasped when the aerial is fully retracted, so that it can be extended.

From the start of the BA-series in June 1984,

all Range Rovers except two-door Fleet Line models were built with speaker wiring, speakers and an aerial; the supplying dealer than fitted the customer's choice of radio. As a result, scuttle panels were pre-drilled to accept an aerial. Fleet Line models had a black rubber blanking plug in the redundant hole. The Vogue models introduced at this time, and their equivalents for overseas markets, had a special aerial. This retracted fully and could only be erected by first disengaging it from its surround with a special key, which was normally kept on the vehicle's key ring.

The DA-series and later Range Rovers have a radio aerial incorporated in the heated rear window element, and a signal booster fitted in the aerial line above the tailgate. There is therefore no mast aerial on the scuttle.

A plate badge was fitted on each side of the scuttle panel on all vehicles up to August 1979. On the earliest vehicles, the Range Rover name was cast into the metal, and the recessed letters were painted black. From October 1973, a simpler type of badge was used, consisting of an alloy plate onto which the Range Rover name was printed. The rear surface of both types of plate had two pins that pushed into friction bushes inserted in holes drilled in the scuttle panel.

Front wings

The front wings have a small section of the under-bumper modesty panel spot-welded to their lower front edges. Their trailing edges are shaped to fit around the lower door hinge (this shaped cut-out is absent from later Service wings, produced to suit later models with concealed hinges). The wings are bolted to the inner wing assembly along their

Early scuttle badges (top) were engraved, but later ones (above) were printed.

Two-door models (right) had edge-pull door handles. Keylock surround is correctly in black. Four-door models (below) had 'letter-box' door handles. This is the later type for the front door, with keylock incorporated.

top edges and just below the sidelamp clusters; they are also bolted at the rear to the bulkhead. An angle-section drainage channel is held to the inner top surface of the inner wing assembly by the bolts which attach the outer wings.

On all vehicles built after September 1979, and on some earlier models, the front wings carry direction indicator repeater lamps. These are covered in the section on 'Lighting' in Chapter 9.

Doors

All doors have an aluminium alloy skin on a steel inner structure, and the window frame in every case is a separate steel structure – finished in satin black – bolted inside the door. This satin black is the same as the paint used on the later body frames. The door seals are attached to the body aperture and not to the doors themselves on two-door models. Four-door versions, however, have rubber seals on the doors as well.

The doors of two-door Range Rovers have black-painted edge-pull outer handles, attached to the handed latches by two stud plates and nuts. Dust and draughts could get through the handle and lock aperture, and so at chassis serial number 60883G, in 1980, a dust seal was fitted between the door panel and the latch assembly. The barrel for the keylock is in the door panel above the edge-pull, and there is a pivoting quarter-light in the leading edge of the window frame. Each door has two hinges at its leading edge, each one with an integral check arm.

On Suffix A models only, the door-to-window rubber seal consists of four separate sections – two sides and two ends. These early seals have been unavailable for many years. Suffix B and later models have a single-piece seal, which was introduced to ease assembly and improve appearance.

The quarter-light is held shut by a black-painted metal catch. Its glass is held in a metal frame, and the whole assembly seats against a large black rubber seal. This seal has a triangular black finisher at its lower leading edge. Suffix A models have a unique quarter-light seal, Suffix B and all later vehicles having a modified type which gives a more positive seal.

Door skins were not available separately until September 1973; before that date, collision damage either had to be beaten out, or the whole door had to be replaced. On the inside surface of each door skin are glued a number of rectangular pads. The three larger ones at the top are anti-drum pads, and the seven smaller ones are anti-rattle pads to prevent the latch linkages and window lift mechanism from rattling against the skin. All door frames up to the end of the AA-series have a stiffener plate welded across the bottom; from BA 14027 in June 1984, however, no stiffener is fitted.

Although bonnet-mounted exterior mirrors were standard on early Range Rovers, some examples were fitted with door-mounted types to special order. These mirrors appear to have had chromed stems and stainless steel heads, and were attached to the door by two screws, with a black seating washer between the door and the base of the stem. Both convex and flat glass types were available. When these mirrors were fitted, the doors were provided with integral nut plates to accommodate the mirror fixings.

Door-mounted mirrors became standard in September 1978, and two different types were used. Both have a plinth which is attached to the door skin by two well-nuts before the mirror itself is attached over the plinth and fixed by a single screw. The earlier type was used up to chassis serial number 59270G in 1979, and the later type thereafter. The later mirrors normally had convex glass (although flat glass was available and was standard on Australian-market Range Rovers), and the glass itself was replaceable.

The front doors of four-door Range Rovers do not have edge-pulls but rather rectangular 'letter-box' handles mounted in the upper third of the door. The pull-handle itself is of satin-finish metal, but the handle surround is made of black plastic. These handles are similar to those used on Morris Marina and Austin Allegro cars of the 1970s and early 1980s, but have plain rather than textured metal pulls. The keylock in the front doors was always mounted below the handle until 1983, when it was incorporated within the frame of the handle itself. From June 1984, two different types of keylock were used, some with barrels of 12mm diameter and others with 14mm barrels.

The basic construction of the front doors of four-door models is otherwise similar to that of the two-door types. The doors have a quarter-light window on all AA-series models. This is smaller than the two-door type (for purely aesthetic reasons) but has the same type of catch. There are no quarter-lights on BA-series and later models, and a modified window frame assembly is fitted, without the stiffener bar welded across the bottom of earlier types.

Door-mounted mirrors are standard on all four-door Range Rovers. On AA-series vehicles, they are the same as the final type found on two-door models, as described above. With the BA-series vehicles, however, came a completely different type of mirror, which was fitted to the bottom leading edge of the window frame. This has a black plastic shell and adjustable mirror glass; on Vogue models (and optionally on others) the mirrors are electrically adjusted and demisted.

The rear doors are similar in construction to the fronts, with an alloy skin over a steel inner structure, and the window frame bolted to this. The frame contains a fixed quarter-light at the rear, which allows the drop-glass to be positioned ahead of the wheelarch cut-out so that it can go down further. Minor changes were made to the frame when the BA-series models were introduced in June 1984. Some early skins appear to have been pop-riveted in position rather than clinched, which became the standard method. There are child-proof locks on these doors, the operating lever protruding from the door shut face at the top of the wheelarch cut-out.

The doors have two hinges, with a single separate check-strap assembly mounted between them. They have the same Allegro/Marina exterior door handles as are used on the front doors, always of course without a keylock. There is a rubber seal around the wheelarch cut-out, and this is fixed differently on doors with pop-riveted skins. All doors have seven anti-rattle pads glued to the insides of their skins, but early doors have

Early vehicles had round mirrors mounted on the bonnet.

Door mirrors were introduced in the late 1970s. At first they had metal bodies (left), but a new design with a plastic body (below left) was introduced for 1985 models.

Two-door models always had a full-height quarterlight, as seen on this 1979 model.

The quarterlight was reduced in size for the four-door models, purely to improve the appearance.

Four-door models (far right) lost their front door quarterlights for 1985.

Front door hinges were always visible on both two-door and four-door carburettor Range Rovers.

only a small rectangular anti-drum pad at the top. Sound-proofing was improved in March 1983, when a full-width rectangular pad with a cut-out for the exterior handle replaced the small one at the top, and an extra rectangular anti-drum pad was added at the bottom. The doors on Range Rovers with central locking have additional anti-drum pads at the top.

Rear wings

The rear wings on all models are made of aluminium alloy, and are bolted to steel corner panels which contain the rear light clusters. The other ends of these corner panels are pop-riveted to the inner body structure alongside the tailgate. The wings on four-door models are much shorter than those on two-doors, terminating approximately half-way across the wheelarch. Two-door wings incorporate the whole of the wheelarch, as well as a short section in front of it.

On both two-door and four-door models, the right-hand wing has a cut-out for the fuel filler panel. The filler surround panel bolts through the wing. Suffix A Range Rovers use a different filler surround panel from all subsequent models, to suit the round, screw-type filler cap (see below). This panel has been unavailable for many years.

The top flange of each wing on two-door models is attached to the body sides by drive screws, and pop rivets secure the flange at the vertical leading edge to the inner body. Each wing has two anti-drum pads glued to its inner surface. On

four-door models, drive-screw fixings are used again for the top flange. On all four-doors up to AA 121295 (RHD automatic) and AA 124860 (RHD manual) in 1982, the wings have a vertical flange at their leading edges like that on their two-door equivalents, and this is attached to the inner body by pop rivets. Subsequent vehicles have modified wings with concealed fixings, which consist of a bolt plate, rivets and pop rivets.

At CA 270023 in 1986, the foam seal between the rear wing and the D-post was modified to improve its appearance.

Fuel filler cap

On Suffix A chassis, the fuel filler cap is a round lockable screw-type, attached to the inside of the filler tube by a chain. This early cap should be painted black. It was no longer available by April 1974, and the later type was recommended for use as a Service replacement.

A second type of filler cap was introduced in January 1973 and is fitted to all Suffix B and later models up to the end of the CA-series. It is a square-shaped lockable type, which has a spring-assisted hinge. At AA 110067 in June 1981, the spring anchorage was strengthened. On Range Rovers with 9.35:1 compression engines built between February 1981 and August 1983, the cap has a yellow warning label to advise of the need to use 97-octane (four-star) fuel.

The two-door carburettor models in the DA-series and EA-series had a new filler neck with a smaller diameter, and with that came a new non-vented locking filler cap. The filler was concealed behind a plastic door in the rear wing panel. This door is not connected to the central locking, as on contemporary four-door turbodiesel and fuel-injected models.

Upper rear body sides

All Range Rovers have the same pressing for the upper rear quarter panel, which contains a black plastic air vent with integral pegs attached to the body by spring spire clips. This quarter panel should be finished in the body colour on early two-doors, and the familiar black grained vinyl covering was not fitted until the start of Suffix C production in October 1973. This modification – which added greatly to the Range Rover's appearance – was supposedly made because it was difficult to get a good finish on the production line with the painted panels, and because vinyl roofs were then fashionable on saloon cars. Four-door models have a sound-deadening block behind the quarter panel, and this block is also fitted to two-doors built from approximately the time of the four-door's introduction in July 1981.

Four-door models have a simple fixed rear side window with a rubber seal. However, two-door models have two-piece rear side windows, the rear section being fixed and the front section sliding. The channels in which the front section slides were finished in bright metal until mid-1972, but were black thereafter. The early channels were fixed to the body sides by nylon nuts, but sealing was a problem because it was difficult to get at the nuts properly on the assembly lines. So from June 1972, steel nuts and washers were used, together with Bostik sealant to cover the elongated holes. This change in fixings may have coincided with the change to black slides. The sliding section of the glass has a black plastic latch block attached to it by two set-screws and collets. The metal

The rear door catch and wheelarch pressing of a four-door Range Rover are seen on a 1983 In Vogue.

framework of the rear window is in several sections, although there is a single-piece rubber seal running around all of it.

From AA 114045 in September 1981, two-door Range Rovers have a simplified one-piece rear window frame assembly. This has aluminium channels and an aluminium frame, to resist corrosion better than the earlier steel type. It also has a different latch block on the sliding section of the glass, with a release lever positioned more accessibly on the top instead of low down at the side.

Two-door models from DA 295585 destined for Denmark have fixed rear side windows with a single pane of glass.

A few very early vehicles had an aluminium-finish type of filler cap (below left), seen on Range Rover number 1. The standard production filler cap on Suffix A models was a lockable screw-off type (below centre), whereas a hinged, lockable filler cap (below right) was fitted from Suffix B onwards.

Rear quarter pillars on early models were painted body colour (right), but black cover panels in grained vinyl (far right) soon became standard.

The rear number plate (right) was designed to hinge downwards when the tailgate was open. On later examples, (below) a helpful decal was applied to show which way the handle had to be moved to lock the tailgate.

Early vehicles carried this oval badge on the tailgate.

Lower tailgate

The lower tailgate is made entirely of steel. It has two hinges bolted to the bottom of the body's rear-end frame. From the start of the 1984 model year in June 1983, torsion bars are fitted to these hinges to provide a counterbalance and reduce the effort needed to lift the tailgate when closing it.

The tailgate also has two supporting stays, each with a pivot in the middle. These stays were always unpainted, and on all vehicles up to the late summer of 1986 they have a star-lock washer and a plain washer in the pivot assembly. From CA 266190, a wavy washer replaces the star-lock type, the plain washer is deleted, and the method of assembling the pivot is reversed. This again

reduces the effort needed to close the tailgate.

The inner surface of the tailgate is ribbed, and has a detachable plate which gives access to the locking mechanism. A galvanised top capping is pop-riveted to the tailgate on all vehicles up to the end of the AA-series. Two rubber buffers for the top tailgate were added at AA 107199 in August 1980 approximately. In June 1984, a black capping with drive-screw fixings was standardised on BA-series models. This had been tried out earlier, on the 1983 In Vogue four-door special edition. Its finish was improved to resist corrosion at CA 265000 in 1986.

A number plate bracket containing the number plate lights (see the section on 'Lighting' in Chapter 9) is attached to the underside of the overhanging upper tailgate lip by hinges. Early brackets are steel, later ones alloy. On the back of the bracket are two plastic clips which locate in plastic sockets in the tailgate to hold the number plate in position. The hinged bracket allowed the number plate to swing down and remain visible when travelling with the tailgate open. This system was not permitted in Germany, so Range Rovers for that market had the number plate bracket riveted to the tailgate. (It is a sign of the times that after the mid-1980s, owners were instructed not to drive with either half of the tailgate open because harmful exhaust fumes would be drawn into the passenger compartment!)

The lower tailgate is released by an external handle on all models to the end of the CA-series. This hangs down just above the number plate and is painted matt black. There is no keylock for this: the lower tailgate could not be opened when the upper tailgate was closed over it and locked shut. With the introduction of the DA-series in November 1986 came an internal release handle. This is incorporated in the access plate for the lock mechanism, and has a bright metal letterbox-type release handle. DA-series and later vehicles also have modified side latches for the tailgate, with round-headed catch pins on the body instead of female location plates.

Tailgate badging varied over the years. The first models have the Range Rover name with separate letters on the upper section, and these letters are the same as those used on the bonnet. In addition, there is a silver oval badge at the bottom left corner of the tailgate, reading 'by Land-Rover'. From September 1979, the silver oval badge was no longer fitted, and black-and-white decal badges were used, as on the bonnet. The BA-series and later models have coloured decal badges to suit the body colour, as on the bonnet. Range Rovers fitted with overdrive were in theory distinguished by a decal reading 'Overdrive' in black-and-white capital letters to match the 1979-84 main badging. This decal was applied on the lower right of the tailgate, but remained rare.

The steel of the lower tailgate was notoriously prone to corrosion, and several modifications were made in an attempt to cure this. Tailgates were wax-injected from AA 100382, and then larger drain holes were specified at AA 103915 in summer 1980. A few months later, at AA 108799, one-sided Zintec sheet was introduced for the manufacture of both inner and outer panels.

The lower tailgate was further redesigned to prevent seam corrosion during 1986. On earlier tailgates, a line of pop rivets is visible where the flange of the upper section is attached over the lower, just above the number plate. The later type was introduced at CA 166727 in March 1986, and has the lower section of the lower tailgate covering the flange of the upper section, and face-welded to it. Pre-coating of the tailgate was further improved at CA 265000, at the same time as the finish of its upper capping changed.

Upper tailgate

The upper tailgate consists of glass in a matt black steel frame. Two hinges at the top corners of the tailgate frame attach it to the top of the body's rear-end frame. These hinges are attached to the tailgate by set bolts; early models have cross-head bolts but later ones – probably beginning in June 1984 – have TorX bolts. From the start of the CA-series, dust sealing of the tailgate was improved.

The steel frame proved as rust-prone as the lower tailgate, and was notorious for rotting and splitting at its lower corner joints. A new cathodic paint process, introduced at chassis serial number 60555 in summer 1979, was supposed to improve corrosion resistance, but no real progress was made until the BA-series models brought plastic protective fillets over the lower corner joints.

A sturdy handle is bolted to the centre of the frame, and this contains the keylock, which operates locking bars that engage in catches in the rear pillars alongside the tailgate. A redesigned lock was fitted from AA 107199, built in August 1980. The keylock barrel doubles as the push-button which releases the tailgate catch, and needs a strong thumb to operate it on early models. From BA 152163 in 1985, improvements led to a reduction in operating pressure, and the pressure was reduced further from the start of the CA-series.

The handle was modified to take a larger lock barrel with the introduction of the DA-series vehicles in November 1986. On all models up to the end of the CA-series, the tailgate is locked by the same small key which fits the fuel filler and the interior cubby box; on DA-series and later models, a single key operates all the locks on the vehicle. From the start of the BA-series, the upper tailgate also operates the vehicle courtesy lights.

Gas struts support the upper tailgate when it is open. On Suffix A and Suffix B Range Rovers, these struts have ring ends which slip over pivots on the tailgate frame and on the body end frame. There is a washer between each end ring and its pivot, and another between the end ring and the press-fit fixing cap which secures it. With Suffix C models, from November 1973, smoother operation was achieved by using different gas struts with simpler ball end fixings; the ball is a snap-fit over a larger pivot and is held in place by a simple wire spring clip. New struts (from three different suppliers) were introduced in December 1977.

From June 1984 and the start of the BA-series, angled pivots replaced the straight type on the tailgate frame. Using the same struts as before, these gave an over-centre action which made closing the tailgate easier. At CA 171500, a modified compression washer within the strut made for easier operation.

All tailgates have a rubber seal at the bottom,

Plain glass was standard on the top tailgate of the earliest vehicles (top). The upper tailgate lock (above) is seen here on a 1983 model. Note the drain hole in the underside of the handle.

Manufacturer's marking on the glass indicates that this is the tinted Sundym type. Security etching was added by the owner. Note the chamfered top leading edge to the window of this 1983 four-door.

held in position by a retaining strip. With the start of the BA-series, a modified strip with fatter end-pieces is used. From Suffix C onwards, a rubber buffer block should be fitted to the inner face of each of the lower tailgate's corners.

Owners of early Range Rovers sometimes had problems with the upper tailgate coming open as the body flexed when the vehicle was being driven over rough terrain. A Service modification was introduced in February 1981 to cure this. It consisted of a crude catch screwed to the rear pillar on either side of the tailgate. The catches were manually operated and had no keylocks. They were listed in later Parts Catalogues as an optional extra, and it may be that they could also be fitted on the production lines to special order. They were never common, however.

Roof panel

The roof is a single alloy panel, strengthened by four pressed-in longitudinal ribs and three lateral roof bows. Rain gutters are welded to all four sides. The roof is held to the body sides, the rear end frame and the windscreen header rail by drive screws and spire nuts. There are 40 of these altogether, of which 10 are in the header rail. There is an additional rubber sealing pad over each A-pillar. Sound-deadening pads are glued to the underside of the panel between the rib pressings, in three rows of four.

From June 1986, two additional clips are fitted to the front rain gutter above the windscreen, just outboard of the drainage holes. The areas behind them are filled with sealant, which prevents water running back and dripping over the front doors. This improvement could also be applied retrospectively as a Service modification! From DA 281665, sealing blocks are glued to the ends of the

rear rain gutter to prevent water dripping into the vehicle when the upper tailgate is opened.

On EA-series models, an electrically-operated sliding steel sunroof – manufactured by Tudor Webasto – became optional. EA-series vehicles without a sunroof have a new roof panel which has no ribbing above the front seat.

Glass

The standard glass in all Range Rovers built up to August 1979 was clear. However, Triplex Sundym green-tinted glass became optional as early as May 1971 and was fitted as standard in some overseas markets. Sundym glass became standard for all markets in September 1979, at about AA 100783.

The windscreen is laminated, and was always supplied by Triplex until a change of supplier was made in 1988 at DA 305128. It has a rubber seal with rubber packing strips which are inserted in a moulded channel after the seal is in place. From EA 339942 in 1988, a modified screen seal was introduced, to cure rippling at the lower corners.

The door drop-glasses are handed. On all vehicles up to the end of the EA-series they are 5mm thick. The 'lightweight' 4mm drop-glasses were not introduced until October 1988, to improve the operation of the electric window lifts.

Tailgate glass initially had no heating element. A heated rear window option was introduced in May 1971, and could be specified with standard glass or Sundym tinted glass, which was made available at the same time. Made by Triplex, the heated rear window has yellow heating elements printed onto the upper half of the glass. The heated rear window was standardised for some markets, but not for all models world-wide until the start of the BA-series in June 1984. At this point, its heating elements were extended downwards to cover a greater area of the glass. On all vehicles with a heated rear window, the wires are protected by two plastic retainers attached to the underside of the roof by drive screws.

Paint

After September 1979, as the Range Rover began to move into the luxury car class, a number of improvements were made to the paint processes used in its manufacture. At AA 101000, a new Electrocoat (ICI 3240) was introduced to improve corrosion resistance. From AA 107280 there was improved paint coverage of the panel edges, and from AA 107399 a new spot repair primer was used to give better paint adhesion to the alloy panels. The whole paint process was further improved in January 1981 when the new North Works paint shop was opened; the first Range Rover to be painted here was AA 110100.

PAINT COLOURS

Jun 1970 to Sep 1974
Bahama Gold
Davos White
Lincoln Green
Masai Red
Sahara Dust
Tuscan Blue

Oct 1974 to Sep 1979
Arctic White[1]
Bahama Gold
Lincoln Green
Masai Red
Sahara Dust
Tuscan Blue

[1] Arctic White replaced Davos White in order to commonise paints with Rover cars. The change took effect at chassis numbers 355-09802, 356-02635 and 358-07722.

Oct 1979 to Jun 1981
Arctic White
Lincoln Green
Masai Red
Russet Brown
Sahara Dust
Sandglow
Tuscan Blue
Warwick Green

In addition, Vogue Blue metallic was available from Feb 1981 on the limited-edition In Vogue model only (see Chapter 11).

Jul 1981 to Sep 1982
Arctic White
Masai Red
Russet Brown
Sahara Dust
Shetland Beige
Silver Birch metallic
Tuscan Blue
Venetian Red
Vogue Blue metallic

Lincoln Green was also available to special order during this period. The two metallic paints were available on four-door models only.

Oct 1982 to Sep 1983
Arctic White
Nevada Gold metallic
Russet Brown
Sahara Dust
Shetland Beige
Sierra Silver metallic
Venetian Red
Vogue Blue metallic

Lincoln Green was also available to special order during this period. The three metallic paints were available on four-door models only. There are indications from Land Rover dealer literature that Sierra Silver may have been the same colour as the earlier Silver Birch metallic, under a new name.

Oct 1983 to May 1984
Arctic White *LRC 273*
Derwent Blue metallic *LRC 999*
Nevada Gold metallic *LRC 321*
Russet Brown *LRC 318*
Sahara Dust *LRC 239*
Sierra Silver metallic *LRC 305*
Venetian Red *LRC 301*

The three metallic finishes were available only on four-door models. Derwent Blue metallic was available only on the In Vogue limited edition.

Jun 1984 to Sep 1985
Arctic White *LRC 273*
Arizona Tan *LRC 341*
Balmoral Green *LRC 340*
Derwent Blue metallic *LRC 999*
Nevada Gold metallic *LRC 321*
Russet Brown *LRC 318*
Sahara Dust *LRC 239*
Sierra Silver metallic *LRC 305*
Venetian Red *LRC 301*

The three metallic finishes were available only on four-door models. Fleet Line models were available only in Arctic White or Venetian Red.

Oct 1985 to Nov 1986
Arizona Tan *LRC 341*
Astral Silver metallic *LRC 364*
Balmoral Green *LRC 340*
Cambrian Grey *LRC 348*
Caspian Blue metallic *LRC 366*
Chamonix White *LRC 998*
Cypress Green metallic *LRC 367*
Savannah Beige metallic *LRC 365*
Tasman Blue *LRC 327*
Venetian Red *LRC 301*

The four metallic finishes were now clear-over-base types and were available only on four-door models. Three of the new colours – Cambrian Grey, Savannah Beige and Tasman Blue – remained uncommon in the UK. All paint from this date was supplied by Berger.

Dec 1986 to Sep 1987
Ascot Green *LRC 001*
Astral Silver metallic *LRC 364*
Cambrian Grey *LRC 348*
Caspian Blue metallic *LRC 366*
Cassis Red metallic *LRC 382*
Chamonix White *LRC 998*
Cypress Green metallic *LRC 367*
Savannah Beige metallic *LRC 365*
Tasman Blue *LRC 327*
Venetian Red *LRC 301*

The metallic finishes were available on both two-door and four-door models. Cambrian Grey, Savannah Beige metallic and Tasman Blue remained rare in the UK. Note that there were two different specifications of Cassis Red metallic. The earlier one is more grainy and metallic, the later one richer and deeper.

Oct 1987 to Sep 1988
Alaskan Blue metallic *LRC 393*
Ascot Green *LRC 001*
Cambrian Grey *LRC 348*
Caspian Blue metallic *LRC 366*
Cassis Red metallic *LRC 382*
Chamonix White *LRC 998*
Colorado Silver metallic *LRC 391*
Cypress Green metallic *LRC 367*
Portofino Red *LRC 390*
Savannah Beige metallic *LRC 365*
Shire Blue *LRC 392*

The metallic finishes were available on both two-door and four-door models. Cambrian Grey, Savannah Beige metallic and Tasman Blue remained rare in the UK. Shire Blue was not available until November 1987 in the UK.

TAPE BADGE COLOURS (BA-SERIES ONWARDS)

The BA-series and later Range Rovers have tape badges in Brown, Green or Silver to suit the body colour. In addition, the BA-series (1985-model) Vogues have tape striping along the top of the lower body flare, in the same colour as the bonnet and tailgate decals. Colour combinations are as follows:

Body colour	Tape badge[1]
Alaskan Blue	Silver
Arctic White	Green
Arizona Tan	Brown
Ascot Green	Silver
Astral Silver metallic	Green
Balmoral Green	Green
Cambrian Grey	Green
Caspian Blue metallic	Silver
Cassis Red metallic	Silver
Chamonix White	Brown
Colorado Silver metallic	Green
Cypress Green metallic	Silver
Derwent Blue metallic	Silver
Nevada Gold	Brown
Portofino Red	Silver
Russet Brown	Brown
Sahara Dust	Green
Savannah Beige metallic	Brown
Shire Blue	Silver
Sierra Silver	Green
Tasman Blue	Silver
Venetian Red	Brown

[1] Includes stripes on 1985 Vogue

AUSTRALIAN CKD PAINT COLOURS

Between 1979 and December 1983, Range Rovers for the Australian market were assembled from CKD kits at the Jaguar Rover Australia plant in Sydney. As the company was also assembling Peugeot 505s at the time, the Range Rovers came to share some of the Peugeot paint colours from about 1982. The known colours used on Australian CKD Range Rovers are:

Bahama Gold (as for UK production)
Charcoal (dark metallic grey)
Coral Glow
Pacific Blue
Paradise Blue (light blue)
Sahara Dust (as for UK production)
Satin Green (light metallic green)
Sebring Red (bright red)
Silver Slate
Snowy White
Vintage Red

There appears also to have been a darker metallic green. In 1980, some vehicles may have been painted in the bright Highway Yellow used on the special-edition 'Game' Land Rover Series III 88-inch Station Wagon, and there may also have been some finished in Olive Green.

There were relatively few changes to the paint colour choices on Range Rovers before the start of the 1980s, when annual changes became the norm as the vehicle was promoted as an alternative to a conventional car. In the accompanying tables, all colours are for UK-built vehicles and dates are approximate. The codes given are those used by British Leyland or Land Rover Ltd.

Decal on the bonnet shut panel are seen on a 1973 Range Rover.

Chapter 4
Chassis

The Range Rover was conceived from the beginning as a sort of luxury Land Rover, and so it inher-
ited from that highly successful vehicle the basic
concept of a box-section ladder-frame chassis with
beam axles. However, its coil-spring suspension
system made for some radical differences from the
older vehicle.

The basic layout of the chassis and suspension
remained the same throughout the production
period covered by this book. The most important
change was to the 'roll-reduced' suspension which
came with the CA-series chassis in October 1985.

Chassis frame

The chassis frame of the Range Rover is a steel
ladder-frame, which in standard form always had

This view of the driveable demonstration chassis now in the Heritage Collection shows
the general layout of the Range Rover chassis. This is not the example built on a pre-
production chassis, but a later, similar one. Note that it has an early aluminium-finish
front bumper and a later black-finished rear one! The roll-over protection hoop,
battery box (behind driver's seat), and wooden ballast box (on right-hand chassis rail)
are all features not found on production models. The blue, white and orange paint used
to highlight various features was also not standard – these items would have been black
on production vehicles.

a wheelbase of 100in. It has box-section side rails
and five box-section cross-members. The second
cross-member is bolted to the side rails in order to
simplify gearbox removal, but the other cross-
members are welded in place. The whole frame is
finished in black enamel, which was applied by
dipping the assembly into a paint bath. Frames

were manufactured by John Thompson (Pressings Division) on a semi-automated assembly line.

The side rails are formed from two channel-section pressings of 0.08in thick steel. The open ends of the two pressings are fitted together so that there is a 0.12in overlap, and the joins are CO_2 welded together to make a box section. The welded joins run along the top and bottom sections of each side rail. The resulting side members are 3in wide, while their depth varies between 3.88in and 6in over the length of the frame.

Welded to these side rails are four body-mounting outriggers and various other mounting brackets. These latter include the spring mountings, the suspension arm mountings, and six more body-mounting brackets, making ten in all. There are two body-mounting brackets at the front, two more to carry the front bulkhead, one on each of the four outriggers, and two more at the rear. In addition, the rear floor is supported by four brackets which are bolted to the side rails; on each side there is one in front of the rear spring mounting and one behind it. When Suffix D chassis were introduced in April 1975, the mounting bosses on the chassis frame were increased in thickness to prevent fouling between body and chassis. Service instructions for fitting a Suffix D or later replacement chassis under an earlier body noted that two additional bottom seat base plates, tie rods, and longer mounting bolts were necessary.

From July 1982, the detachable second cross-member changed, initially to make room for the then-new automatic transmission. The revised cross-member was standardised for both manual and automatic models at this stage. The rear cross-member, always welded to the frame, proved vulnerable to corrosion in service, and was made available as a replacement part.

Four eye brackets for lashing or towing are also bolted to the inner faces of the chassis side rails, two at the front and two at the rear. On early vehicles, the front eyes have a two-bolt fixing, being attached to the dumb irons by the bolts which hold the main bumper support brackets. When the bolts were found to shear in use, the eyes were changed for the single-bolt type used at the rear, and were attached by the lower of the two bumper-support securing bolts. The rear eyes always had a single-bolt fixing, and are attached to a bracket welded to each side member just behind the spring mounting brackets. These brackets are also used to anchor the stay bars of the towing drop-plate when one is fitted.

The side rails sweep up to clear the rear axle, and a damper mounting bracket is bolted to each side. On all Range Rovers built up to the end of the BA-series in September 1985, the left-hand bracket is positioned ahead of the axle and the right-hand bracket behind it; the left-hand

Early front bumpers had a shaped cut-out for the starting handle.

damper is thus angled towards the front of the chassis and the right-hand one towards the rear. This arrangement, usually described as the 'staggered damper' layout, was intended to prevent axle tramp under hard acceleration. On CA-series and all subsequent vehicles, both brackets are located ahead of the axle, and both dampers are angled towards the front of the chassis.

It is worth noting that Land Rover introduced a retro-fit kit of anti-roll bars in 1992. These were designed for vehicles built after October 1985, with the forward-pointing rear dampers. The mounting brackets for the anti-roll bars were supplied with Riv-nuts so that they could be bolted to the chassis side rails, although some garages preferred the security of welding. The anti-roll bars could be fitted to the chassis of earlier vehicles only if the right-hand damper was changed to the forward-pointing type. Changing the location of the mounting bracket on the side rail was straightforward, but the job also demanded a prohibitively expensive change of axle and so was never made an authorised modification.

Axle bump stops made of rubber and bonded to steel carrier plates are bolted to the underside of the chassis side rails above the axles, front and rear. Although these bump stops are similar in appearance, the fronts are not the same as those used at the rear. Neither type changed during the production life of the carburettor Range Rovers.

Front bumper

On models up to the end of the CA-series, the rolled-steel front bumper is bolted to the chassis frame by four brackets. Two are located towards the centre, and these in turn fit over the chassis dumb irons and are each secured by two bolts. These bolts should have their heads towards the centre of the vehicle, while their securing nuts are on the outside of the dumb irons. The other two

Early bumpers had an aluminium paint finish. Over-riders were always fitted at the rear.

Plastic front bumper ends were introduced for 1983.

brackets are made of flat steel with an angled section at each end. One end is bolted to the back of the bumper at its outer end, and the other bolts to the chassis side rail behind the dumb iron. All four bumper brackets are finished in chassis black.

All front bumpers have an angled number-plate mounting bracket bolted to their undersides. This bracket was normally painted black. Parts catalogues list a special bracket for the US market, but it is unlikely that this ever went into production because the plan to sell Range Rovers in the USA did not materialise during the lifetime of the carburettor models.

Three different types of bumper were used on these vehicles, and a fourth on the later DA-series and EA-series chassis. The earliest type has closed ends and is painted in aluminium enamel. The second type, introduced on the 1980 models in September 1979 at AA 100783, also has closed ends but has a chip-resistant satin-black polyester finish. Both these types of bumper have a shaped cut-out for the starting handle. Range Rovers destined for Germany had black rubber over-riders on the bumper ends to meet TUV regulations. The third type was introduced in July 1982, at about

AA 123568, and is once again finished in satin-black polyester. It has shaped ends to accommodate the over-riders which were fitted from that date and, unlike the first two types, has no cut-out for a starting handle. Black plastic over-riders are fitted to each end of the bumper for all markets.

The fourth type of bumper was introduced in November 1986 with the DA-series models. It is pre-drilled for the headlamp power wash system used on high-line models, and when this is not fitted the holes are plugged with plastic blanking plates. The number-plate support bracket is the same as that used on earlier bumpers, but not the same as the one used on contemporary high-line models with the under-bumper spoiler. The power wash system consists on each side of a moulded plastic jet support with a threaded section which passes through the bumper bar and is secured underneath by a nut and washers. The two-piece flexible hose for the power wash system is push-fitted onto the ends of these jets and clipped underneath the bumper. There is a T-piece in the hose on the passenger side, where the main feed tube comes from the washer reservoir.

The two bumper-to-chassis brackets are the same as on earlier vehicles, but there are different brackets at the outer ends for the over-riders. All DA-series and EA-series Range Rovers have large plastic over-riders which wrap around the sides of the front wings. On early models, the over-riders have threaded brass inserts and are attached to black-painted angle brackets. This early type of fixing gave trouble in service: typically, the over-rider would catch on some undergrowth while the vehicle was reversing, and when it was pulled away from the body the bracket would come with it and distort the wing. So from DA 268576, plastic brackets of a different design were fitted, and spring clips were used to hold the over-rider to the bracket.

The paint used on all black bumpers is Berger matt black air-drying enamel, with reference number 416-5108-6.

Rear bumper

The rear bumper is a single-piece steel bar, with two brackets welded on its concave inner surface. A bolt passes through each bracket and attaches the bumper bar to a mounting bracket welded on each side of the rear chassis cross-member.

The rear bumper on all models up to and including the CA-series has an over-rider at each end, bolted through the bumper bar. These over-riders are made of steel except on German-market vehicles (see below). Bumpers and over-riders were finished in aluminium enamel up to AA 100782, and thereafter switched to the same black polyester as the front bumpers. The DA-series and

EA-series vehicles have longer black plastic over-riders to match those at the front. The method of attaching these changed at DA 268576, in the same way as on the front bumper.

A dust seal was added to the rear bumper of the Range Rover Vogue from June 1984, and was probably also fitted as standard on all Range Rovers for markets where dust was prevalent. This seal is a black rubber strip which is held to the bumper by a black retaining strip. The underside of this retaining strip has six pegs which pass through holes drilled in the bumper and into push-fit plastic retainers. The specification of this retaining strip was changed at EA 308282 to counter corrosion troubles with the earlier type.

German TUV regulations demanded rubber over-riders instead of the steel type fitted to Range Rovers for other markets. German lighting regulations in the 1970s also demanded a rectangular red reflector lower down than that on the tail lamp cluster. As a result, Range Rovers for Germany were fitted with special black rubber rear over-riders, with a rectangular reflector plate glued into a recess in the moulding. From AA 100783, when revised tail-lamp clusters were fitted, German vehicles had black rubber over-riders without the reflector.

Fuel tank, pump & pipes

The Range Rover's fuel tank is mounted between the chassis side rails behind the rear axle, and is bolted to the rear cross-member and to the cross-member behind the rear axle. From October 1972, a steel guard plate was made available as an option, but remained rare. The guard plate bolts to the underside of the rear chassis cross-member, and its front fixings are shared with those of the fuel tank, although longer bolts are used.

The outlet pipes are incorporated in the fuel gauge sender unit, which is on the left; the filler neck is on the right. The tank is pressed from steel and holds 19 Imperial gallons (86 litres); it was always painted black. None of these components changed during the production life of the carburettor Range Rover. Suffix F Australian-market models in the 398 chassis series have an additional fuel catch tank at the rear between inner and outer right-hand wings, and this was fitted as standard to all models from EA 308803, except those with an Evaporative Loss Control system.

The filler tube is attached to the tank neck by a rubber hose. Suffix B and later chassis have a different filler tube from Suffix A types; some tubes have one-piece construction, others three-piece. DA-series and later chassis have a different filler neck with a smaller diameter. Petrol leaks from the filler neck were a problem on early vehicles, and in January 1977 a shorter filler tube assembly

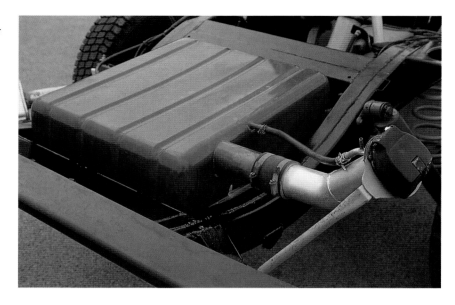

The later type of locking fuel filler cap is seen here on the driveable demonstration chassis. The fuel tank breather pipe is also clearly visible.

The Facet electric fuel pump was normally mounted to the heelboard on the body, but has its own bracketry on the driveable demonstration chassis.

with a spigot location for a thicker seal was fitted, together with a longer rubber connecting sleeve. Then in February 1981, at AA 110552, the end of the breather pipe was swaged to improve the seal between the tube and tank connection.

Vehicles for Italy and (from the early 1980s) Finland have a special breather pipe system for the filler neck, incorporating anti-surge valves.

The fuel pipes run forward from the tank and are clipped to the left-hand chassis side rail. On Range Rovers destined for Sweden, additional securing clips were fitted at all hose and pipe joints. From February 1980, a bracket and clip were mounted to the exhaust tailpipe fixings, in order to maintain the clearance between the fuel pipe and the exhaust tailpipe.

On Suffix A and B chassis for the home market, the fuel pipes run up to a disposable-element fuel filter bolted to the left-hand inner wing close to the coil, and then to an AC-Delco

The Panhard rod which locates the front axle laterally is seen here behind the steering connections.

mechanical pump which is bolted to the engine front cover and operated by the camshaft. From the pump, the pipes run to the left-hand carburettor. On very early vehicles, a plastic-bodied, in-line fuel filter is fitted between pump and carburettor, but this was later deleted as it was deemed unnecessary.

Suffix A and B export chassis, as well as Suffix B home-market chassis with power-assisted steering, have a Bendix electric fuel pump, which is mounted horizontally on a bracket bolted to the left-hand chassis rail. This pump has an integral fuel filter, so there is no separate filter on the inner wing. A radio interference suppresser is also fitted, and foam covers reduce noise.

From Suffix C chassis until the end of the BA-series, all models have an electric fuel pump mounted vertically to the rear face of the rear seat heelboard. Three different types of pump were fitted, probably all made by Facet. The first lasted until August 1981, and the third was introduced on BA-series chassis in June 1984. At AA 116742, shortly after the introduction of the second type, an independent earth tag was added to the pump body with a secondary earth lead to the chassis frame; this doubled up the existing earthing braid. All three types of pump have an integral fuel filter and are fitted with a radio interference suppresser. However, a different type of suppresser is used with the third type of pump.

From the start of the CA-series chassis in October 1985, the fuel pump was mounted inside the tank itself. This is a low-pressure electric type made by AC-Delco.

Since the terminals on the fuel tank sender unit of very early Range Rovers tended to corrode, Bostik 772 was applied to the tank unit and surrounding area from September 1971 approximately. This blue-grey rubberised compound sealed the area and prevented rust forming, and

dealers were encouraged to use it on earlier vehicles as well. The first production vehicles so treated had chassis numbers 355-0937A, 356-00012A and 358-00161A.

For details of the fuel filler cap, see Chapter 3.

Front axle & differential

The same front axle is used on both RHD and LHD Range Rovers. There were several detail modifications during the production life of the carburettor models, and some changes to the differential housing which bolts to the axle casing.

However, the most important change occurred in 1981 with the introduction of the so-called universal hubs on Suffix G axles, beginning with axles numbered 355-37516G and 358-56735G. These hubs have longer wheel studs to suit both steel and alloy wheels; the studs have a larger head and are identifiable by a shallow groove stamped at their thread ends, although the studs on approximately the first 100 axles have a triangle in place of this groove. The new hubs were fitted first to LHD four-door models (at AA 115578), then to RHD two-doors (at AA 115596), LHD two-doors (at AA 115604), and finally to RHD four-doors (at AA 115609).

Another important change took place with the introduction of Suffix H axles. At this stage, metric fixings replaced the Imperial type used on all earlier axles. Note, however, that metric threads for the brakes were introduced earlier, with Suffix F axles. Thus, an axle with Suffix E is all-Imperial; axles with Suffix F or G have Imperial fixings but metric brake components; and an axle with Suffix H or later is all-metric.

The banjo casing, which is offset to the right of the axle, has two threaded plugs. The one in its underside is the oil drain plug, and the one in its face is the filler and level plug. Early axles have a 16-TPI flange-type drain plug and a 14-TPI square-head taper plug for the filler. Later types have the same type of plug in both positions, and this is a BSP taper plug with a recessed head. From axles numbered 355-00574A (RHD) and 358-00036A (LHD) in early 1971, the filler plug was relocated lower down to reduce the oil capacity and thus prevent leaks through the axle breather.

This breather is screwed into the top of the left-hand (longer) side of the axle casing, and on most carburettor models this is a simple vertical metal assembly. However, from vehicle number AA 141700 in January 1984, a remote axle breather is fitted. This has a much shorter plug inserted through a collar connected to a plastic pipe. This pipe runs along the top of the axle and is clipped outside the chassis rail; its open end is curved over and emerges above the chassis.

The differential housing bolted to the rear of

the banjo on the axle casing changed on Suffix H axles, to suit the newly-introduced metric fixings. This housing also has a brass filler plug, which changed from a 14-TPI square-head taper type to a BSP taper plug with a recessed head, at the same time as these plugs were standardised for the axle casing. Behind the differential input flange which bolts to the propshaft are an oil seal and a mud-shield, both of which were improved in July 1985.

At each end of the front axle casing is a swivel pin bearing housing, which looks like a large chromed ball. Its outer end is partially covered by the swivel pin housing, which is the element that actually turns with the steering. On top of this second housing is the upper swivel pin, which is screwed into the steering lever; the bottom swivel pin is fixed. Inside the swivel pin bearing housing, the axle drive-shaft is divided into two by a Hardy Spicer joint. Drive is taken to a hub assembly, to which the road wheel is bolted.

Pre-packed hub bearings were introduced in about September 1971 after there had been some early cases of leakage. These entered production at axle numbers 355-01947A (RHD) and 359-00232A (LHD). Slightly earlier, at axle numbers 355-01600A (RHD) and 358-00232A (LHD), the front hub oil seals had been fitted with a mud shield, which also acted as a lock washer and superseded the separate lock washers and plain washers on earlier axles.

A single hub oil seal is fitted to all vehicles built before October 1979. The earliest type of seal proved unsatisfactory and was replaced by a leather type in June 1972, at axle numbers 355-03865A (RHD) and 358-01045A (LHD). The leather seals then gave way to dual-lip types made of nitrile rubber in November 1979 at axles 355-30456 (RHD) and 358-43899 (LHD). A further change was made in September 1985, with effect from axle numbers 355-54972J (RHD) and 358-88282J (LHD), when a new Simrit dual wiper lip inner hub seal was used in conjunction with an outer seal, while a seal track spacer, adjusting nuts and tab washers were all added. These changes coincided with the introduction of new stub axles and hub assemblies.

The internals of the differential were modified when the Suffix C chassis entered production in November 1973, in order to improve fatigue resistance. The shapes of the differential wheel and pinion were modified and the wheel's retention on the cross-shaft was improved. Better lubrication was also provided, and the clamping of crownwheel to casing was improved. Much later, in January 1983, the differential carrier bearings were changed as part of a rationalisation scheme. From axles 355-37737H (RHD) and 358-57253H (LHD), they were commonised with those used in Land Rover axles.

The front axle locating arms are known as C-spanners because of the distinctive shape of their forward ends, which fit around the axle casing. The right-hand one is seen here in place.

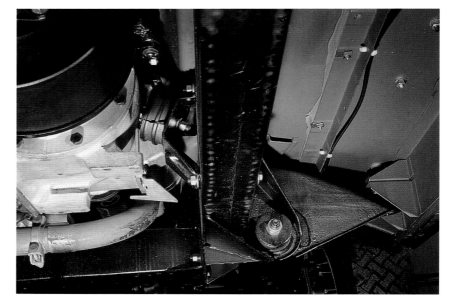

Front suspension

The front axle is located fore-and-aft by two leading links or radius arms, and sideways location is provided by a Panhard rod. The C-shaped front ends of the radius arms are bolted to the axle casing at two points through rubber bushes. Their rear ends are bolted through a rubber bush to a bracket welded to the chassis side rail. With the introduction of the DA-series chassis in November 1986, new mounting bushes were introduced at the axle end of the radius arms. These had a stiffer inner tube, designed to reduce knocking noises from the suspension. An earlier Service modification, announced in February 1986, also suggested using the shorter Land Rover type of fixing bolts to give better access to the securing nuts for these bushes.

This view – of YVB 151H – shows the right-hand gearbox mounting and the rear mounting of the front axle locating arm.

FRONT SPRING SPECIFICATIONS

Application	Type	Part no	Rating	Identification
All RHD	Standard	572315	133lb in	Blue stripe
	Heavy duty	NRC 2119	150lb in	Green stripe
LHD to 358-55584F	Standard	572315	133lb in	Blue stripe
	Heavy duty	NRC 2119	150lb in	Green stripe
LHD from 358-55585F	Standard, RH side	572315	133lb in	Blue stripe
	Standard, LH side	NRC 4306	133lb in	Blue & white stripe
	Heavy duty, RH side	NRC 2119	150lb in	Green stripe
	Heavy duty, LH side	NRC 4305	150lb in	Red & yellow stripe

acts as the top mounting point for the damper. The tower is attached to the chassis by nuts on the studs welded to a ring which is fitted to the underside of the spring mounting point. The top of the coil spring engages in the spring mounting point, and its bottom is located by a spring seat bolted to the axle casing; the damper bottom mounting attaches to the axle casing here.

The first change to the front dampers was made when roll-reduced suspension was introduced on CA-series chassis: new dampers accompanied a change in the front springs. Only one further change was made to the front dampers, and that was at DA 313049 when improved internal seals were fitted to reduce noise.

There were several different types of road spring, as detailed in the accompanying table. Note that heavy-duty springs were normally used only when the front axle load regularly exceeded 1200kg (for example, when a winch was fitted).

Rear axle & differential

The rear axle uses the same differential and differential housing as the front axle, but is otherwise different. Its banjo housing is on the right, and there is a large welded mounting for the self-levelling strut. The leading face of the casing carries brackets for the trailing arms, and there are damper mounting brackets welded to the outer ends of the casing. On axles up to and including 355-25693G in October 1985, the left-hand bracket is in front of the axle and the right-hand bracket behind, to suit the staggered damper arrangement. On later axles, both brackets are welded to the front face of the axle.

Rear axle suffixes do not match those used on the front axles. The change to universal hubs in 1981 was made as the axle suffix changed to E; the first axle to have them was 355-94371E, and the change took place at the same vehicle numbers as the corresponding change to the front axle.

Metric fixings replaced the Imperial type at axle suffix F. Metric threads for the brakes, however, were introduced on suffix D axles. Thus, a rear axle with suffix C is all-Imperial; axles with suffixes D and E have Imperial fixings but metric brake components; and an axle with suffix F or later is all-metric.

As on the front axle, the filler and level plugs changed from 16-TPI types to BSP types with a recessed head. The same plug changes took place on the differential housing, and the remote breather arrived at the same time in January 1984. The breather tube runs along the left-hand side of the suspension. A-frame, emerges on the crossmember ahead of the axle, and is clipped in place.

Very early on, at axle number 355-01842A, the mudshields at the outer ends of the axle were

The Panhard rods used on RHD and LHD vehicles are mirror images of one another, and are fitted on the same side of the chassis as the steering. The axle end of the Panhard rod bolts into the radius arm mounting on the axle casing, leaving the corresponding mounting on the other side of the axle unused. The chassis end of the rod is mounted to a drop bracket attached to the side rail on the appropriate side of the chassis; on later vehicles this drop bracket also incorporates the steering box stiffener tie rod. All chassis were made with a mounting for this drop bracket on both sides to simplify manufacture, so there is always one mounting tube left unused. From the start of CA-series production, the Land Rover 110 type of Panhard rod is used, as part of the so-called roll-reduced suspension.

The front coil springs and dampers are concentric. A conical tower is bolted to the spring mounting point on the chassis, and the top of this

The front suspension turret and its fixings are visible in this view of the left-hand front road wheel. Note the early type of power steering reservoir, just visible on the left.

changed to a type which incorporated lock-washer tabs. The three separate lock-washer plates used at each end of early axles were therefore no longer needed. This change was made at the same time as the corresponding one affecting the front axle. Two types of rubber axle oil seal were used, one 8mm thick and the other 12mm thick. The 8mm type was used on early axles with a sleeve between bearing and oil seal. This sleeve is not present when the later 12mm type is used.

Pre-packed hub bearings were introduced at the same time as they became standard on the front axle, in about September 1971 from axle number 355-02037A. Leather hub seals were introduced at axle number 355-04904A in June 1972, and they were replaced by nitrile rubber seals at the same time as this change was made for the front axle; the first rear axle to have the new seals was 355-74564 in November 1979. As on the front axle, Simrit inner seals with additional outer seals and new hub assemblies were fitted in September 1985, from axle number 355-43042H.

The internals of the differential were modified in the same way as those of the front axle differential when the Suffix C chassis entered production in November 1973. The differential carrier bearings were commonised with the Land Rover type at axle number 355-95080F in January 1983. Then, in July 1985, various changes affected the rear axle: hubs, stub axles, mudshields, inner and outer hub seals, lock-washers and lock-nuts were all changed, and seal track spacers were added.

Rear suspension

The rear axle is located fore-and-aft by two trailing links or radius arms, and sideways location is provided by an A-bracket or wishbone assembly. The leading end of each radius arm is bolted to a bracket on the chassis through a rubber bush, and its trailing end is bolted to the axle casing with a single cylindrical rubber bush. A Boge Hydromat self-levelling strut mounted between the rear axle and the chassis maintains a constant ride height at the rear even when the vehicle is heavily laden, thus permitting softer rear springs and consequently a more comfortable ride.

With the arrival of roll-reduced suspension on CA-series models in September 1985, revised bottom link assembles were used, together with dual-rate springs and new dampers. The right-hand damper, which points backwards on models to the end of the BA-series, was also changed to point forwards in parallel to the left-hand damper.

The A-bracket actually consists of two separate arms, joined at the point of the A by a fulcrum bracket attached to the axle casing. The other ends of the A-bracket arms pivot from the third chassis cross-member. Between a bracket on this

Clearly visible here are the rear suspension A-frame (in blue), the Boge self-levelling strut (orange) and the early type of staggered damper arrangement, with the upper mounting of the left-hand damper ahead of the axle and that for the right-hand damper behind it.

The damper mounting on the axle casing was ahead of the axle on the left-hand side; also visible here is the disc brake.

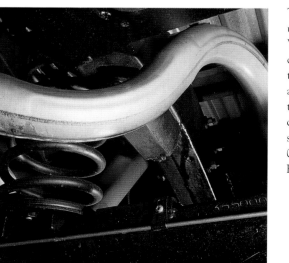

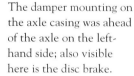

The exhaust pipe loops up to clear the rear axle. Visible here are the corrugated underside of the load area floor, the axle bump stop bolted to the underside of the chassis rail, and the axle serial number (355-00001A – this is Range Rover number 1).

In real colours this time on Range Rover number 1, this is the forward mounting for the right-hand trailing arm on the rear axle. Note also the outrigger which carries the body mounting.

The rear right-hand road spring, upper mounting and lower clamping plate are seen here, as is the trailing arm attachment on the rear axle.

cross-member and the fulcrum bracket at the point of the A on the axle is the self-levelling strut. A rubber bellows-type seal at the lower end of the strut is held in position by spring rings, while the rubber seal at the top of the strut has a spring ring at its top end but a large Jubilee clip where it meets the body of the strut. The bonding between the lower (rear) link flexible bush and the centre plate was improved at EA 309201, and

a sealed-for-life ball joint on the upper link was introduced at EA 329885 in 1988.

The early self-leveller has a black body and was used on all models up to chassis serial number 53045F in 1979; thereafter a different type with a blue body was fitted. A further change to the self-levelling unit was made at axle number 355-55585F in July 1979, to suit the higher-rate rear springs and new tyre pressures introduced then.

Rear springs are located at the top in mounting brackets on the chassis, and at the bottom on spring seats bolted to the axle casing. These spring seats are the same as those used on the front axle. As on the front, there were several different springs, as detailed in the accompanying table.

On all models to the end of the BA-series, the rear dampers are 'staggered': the left-hand damper points forwards and the right-hand damper points rearwards. This design was adopted to prevent axle tramp under hard acceleration.

Damper locations were altered on CA-series and later models, starting in October 1985 (it has been impossible to verify an assertion in Service literature that the change was actually introduced in January 1985). On these later chassis, both dampers point forwards. The change was made to improve the life of the damper bushes and to reduce axle twist through bump and rebound conditions. As on the front axle, the rear damper seals were improved to reduce noise at DA 313049.

Steering

Range Rover steering was always a recirculating ball, worm and nut system, initially without power assistance. As it was unacceptably heavy on the earliest models, the ratio was lowered in April 1972. Power assistance then became optional in January 1973 with the introduction of the Suffix B chassis, but did not become standardised until

REAR SPRING SPECIFICATIONS

Application	Type	Part no	Rating	Identification
To 9/76	Standard	90 575625	?	Yellow stripe
	Heavy duty	620101[1]	170lb in	Yellow & white/& red, or/& blue stripes
9/76 to 358-55584F	Standard	NRC 2119	150lb in	Green stripe
	Heavy duty	NRC 4304	170lb in	Red & white stripe
RHD, from 355-55585F	Standard	NRC 4304	170lb in	Red & white stripe
LHD, from 358-55585F	Standard, LH side	NRC 4304	170lb in	Red & white stripe
	Standard, RH side	NRC 4234	170lb in	Green & yellow stripe
RHD, from AA 112533 (4-door), and AA 113743 (2-door)	Standard	NRC 2119	150lb in	Green stripe
	Heavy duty	NRC 4304	170lb in	Red & white stripe
LHD, from AA 112533 (4-door) and AA 113743 (2-door)	Standard, LH side	NRC 4305	150lb in	Not known
	Standard, RH side	NRC 2119[2]	150lb in	Green stripe
	Heavy duty, LH side	NRC 4304	170lb in	Red & white stripe
	Heavy duty, RH side	NRC 4234	170lb in	Green & yellow stripe
CA-series	Dual-rate springs	Not known	127/180lb in	Not known
RHD DA-series and later	Standard	NRC 8113	178.2lb in	Pink & purple stripe
LHD DA-series and later	Standard, RH side	NRC 8113	178.2lb in	Pink & purple stripe
	Standard, LH side	NRC 8477[3]	178.2lb in	Green & pink stripe

[1] Spring number 620101 was supplied in three grades: Low grade springs had a yellow vertical stripe with a red horizontal stripe; Medium grade springs had a yellow vertical stripe with a white horizontal stripe; and High grade springs had a yellow vertical stripe with a blue horizontal stripe. These springs were all replaced by NRC 4304, which represented the Medium grade and carried its colour coding.
[2] Recommended replacement in later years. [3] Early LHD models have NRC 8113 on both sides. NRC 8477 was replaced in May 1988 by NTC 3285, with the same colour coding and rating.

September 1979. Although the basic layout of the steering remained unaltered during production, most components were changed more than once.

The basic layout uses a steering box mounted on the side rail at the front of the chassis, on the same side as the steering wheel. Inputs from the steering column are transferred to a drop arm underneath the steering box, movement in turn being transmitted to a cross-rod running below the chassis. This cross-rod has adjustable ends to facilitate assembly, and is connected to the wheel hub on the opposite side. The track rod runs behind it and connects the hubs on opposite sides; this also has adjustable ends, which in this case are used to set the correct tracking or toe-out of the wheels. All connections on the steering rods are made by ball joints. Mounted horizontally between track rod and final drive housing is a hydraulic steering damper, an item that did not change during production of carburettor models.

Imperial (UNF) ball joint fixings were used on the steering drop arm of Suffix A and Suffix B chassis. From the beginning of Suffix C production, however, metric ball joint fixings were used. The drop arm changed again at AA 132294 (LHD) and AA 137736 (RHD) during 1983. The steering cross-rod and track rod ends also changed from UNF to metric, but this time the change was made at axle suffix C rather than chassis suffix C. With the introduction of the suffix D front axles in August 1979 came a new cross-rod end which was not interchangeable with earlier types, and the Service recommendation was therefore to replace the complete cross-rod assembly in cases of need. The new cross-rod end had a 2in plain portion on the threaded shank of the cross-rod eye and a new cross-rod was introduced to suit.

Other minor modifications were made over the years. Very early in production, in November 1970, the material specification of the steering rod ball joint clip was changed to prevent distortion, and slots were added to all steering linkage tubes. The original track rod adjusting shaft had a machined thread and a single groove machined in the shank, but this was changed in September 1979 for a shaft with a rolled thread and two grooves machined in the shank.

The early manual steering box was made by Burman and had an 18.2:1 ratio, giving 3.75 turns of the steering wheel from lock to lock. It was characterised by a square-headed oil filler plug, and had no tie-bar to steady it against the chassis. The later, lower-ratio box had a 20.55:1 ratio which gave 4.75 turns of the wheel from lock to lock, and this became the recommended Service replacement for the earlier type. This lower-ratio box has a hexagon-head oil filler plug, and is steadied against the chassis by a tie-bar. The tie-bar differs between RHD and LHD vehicles, and

the worm-shaft and main nut assembly on both types of box also differ between RHD and LHD.

This second type of steering box was used on all Range Rovers without power steering up to AA 135737 in 1983. Thereafter, supplies of Burman manual steering boxes were supplemented by a ZF Gemmer type. This German-made box has a very different appearance, with a lid strengthened by external flanges and with a hexagon-head filler plug on top. It was possible to fit the ZF steering box retrospectively to earlier vehicles (up to AA 101677) only if the lower steering column was changed to the later type.

The power-assisted steering system for the Range Rover is made by Adwest, and consists of a special steering box with hydraulic connections, a pump mounted on brackets on the left-hand side of the engine, an oil reservoir mounted on the left-hand inner wing, and a series of high-pressure hoses connecting these components. The steering box is handed to suit RHD or LHD, and has a tie-bar to steady it against the chassis. Some boxes have their lids attached by nuts on studs, while others have bolt fixings. All the early boxes have Imperial dimensions, and are recognisable by the four bolts that retain their top covers. They were replaced on later models by metric steering boxes, which have only three bolts.

Fluid leaks from these steering boxes were a perennial problem. Early in 1986, at CA 264760, a polished sector shaft was introduced in an attempt to cure the problem. Then at DA 293802, the material specification of the seals was changed to improve their durability.

The power steering pump is driven by a second rubber belt from the crankshaft pulley, and its upper bracket is adjustable to maintain the correct belt tension. On vehicles with air conditioning, the pump has a dual pulley, and a third drive belt runs from this to the air conditioning compressor. The early type of pump is a 30-series, and is used on all carburettor models up to the start of the 1988 model year approximately. The final engine numbers for this pump are 26D-01083C, 27D-00249C, 28D-00129C, 29D-00029C and 30D-00014C. Later carburettor models presumably used the 200-series pump, which by then was

Normally black rather than green, the early Imperial steering box (far left) has four bolts on its lid. The later power steering box (left) has only three bolts.

already standard on fuel-injected models.

The oil reservoir on early models is a black metal cylinder with its knurled filler cap offset to one side; it is mounted on a bracket attached to the left-hand inner wing. Later models have a different type of reservoir, which is once again a black metal cylinder but has a much larger filler cap in the centre. In October 1984, at BA 149766, the manufacturing process was changed, and the reservoir was sprayed with its cap in place, so that paint did not clog up the threads and cause the cap to stick. From CA 266319, a third type of reservoir was introduced; this is made of plastic and has a black screw cap with moulded ZF logo.

Black hoses run from reservoir to pump, from pump to steering box, and from steering box to reservoir. These hoses are held together by two black rubber 'Christmas tree' cleats, and are attached to the inner wing by three P-clips. Fluid tended to leak from a fibre sealing washer on the banjo connection at the pump on early vehicles, so this sealing washer was replaced by a copper crimp type at chassis number BA 158317.

The steering column consists of top and bottom shafts linked by a universal joint assembly. In January 1975, the steering column top bearing and housing were changed, the later type not having the locating lugs that are evident on the early type. A larger-diameter top bearing was fitted in March 1980 at AA 101678, and at the same time there was a new steering shaft assembly incorporating a flexible rubber coupling.

The lower steering column provides the inputs to the steering box, and three different types were used. The earliest type has all-metal universal joints at both ends, and was used on vehicles with power steering up to AA 101677 in 1979 and on those with manual steering up to AA 105755 in 1980. Subsequent lower steering columns have an upper universal joint assembly with rubber couplings, which were introduced either to allow more longitudinal deflection of the shaft (according to Service literature) or to reduce the transmission of hydraulic hiss into the passenger compartment (according to Range Rover Project Engineer Geof Miller). The length of the rubber coupling and UJ assembly for manual steering is 324mm, but the power steering equivalent is longer, at 365mm. This longer third type was then fitted to vehicles with manual steering as well from some time in 1983.

Braking

Disc brakes are fitted on all four wheels, with vacuum servo assistance. The front brakes have a dual hydraulic circuit, the primary circuit operating with the rear brakes and the secondary circuit providing fail-safe operation. There is a pressure-apportioning valve in the circuit to the rear brakes. The parking brake does not operate on the rear wheels but rather on the rear output shaft of the transfer gearbox. It is an expanding drum-type brake. Except where otherwise stated, all braking components are of Lockheed manufacture.

Imperial threads were used until about May 1981, when all braking components changed to metric threads. The metric brakes were fitted to four-door Range Rovers from the start of production, but did not reach two-door models until shortly afterwards. The commencing VINs were as follows: AA 112529 (RHD, four-door), AA 112532 (LHD, four-door), AA 112612 (LHD, two-door) and AA 112672 (RHD, two-door). These coincided with the introduction of suffix F front and suffix D rear axles.

From the start, the Range Rover was intended to have a Lockheed 2/50 servo. However, the first 569 vehicles built actually had an American-manufactured Bendix servo, which quickly became unavailable as a service replacement. The Bendix servo can be recognised by the style of its casing, which has four 'spokes' on the front, crenellations around the circumference, and a square flange for the master cylinder mounting.

The Lockheed servo (latterly manufactured by Automotive Products as a Type 100) is finished in aluminium colour, and there are minor differences for LHD and RHD. The tandem master cylinder is bolted to a circular flange on the nose of the servo, and carries a translucent plastic reservoir on top. On vehicles fitted with an Imperial-thread braking system, the flange on the master cylinder is oriented vertically, so that it bolts to the servo above and below. On vehicles with a metric braking system, the servo is turned through 90° and the master cylinder flange is oriented horizontally, so that the bolts are on either side. The servo has a yellow label reading 'Warning. This Equipment has Metric Fixings'.

The metric master cylinder has a bronzed finish, as a further aid to prevent Imperial and metric components being inadvertently mixed. It also has a Pressure Differential Warning Actuator in its nose, under a hexagon-headed cap. A larger-bore master cylinder was introduced at AA 116654 in October 1981.

Just before the start of the 1988 model year, at DA 301158, a Girling type 115 servo and master cylinder were introduced. This servo is much slimmer, and has a black-painted casing.

On all models with Imperial brake threads from September 1979, and on some earlier export types, the servo is fitted with a vacuum loss indicator switch, which is connected to a warning lamp on the dashboard. Range Rovers with metric braking systems were not fitted with this switch and warning lamp. On vehicles up to AA 100782, the switch is connected to the main harness by a separate cable which is held to the bulkhead by two P-clips. From AA 100783, however, the wiring for the vacuum loss switch is incorporated in the main harness.

On Australian-market models up to AA 100782, the vacuum loss indicator and parking brake warning lamp circuits are integrated, so there is a different and more complex wiring harness for the system. When the wiring for the vacuum loss switch was incorporated in the main harness, however, the parking brake lamp was separated from it and was operated by a plunger switch under the handbrake lever. Australian Design Regulations (ADRs) also demanded a diverter valve in place of the standard non-return valve at the manifold end of the servo vacuum pipe, and this was fitted from engine suffix F.

The brake discs are solid, the front ones being of 11.75in (298mm) diameter and the rears 11.42in (290mm). Front and rear calipers are both Lockheed 26C types, but those at the front have four pistons to suit the dual-circuit hydraulic system, while those at the rear have only two pistons. The lock-washers on front and rear brakes were replaced by spring washers in March 1976 during a temporary supply shortage.

The original brake pads had Ferodo 2430F friction material, but an improved pad with a new synthetic rubber mix friction material was introduced at AA 196165 in summer 1980, and Don 230 pads were used after the metrication of the braking system in May 1981. On early vehicles the rear pads had clip-on anti-squeal shims, but from September 1984 production pads had an anti-squeal gasket bonded to their rear faces. Brake pad wear indicators were standardised at the start of CA-series production in October 1985. Wired to a warning lamp on the instrument panel, these consist of metal contacts buried in the pad which are not exposed until the pad is well worn: the circuit is completed when the exposed contacts touch the brake disc, and the lamp illuminates. The front indicator is always on the inboard right-hand pad, but the rear indicator is on the inboard right-hand pad on RHD vehicles and on the inboard left-hand pad on LHD models.

The brake pipes and flexible hoses are identical on RHD and LHD models, but the pipes from master cylinder to front brake cylinders differ to suit the different position of the master cylinder. All pipes and hoses differ between the Imperial and metric braking systems.

A distribution block is fitted into the hydraulic lines for the right-hand front brakes. On early Range Rovers, the block is a five-way distributor with an electrical connector, and it is mounted horizontally on the right-hand inner wing panel. Vehicles with Imperial-thread braking systems

The front right-hand brake, ball swivel and dual brake pipes are seen here. Also visible are the road spring with its concentric damper and the steering track rod.

Brake pipes are clipped to the rear axle casing, and the springs have colour-coded paint stripes. This shows the left-hand rear of YVB 151H.

from 356-39517D (Australia) and 358-40905D (all other markets, including RHD) have a different block, which is mounted vertically and has a pressure-loss switch screwed into its top surface.

From March 1979, at chassis serial number 48402, the rear hydraulic circuit on Range Rovers with the Imperial-thread braking system incorporates a pressure-reducing valve, which is designed to prevent a skid by reducing pressure to the rear brakes when there is a heavy load on the front. This valve had earlier been standard on vehicles for Holland and Germany. On models for Sweden,

The flange by which the Imperial master cylinder (right) is secured to the servo is oriented vertically, while the Metric type (below right) has the flange oriented horizontally to avoid confusion.

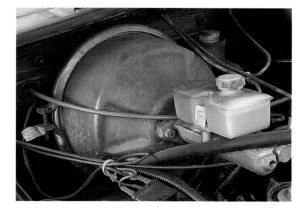

an additional retainer plate for the main front-to-rear hydraulic pipe is pop-riveted to the chassis.

On vehicles with the metric braking system, the distribution block is combined with a pressure-reducing valve, and the new unit is once again mounted on the right-hand inner wing panel. An O-ring seal was added between the body and end seal of this valve at AA 101853 in March 1980, and a new type of valve was introduced at the start of the DA-series in November 1986. Range Rovers with metric braking systems also have two push-fit rubber buffer blocks on the hydraulic pipes running across the bulkhead, in place of the metal clips used with the Imperial braking system. These pipes changed slightly at the introduction of BA-series chassis in June 1984, as did the main front-to-rear hydraulic pipe.

Mudshields are fitted behind all four brakes, and should be finished in black paint. Both front and rear types are handed, the fronts being very much smaller. Early rear mudshields are attached with nuts and bolts; later examples have nuts welded on their insides and therefore are attached with bolts only. Suffix A chassis have shields which only partially envelop the disc, but Suffix B and later chassis have shields which are all-enveloping, mainly as a way of extending pad life.

Two-piece shields, offering better protection from abrasive spray and slurry, were fitted from approximately November 1974 on Range Rovers for Finland, Norway and Sweden. They consist of

The early type of rear brake splash guard is seen here on YVB 151H.

a flared disc shield with a Durestos caliper side cover. These two-piece shields were also fitted to UK Police-specification models. Three-piece shields, which completely encircled the brake disc, were fitted on all vehicles for Iceland, and these three-piece shields were later also fitted to Range Rovers sold in Sweden. The three-piece shields could not be used in warm climates because they reduced the airflow around the brakes, which led to excessive heat build-up.

The transmission brake on all four-speed models is a 7.25in (184mm) diameter drum with a width of 3in (76mm). The later automatic and five-speed types have a completely different transmission brake, with no common components.

Wheels

The standard steel wheel on all Range Rovers of this period was a Rostyle design of size 6Kx16. This was finished in Polychromatic Aluminium paint; an alternative recommended for Service use was BLMC Light Silver. Early and late versions of the wheel differ. Early wheels, for use on axles not designed to take the alloy wheel option (ie, front axles with suffixes A to F and rear axles with suffixes A to D), have a central hole of about 60mm diameter; these have part number 598690. Later types, with part number NRC 3283, have a larger central hole, of about 70mm diameter.

These central holes were never filled on the earlier wheels. However, on the In Vogue two-door limited edition introduced in February 1981, they were fitted with black plastic caps bearing the Range Rover name. These same caps were always fitted to the alloy wheels which became optional shortly afterwards and were standard on some models. The name on these caps was not picked out in white paint as it was on some later vehicles.

A three-spoke alloy wheel option was announced in summer 1981, and could be fitted to all models with the universal hubs which were introduced at AA 115578. The original plan had been to fit these wheels to the In Vogue special edition, but supplies were not available in time. These wheels were size 7Kx16, and had a polished metal finish when supplied as optional equipment. However, for the In Vogue special editions of 1982 and 1983, and for the line-production Vogue introduced in June 1984, they were finished in light grey enamel.

In October 1985, at the start of CA-series production, a second version of this wheel was introduced, with an asymmetric rim hump intended to improve the retention of a deflated tyre. This wheel was designed to suit tubeless tyres only, and had a smaller hole for the tyre valve to suit the type normally specified with tubeless tyres.

All wheels have a five-nut fixing. Steel wheels

Early Rostyle steel wheels have a small central aperture (far left), whereas the later type (near left) was designed for the 'universal' hubs. The visible part of the hub would not have been painted to match the wheel when the vehicle was new.

always have the same 16mm nuts with a convex face on the side next to the wheel. However, the alloy wheels have much larger nuts, with a long hexagonal head, a rotating captive washer, and an insert that passes through the wheel and locates it. Locking wheel nuts for the alloy wheels were made available through Land Rover Parts in 1990. These consist of a nut body and a dummy press-fit head made of sheet metal, and are fitted one per wheel. The nut body is shaped to fit an insert or 'key' with a hexagonal head like that of a standard wheel nut, and cannot be removed without this insert. Several different 'key' patterns were used, to maximise the theft deterrent.

Tyres

The carburettor Range Rovers were supplied with 205x16 tubed radial tyres; tubeless tyres were available as original equipment on fuel-injected models with alloy wheels.

From the beginning, the original equipment tyres were either Michelin X M+S or Firestone Town and Country. For Sweden, the standard tyre was a Michelin X M+S reinforced type. From approximately September 1979, Goodyear G800 Wingfoot tyres were introduced alongside the earlier types as original equipment, although by July 1983 these were listed as optional equipment for overseas markets only.

Tyre pressure recommendations varied over the years, partly for safety reasons and partly because of the changing weight of the vehicle. The original recommendation in 1970 was 25psi front and rear, with 35psi in the rear tyres when travelling fully laden. In July 1979, the recommendations were changed to 25psi at the front and 35psi at the rear under all conditions – mainly because owners rarely bothered to pump up the rear tyres before loading the vehicle to its

Three-spoke alloy wheels were introduced in 1981. This is the grey enamelled type; standard wheels of the time were unpainted and their centre caps did not have the Range Rover logo picked out in white. The stamping on the rim just above the tyre valve makes clear this wheel is for use with tubed tyres; a different stamping (below) is found on a wheel that can be used with tubeless tyres.

maximum. In July 1982, Service literature recommended reducing the rear tyres to 25psi for comfort if the rear axle load did not exceed 1250kg. Finally, in June 1984, the recommended pressures were increased to 28psi (front) and 38psi (rear) for sustained motoring at 60mph or more – in other words, for all practical everyday uses.

Chapter 5

Interior Trim

The interior underwent more changes than any other area as the Range Rover moved from the glorified Land Rover of 1970 to the luxury car of the mid-1980s. These changes are extremely complicated to follow, so to avoid confusion this chapter – as with the next chapter about the facia, instruments and controls – sets out the original Suffix A specification in detail and follows with the changes made for each successive variant.

Suffix A

Seats & safety belts

The seats on Suffix A Range Rovers are upholstered in PVC, in a beige colour called Palomino. The front seats have just three large pleats running front to back on the cushion and vertically on the squab. Although it looks tough, this PVC material is notorious for cracking and splitting. New seats have been unavailable for some time, and replacement secondhand seats in good condition are extremely hard to find.

Each seat is mounted on a metal plinth, painted in Palomino to match the upholstery. The outboard edge of each plinth has a moulded Palomino PVC finisher. On the outboard side of the metal seat slide is a black label which gives details of the safety belt's compliance with regulations in force at the time.

The front seats have fixed backrest rake, but the backrest folds forwards to allow access to the rear seats. The backrest pivots are concealed on both inboard and outboard sides by moulded plastic covers, again in Palomino. The detachable rear panel of the backrest is covered in Palomino PVC, and is retained by plastic peg fixings. There is fore-and-aft adjustment of the cushion on slides that are locked and released by a bar under the cushion. A single black release handle, on the inboard edge of each seat, releases the backrest and allows the seat to slide forwards. Note that a November 1971 Service Bulletin advises that the pivot bolt can be removed from the fixed passenger seat to allow normal fore-and-aft adjustment; alternatively, the bolt can be moved to the rear hole to give more legroom.

Static safety belts are fitted, with black

Upholstery changed several times over the years. This is the original PVC type, with broad pleats.

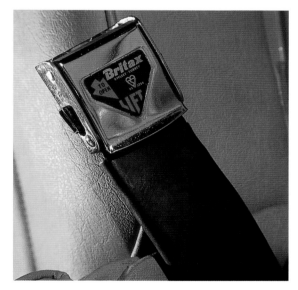

Early Britax seat belts needed both hands to buckle and unbuckle.

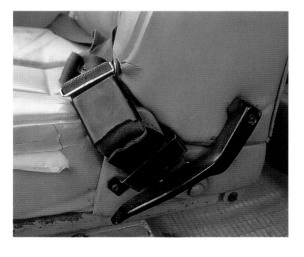

Belt guide is screwed to the seat, and belt has a plastic sheath – which has broken. The cracking and tearing of the PVC seat material on this 1973 model is typical.

webbing. The belt buckle is carried on a long tongue of webbing which is sheathed in black plastic and runs through a guide attached to the seat. These belts need both hands to be buckled or unbuckled. When not in use, the belt tongue fits over a plastic peg on top of the seat, and this acts as a keep for the belt.

Three different types of belt were fitted. The first type was specified for the UK, Austria, Eire, Greece, Italy, Portugal and Switzerland; the second for Denmark and Germany; and the third for Belgium, Holland and France. It is not clear what the differences were.

The rear seat is designed to fold forwards to increase the rear load space. Its backrest pivots on

the cushion, and the cushion pivots forwards on brackets attached to the floor on either side. Backrest and cushion are carried in metal trays that are painted in Palomino to match the interior. In the lower centre of the cushion is a webbing strap with a hook, which holds the seat still when it is folded forwards. There are three rubber buffers under the cushion tray. Under a metal cover plate running across the rear of the backrest is the locking mechanism, with an operating lever in the centre. A striker on each end of long bars running under this cover plate engages with a catch plate screwed to the body side, and the backrest is supported by a bracket on each side of the body, with a housing and a rubber stop.

Seats on Suffix A models had only inboard release handles. Note the 'tram lines' on the side panel of the nearer seat, where the door handles have pressed against it. The fire extinguisher was not a standard fit.

Early type of seat backs, (left) seen on Range Rover number 1, are plain. In the view of the PVC-upholstered rear bench seat (below), note how the black boot floor trim is visible under the front edge, while the leading edges of the wheelarches remain untrimmed. The early type of PVC floor covering is also visible, with its metal retaining bar held to the floor by plastic studs.

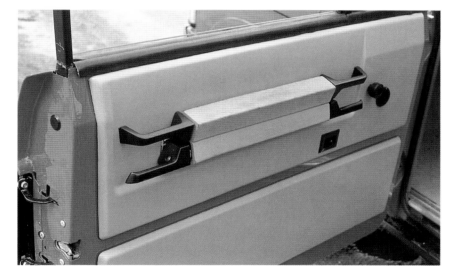

Two-door models had this arrangement of interior handles: the upper two are fixed, the lower two release the catch. Seen here on a pre-production model, door trim pads rarely fitted this well in production. Later vehicles had carpet on the lower section.

Doors

The door trims consist of two pieces, these being upper and lower sections. The metal of the inner door structure is exposed to a large extent, and is painted to match the exterior of the body. Both upper and lower door trim pads are trimmed in Palomino grained leathercloth, and both are attached to the door by plastic stud-type fixings. Behind both upper and lower trim pads, a clear polythene membrane (for water- and draught-proofing) should be stuck to the metal of the door. Door seals are moulded from black rubber and are a push-fit into retaining channels on the body side frame. The bottom of each seal has an additional moulding which fits under the sill kick-plate.

There is a one-piece plastic moulding over the door handles, and this moulding is the same on both doors. Pairs of handles protrude from the front and rear of this. All four are made of alloy and are painted black. The upper handle is fixed and acts as a door pull, while the lower is moveable and releases the door catch. Located just ahead of the door release handle, the window winder has its shank and knurled knob made of black plastic. The locking catch is a sliding knob in a black plastic bezel, below and ahead of the front pair of handles.

Headlining & pillars

The headlining is in two pieces, with a Palomino PVC covering on a moulded backing pad. The two sections meet around the single interior lamp, just above the front seats. The rear section of the headlining has a cut-out in the centre to clear a lip on the tailgate frame, and the front section is held in place by a black plastic grab handle above each door. Each handle has a movable coat hook and is retained by four screws, which are concealed by sliding covers. The interior light and courtesy switches are covered in Chapter 9.

The sun visors are covered in Palomino PVC to match the upholstery. Each has a black metal pivot attached to the outer corner of the roof by a triangular plate with three screws. There is an additional black plastic mounting in the middle, behind the rear-view mirror. Vehicles for Australia and New Zealand have special sun visors. The windscreen pillars each have a dark grey moulded plastic cover panel, which is secured on all models by three metal spring clips. The B/C-pillar has two trim pads, one above waist level and the other below it, both secured by plastic stud fixings and trimmed in Palomino grained leather-cloth. Moulded ABS plastic covers in Palomino beige are fitted over the rear quarter pillars and air vents. They have two screw fixings and a black sliding knob to open and close the vent louvres behind the panel.

Further trim pads are fitted to the rear body sides, on either side of the rear seat. These are once again covered in grained Palomino leather-cloth and secured by plastic stud clips.

Floor coverings

The Range Rover interior was originally designed so that it could be hosed out, and to that end the floor trims were made of PVC to match the seats. The passenger compartment flooring is in four sections: two footwell mats, a rear floor mat and a transmission tunnel cover.

The three floor sections have a grid pattern moulded into the main wearing area. The footwell mats are differently shaped to suit LHD or RHD vehicles. The rear section is moulded to include the heelboard cover, and is held to the floor by a metal retainer plate under the leading edge of the rear seat. This plate and the rear floor covering are held to the vehicle's floor panel by 26 plastic inserts. The front sections of the rear wheelarches alongside the seat cushion remain uncovered, and are painted in the body colour. The front mats fit under the door kick-plates, which are screwed to plastic inserts in the top surface of the body sill. These kick-plates, which are handed, are made of aluminium alloy and have a dull finish.

The tunnel cover differs between RHD and LHD vehicles, to suit the different position of the handbrake and the different shape of the tunnel itself; both types have been unavailable new for many years. There is also an ashtray on the top of the transmission tunnel. It has a spring-loaded lid of bright metal with a ribbed pattern, and is the same as that found in contemporary Rover saloons. The ashtray fits into a metal insert, which is fixed to the tunnel by four drive-screws. A dark grey plastic bezel around the ashtray is held in place by this metal insert.

Load area

The load area is covered with black rubber matting, which is in three sections. The centre section is shaped to fit into the corrugations of the load floor. The two side sections are shaped to fit around the wheelarches and, on the left, the spare wheel. The 'corrugated' matting is visible in the passenger compartment, under the front of the rear seat cushion.

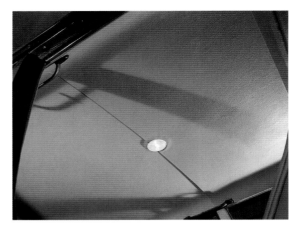

Headlining on the earliest Range Rovers was covered in PVC and had a single light.

Early rear quarter-panel trims had a sliding vent arrangement.

The early PVC tunnel covering, complete with the usual discoloration caused by heat from below! The dark grey plastic of the ashtray surround is clear.

The right-hand side of the load area is untrimmed, and the metalwork of the inner wing is painted to match the body. This area is used for tool storage, and the tools are concealed by a top-hung curtain made of felt material faced with PVC. The spare wheel stands upright in the left-hand side of the load area, in a shallow well behind the wheelarch. Its front face rests against two rubber buffers on brackets bolted to the inner wing. The wheel is secured by a metal disc through which the threaded end of a cranked handle passes and screws into a captive nut on the inner wing. The spare wheel has a cover made of the same material as the tool curtain, with a circular cut-out to give access to the cranked securing handle.

Tools

Range Rovers were provided from the beginning with a comprehensive set of tools. On Suffix A models, the tools consist of a starting handle, a tool roll containing small items, a screw jack with handle and shaft, a wheel nut wrench, a grease gun and a foot pump. The starting handle, jack shaft, jack and nut wrench are all painted gloss black. The nut wrench has a cranked handle and fixed socket head. The foot pump is painted light green, and was supplied in a clear plastic bag.

The tool roll is made of black rubberised canvas and has canvas ties. It contains pliers, a screwdriver with reversible shaft, an adjustable wrench, a box (spark plug) spanner and tommy bar, a tyre pressure gauge and six spanners. The pliers appear to have been sourced from more than

Load area in an early vehicle has a ribbed floor covering of black rubber, and no wheelarch trim. The black spare wheel cover was made of grained PVC over a felt base, and degraded quickly. This is a pre-production model with certain differences from production: tools and tool curtain are not fitted at the right, and the jack handle is clipped to the underside of the seat.

Tool board is seen here on Range Rover number 1. This installation is not quite correct: the tool roll should be stowed on the left of the jack, and the foot pump should be secured by the two spare clips visible on the right.

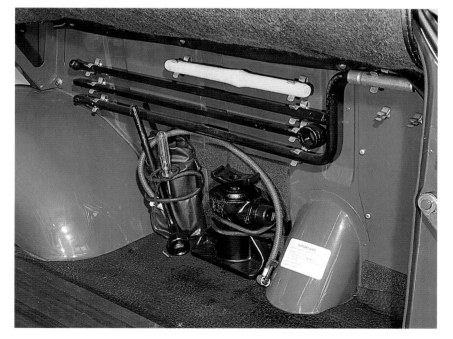

one supplier; some have plain metal handles while others have them sheathed in blue or black plastic, and there may have been other varieties as well. The tyre pressure gauge is a pencil type in bright metal, the adjustable spanner is made by King Dick, and the reversible screwdriver normally has a yellow plastic handle. The plug spanners sometimes did not fit the recesses in the cylinder head, and a March 1973 Service Instruction advised grinding where necessary. One spanner is a single-ended ⅜in Whitworth type,

while the other five are double-ended types of sizes ⁵⁄₁₆in x ¼in Whitworth, ⁵⁄₁₆in x ⁷⁄₁₆in Whitworth, ½in x ⁷⁄₁₆in AF, ⅝in x ⁹⁄₁₆in AF and ¹¹⁄₁₆in x ¾in AF. In addition, the tool kit includes a two-pin plug for the inspection socket on the steering column shroud; this is rolled up with the small tools.

On Suffix A models, all tools are clipped to the right-hand inner wing panel in the load area. They are securely held by 11 spring clips and two brackets with black rubber elastic rings. Clips and brackets alike are held to the inner wing by pop rivets, and a black sponge rubber anti-rattle pad is glued behind the two brackets. The bracket nearer the front of the vehicle holds the tool roll and wheel nut wrench, while the rearward one is for the jack. In addition, a safety warning label (part number 595017) alongside the fuel filler tube explains the correct jacking procedure.

Suffix B (from Jan 1973)

Although the seat upholstery remains Palomino PVC of the same pattern, there are now release handles on the outboard as well as inboard edges, and a spring mechanism that allows the seat to return to its original position after being tilted to give access to the rear. The inboard release handles are spaced further from the squab than before, to give more clearance for the buckles of the new safety belts.

These belts are still static types, but have a rigid buckle mounting that allows one-handed operation. Two types of belt were used. The first was for the UK, Austria, Belgium, Eire, France, Greece, Holland, Italy, Portugal and Switzerland. The second, which has a different layout and different material specification, was for Denmark, Finland, Germany, Norway and Sweden.

Range Rovers sold in Australia and Sweden had fixed head restraints on their front seats, and the trim pads on the seat backs had a cut-out to fit round these. There were special front seats for Germany, with a limited amount of rake adjustment for the backrest on the driver's side. The release lever for the rake adjustment is a black handle, located on the inboard edge above the seat release handle.

The rear seat is unchanged except for the deletion of the three buffers from the cushion tray. In addition, vehicles for Germany have a special striker plate with a guide pin to ensure correct engagement (this is the same as the one which became standard for all markets from Suffix F).

Rear seat belts were an optional extra. They are static types with square, flat buckles in unpainted metal, and a square black release push in the centre. The two outer belts are three-point types, but the centre belt is a lap type. Mounting points are on the wheelarches, on the rear floor behind the seats, and on the rear quarter panels.

The door armrest pulls differ from those on Suffix A models, and allow clearance for the outboard seat release handles introduced for Suffix B.

The headlining is in two pieces like the Suffix A type, but trimmed in beige brushed nylon rather than PVC. The fixings for the rear section differ, and there is a retaining lip above the tailgate; in theory revised rear quarter panel trims also help to keep the headlining in place. Each of these trims has a similar sliding vent arrangement to the Suffix A type, but the panel has an extension at the top and an additional fixing, which is covered by a plastic blanking plug. The fixing points for the optional rear safety belts are covered by plastic plugs in the headlining, above the quarter panels.

The floor coverings are the same as on Suffix A models, but the transmission tunnel is covered by dark brown carpet. There are different versions of this to suit LHD and RHD models; it was also possible to buy a tunnel carpet to fit to Suffix A models, but this differed slightly from the Suffix B production type. The carpet has a clear plastic backing, which allows the material to be heat-moulded to fit the tunnel. The underside of the transmission tunnel was undersealed as an additional sound-insulation measure.

The original 'corrugated' floor covering for the load area was not liked, particularly by Range Rover owners with dogs. The new covering, which provided a flat surface, comprised two dark grey PVC sections for the left and right sides of the vehicle, and its underside was ribbed to fit into

Headlining became brushed nylon for Suffix B vehicles, but there was still a single interior light.

the corrugations of the load floor. The rear edges of the two panels were secured at the bottom of the tailgate opening under a bright metal capping plate, which was fixed to the body by ten rivets.

The tool kit is similar to the Suffix A type, except that the grease gun was deleted and the jack shaft is in two pieces, to facilitate stowage behind the wheelarch.

Suffix C (from Oct 1973)

From the start of production, the sliding vent arrangement in the rear quarter pillar trims was replaced by an automatic flap valve. As stocks of the old trims became exhausted by September 1976, the Service recommendation thereafter was to replace them with this 'through-flow' type.

In hot climates, the brushed nylon trim of the earlier headlining tended to come away from the moulded glass-fibre backing pad, so the adhesive was changed in approximately May 1974, at 355-07247C, 356-01587C and 358-04430C.

As the result of a steel shortage, some early Suffix C models for the home market were despatched without the roll of tools. Rover sent the missing items on to supplying Distributors as soon as supplies became available again, so in theory no vehicle should have remained without the proper tool roll.

Suffix D (from Apr 1975)

The arrival of Suffix D models in approximately April 1975 brought a change from PVC to Ambla leathercloth for the standard upholstery. At the same time, brushed nylon seat facings with a herringbone pattern were introduced as an extra-cost option, which most British buyers specified. Seats in either of these materials, which are much more hard-wearing than the earlier PVC, have nar-

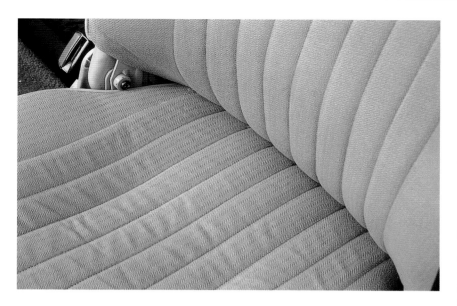

Upholstery for Suffix D models had narrower pleats to give better wearing properties. Standard trim material was now Ambla (right), but brushed nylon with a herringbone pattern (above) was an extra-cost alternative.

rower pleating (with six pleats on each front seat), but the existing PVC-covered back panels were retained. With brushed nylon, the side panels are in matching leathercloth.

The standard seat belts are the same static types as on Suffix B and C models, although inertia-reel belts were now optional and became increasingly popular. For the rear seat, which was unchanged in construction and fixings, the same static belts as before remained optional.

German-market Range Rovers continued to

have special front seats, with backrest rake adjustment for the driver's side. Ambla upholstery was never available on Range Rovers for Germany, and the special seats for that market were always upholstered in brushed nylon.

At chassis numbers 355-10723D, 356-03172D and 358-10179D in April 1975, the headlining was modified at the rear to suit the new rear-end structure of the body. If the new headlining was fitted to an older vehicle as a Service replacement, an additional angle bracket had to be fitted at the rear to support it.

Suffix E (from Oct 1975)

Suffix E models were the first to be fitted with two courtesy lights, and the headlining is modified to suit. It is still in two sections, but both front and rear sections now have separate cut-outs to fit around the two lights. Plastic stud fixings are used to hold the headlining to the roof cross-member where the two sections meet.

In June 1976, supply difficulties caused the covering for the sun visors to be changed from Palomino to Chamois material, which looks similar and was already in use for Rover cars.

By February 1977, the gear lever had a long gaiter made of carpeting material, which was sewn to the transmission tunnel carpet.

Suffix F (from c. May 1977)

Front seat head restraints probably became optional with Suffix F, requiring the tops of the seat back panels to be shaped to suit. Head restraints are always covered in Palomino leathercloth, irrespective of whether the upholstery is Ambla or brushed nylon. Suffix F vehicles also have different finishers concealing the backrest pivots, and brushed nylon seats have minor changes to the cushion. The optional inertia-reel safety belts also differ from earlier types.

There were minor changes at Suffix F – and Suffix G – to the special front seats for German-market Range Rovers.

Suffix G (from c. Sep 1978)

Both the front seat squabs and the finishers changed. Front seat head restraints were standardised for most markets and the rear panel of each front seat had an appropriate cut-out. When head restraints were not fitted (as on Fleet Line models, for example), the cut-out was filled with a black plastic plug. The inertia-reel belts also changed once again.

Changes to the tool kit were probably made with the introduction of Suffix G models, but it is not possible to be certain. What is clear, however, is that by the time Suffix G chassis gave way to AA-series vehicles with VIN identities, certain changes had already taken place. The upper section of the jack shaft now had a smaller eye to accommodate a steel handle in place of the wooden type, although the earlier shaft and handle may have been available as well. In January 1979 the wheel nut wrench was given a folding extension handle to provide greater leverage; it is not clear whether the alternative type, with a box-type socket on a straight handle with a similar folding extension, was introduced at the same time or later. Although the foot pump was still not supplied as standard, it was available as an optional extra. By the end of Suffix G production in September 1979, two different types of foot pump were being used, one manufactured by Sutty and the other by Desmo.

AA-series (from Sep 1979)

Two-door models

This section describes the interior trim of two-door AA-series models produced between September 1979 and May 1984. Note that 782 Range Rovers with AA-series VINs (100001 to 100782) were built before the full 1980 model-year specification was introduced: some of these probably had Suffix G specification while others were certainly hybrids. An example of a hybrid is HAC 415V, which appeared in publicity photographs for the 1980 models but actually had 1979-model tail light clusters. It is not clear what variations of interior specification may exist within this sequence of 782 vehicles.

The standard upholstery on 1980 models was initially brushed nylon, as on Suffix G types, but this was changed to Bronze velvet in February 1980 at AA 103441. Vehicles with the new upholstery, which is generally considered to be a 1981 model-year feature, went on sale in summer 1980. Fleet Line models (see Chapter 13) continued to use Ambla upholstery. Bronze velvet seats have ribbed velvet facings and plain velvet side panels, but their rear panels are in PVC, as before. From July 1981, the back panels have ruched map pockets. Fixed head restraints were standard, but they differ from the earlier type by having a detachable cushion secured by two press-studs on each side. The body of each head restraint is covered in leathercloth, and the cushion is covered in velvet to match the seats. German-market vehicles again have special seats with an adjustable backrest for the driver.

A rounded contact edge was added to the seat belt guide on each front seat at AA 100593, before the full start of the 1980 model year. There was also a new belt with a moulded plastic tongue cover, plastic dipped brackets, and shorter

This 1977 Suffix F model with herringbone cloth upholstery has the newly optional head restraints, correctly trimmed in PVC. The rear seat belt installation dates from later, but shows the early 1980s mounting position on the tailgate frame. The rear floor is now carpeted and the load area mat, visible ahead of the back seat, is grey.

Vehicles from Suffix E had two interior lights, as seen on a 1977 model.

A new type of velour upholstery (right) was introduced in 1980 for AA-series models. Head restraints (far right) now have detachable cushions; the body of the restraint has a fabric front panel but PVC sides.

Velour rear seat in a two-door AA-series model: carpet and retaining arrangements are the same as before, and once again the load area mat protrudes forward of the seat. Black rubber floor mats and dog guard are later additions, dating from the mid-1980s.

anchorage bolts. These measures were taken to prevent the belt webbing from fraying at the top corner of the unprotected guide slot. Further changes were made at AA 136112 in February 1984, when the front belt webbing gained a softer edge and the reel spring tension was decreased by 10%. A new 'lie-flat' buckle was also specified, to prevent the belt tongue twisting.

The rear seat is the same as on earlier models, except for the upholstery material. However, from August 1982 (when the two-door Range Rover's rear floor was commonised with the four-door model), the cushion pivots are under the seat tray instead of on either side of it. The seat itself nevertheless remains different from the four-door type, lacking a central armrest.

When inertia-reel rear safety belts are fitted on models up to August 1983, they are mounted on brackets bolted to the tailgate frame, as before. From September 1983, however, the mounting changes to the rear quarter panel, but with the reel still exposed (unlike later models). The later belts are new types with pointed tongues. On Range Rovers for France, Germany and Switzerland, the tongues can be stowed in black plastic 'flower-pot' keeps bolted to the side panels alongside the seats. These keeps were optional (but almost non-existent) in other markets.

With the exception of the Monteverdi four-door models (see Chapter 10), the first Range Rovers to have a cubby box were the In Vogue two-doors released in February 1981. The same cubby box was standard on two-door vehicles with air conditioning from July 1981, and was available as an optional extra on other two-doors except those destined for Germany. This early cubby box is a square-rigged item which fits over the rear of the transmission tunnel and incorporates a keylock in its lid.

When automatic transmission was introduced in August 1982 (for 1983 models), it was accompanied by a transmission tunnel finisher or console, and by a new type of cubby box that is shorter than the early type, with an angled front face and an ashtray in its rear wall. As before, it has a keylock in its lid. The same cubby was also fitted to the five-speed models introduced a year later. On 1983 and 1984 models, it is always finished in brown to match the upholstery.

Both the automatic and the five-speed manual models built in this period use the same tunnel finisher, with different blanking plates to suit. The transfer gearbox lever is always in the same place, with a grey leathercloth gaiter incorporating a stiffening surround which is clipped to the underside of the tunnel finisher. On automatic models, the main gearbox selector is behind this, and the aperture for the five-speed gear lever in front of it is blanked off. On five-speed models, the aperture for the automatic selector is filled by a blanking plate which is covered by an anti-slip mat for use as a coin tray.

On both automatic and five-speed manual models, the tunnel finisher incorporates a black metal ashtray on either side, and a coin tray angled inwards, with an anti-slip mat, on the right at the front. There are five cut-outs for electric window switches in the rear, just ahead of the cubby box; as two-door models never had electric windows in this period, they always have a blanking plate fixed over these cut-outs.

The lower door trim pad is in Palomino leathercloth on 1980 models, Bronze velvet (to match the upholstery) on 1981 and 1982 models, and Ambla from November 1982. Later models have a speaker in the leading edge of each trim pad when a radio is fitted. This installation was first seen on In Vogue models in February 1981, and seems to have become standard in July 1981.

AA 105818, in spring 1980, saw the introduction of a new window winder handle (part number MRC 9390), which has a thicker section around the boss – to prevent cracking – and an identifying triangle embossed on the rear face. A minor change made on the assembly lines in summer 1980 affected the positioning of the plastic waterproof sheet behind the upper door trim pad. There had been problems with this sheet obstructing the lock and linkage mechanism, so from AA 107709, in summer 1980, it was fitted before – not after – assembly of the centraliser and rod mechanism.

The windscreen pillars have the same design as earlier types, but are in a lighter grey to match the facia. The B/C-pillar has separate trim pads above and below waist level, as before, with fir-tree plastic fixing clips on the upper section and plastic studs on the lower. The pads are trimmed in Palomino grained leathercloth, but on 1981 and later models with Bronze velvet upholstery, a Bronze velvet facing panel covers their lower ends and extends onto the rear side trim panels as well. A minor change was made to the quarter pillar trims in September 1982.

As before, there are trim pads fitted to the rear body sides, on either side of the rear seat. These are covered in grained Palomino leathercloth, but their lower sections are faced with Bronze velvet cloth on 1981 and later models with this type of upholstery. The cloth panel is also attached to the lower B/C-post trim. The trim pads are secured by plastic fir-tree studs. On the 1981 In Vogue models only (see Chapter 11), a wood veneer capping is screwed to the inner body frame and overlaps the top of the trim panel.

When Bronze velvet upholstery replaced brushed nylon on 1981 models, Nutmeg carpets were fitted to all vehicles as standard. The floor carpets have bound edges and match the tunnel carpet, which once again has a sewn-in gear lever gaiter. They consist of three sections – left and right front footwells, and rear floor. The front carpets, which are secured by brown plastic pegs, are handed to suit LHD and RHD models, and only the driver's side carpet has a black heel-pad sewn into it. There are matching moulded carpet sections on the front faces of the rear wheelarches, beside the seat cushion. When the rear seat and load areas of the two-door body were commonised with the four-door version in September 1982 (for 1983 models), the rear floor mat and carpet changed to the larger four-door types, and the floor covering in the load area changed to the shorter four-door type (see below).

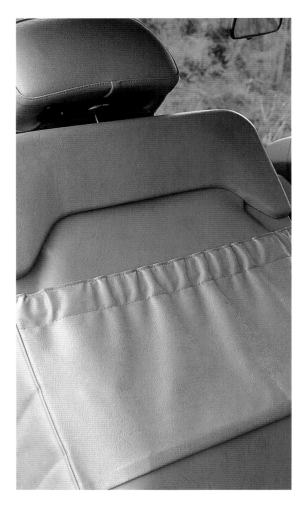

From July 1981 map pockets featured on the seat backs, seen on an In Vogue limited-edition two-door model.

Again seen on an In Vogue two-door, each front seat has an outboard release handle in addition to the original inboard handle; the outboard handle was introduced in 1973.

A number of changes to the load area trim and spare wheel cover were introduced together for the 1982 models, starting at AA 114957 in July 1981. The floor covering changed from grey to Palomino beige, as previewed on the In Vogue limited edition of February 1981 (see Chapter 11), and one-piece moulded carpet sections were glued to the wheelarches. The tool curtain and the spare wheel cover also changed from black leathercloth

Front quarter-lights were secured by rather crude catches.

Early style of door trim on four-door models has ribbed release catches and a large circular cut-out for the window winder.

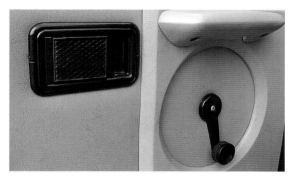

Four-door models have an engagement lever for the childproof locks protruding from the lower face of the door. This 1983 model also has the early style of weatherseal around the wheelarch cut-out; a much larger type was introduced later.

to bound Nutmeg carpet. However, there is no carpet on the load floor itself. The spare wheel is no longer retained by a cranked handle, but by a system of three straps, of which the one at lower left has a ratchet tensioner.

A modification to the tools occurred when the starting handle and its stowage clips were deleted from 1983 models at AA 123568 in August 1982.

Four-door models

The earliest factory-built four-door Range Rovers have the same Bronze velvet upholstery as contemporary two-door models. The 1982 models (July 1981 to July 1982) have front seats which are visually identical to the two-door type, but have fixed backrests. The 1983 and 1984 models (August 1982 to May 1984) have adjustable armrests added to the inboard edges of these seats. All models through to May 1984 have fixed head restraints with detachable velour cushions. The front safety belts are inertia-reel types mounted on the seats, and the 1984 models (from September 1983) have a new type with pointed tongues.

The rear seat on 1982 models has the same cushion and backrest as contemporary two-door models. However, it is mounted nearer the rear of the vehicle, in order to give more legroom, and the pivots for the seat base are underneath the tray rather than on either side of it. From August 1982, the rear seat of all four-door models has a folding centre armrest. The special edition models (In Vogue types in the UK) have a special rear seat with centre and side armrests, and two removable head restraints with detachable cushions like those fitted to the front head restraints.

Rear safety belts remained optional during this period except on certain special edition models (see Chapter 11). They were probably always inertia-reel types when fitted, mounted on brackets on the tailgate frame on 1982 and 1983 models. On 1984 models (built from September 1983), new belts with pointed tongues were fitted, and their reels were mounted to the rear quarter panels at an angle. No cover was fitted, unlike later models. When these belts were specified on Range Rovers for France, Germany and Switzerland, the 'flower-pot' tongue keeps were fitted alongside their outboard edges. These keeps were optional, but probably very rare, on vehicles for other markets.

All four-door models built in this period have one-piece door trims in Palomino, with a large circular moulding around the arc prescribed by the window winder handle. Each door trim carries a carpeted lower kick-panel, and a radio speaker is fitted in the leading edge of this. The door trims are held to the doors by plastic studs. There are minor differences at the top of the trim to suit either the early two-piece or later one-piece waist

seals. There are also differences between the trims on vehicles with manual locking and those with central locking. The optional wood capping is held to the top of the trim by three screws on some models, and two on others. Dark wood cappings with a boxwood inlay were used only on the 1982 In Vogue Automatic special edition models (see Chapter 11), and these have two screw fixings on both front and rear doors.

Each door has an armrest which doubles as a door pull and is attached by two set-screws. The front and rear armrests differ, but are not handed. Black plastic is used for the sill locking buttons and release handles, which have a diamond-pattern rubbing plate.

The headlining used on 1982 and 1983 four-door models is broadly similar to the contemporary two-door type. A special rear section is used on the 1983 In Vogue special edition, which has two forward-facing radio speakers above the tailgate. The 1984 four-door models differ again, the

rear headlining section being moulded to accept speakers on all models, but pierced only when they are fitted. Four-door models have a two-door style of grab handle above each rear door.

The B/C-pillar trim is a single ABS plastic moulding in Palomino; the trims are handed. The upper D-pillar is trimmed with grained Palomino leathercloth, and the lower section, alongside the seat and above the leading edge of the wheelarch, is trimmed separately in the same material.

Floor carpets are fitted as standard. The front carpets are the same as those of contemporary two-door models, but differ on automatic and five-speed models to suit the different transmission tunnel shapes. The rear carpet differs to suit the repositioned rear seat and has two sections, one covering the floor and the other the heelboard; the heelboard carpet is secured by a metal strip fixed to the floor by four plastic studs. There are also short moulded sections of carpet covering the bottoms of the B/C-pillars. There are, of course,

This view inside one of the first four-door models shows the beige floor covering in the load area, and the carpet material used for wheelarches, spare wheel cover and tool curtain.

The centre console on a five-speed model is seen with the blanking plate used when no electric windows were fitted (top), and with the window switches (above).

BA-series (1985 models)

With the introduction of the BA-series in June 1984, a new top-of-the-range four-door model became available. This was called the Vogue in most markets, but the Highline in Australia. These models have Silver Grey upholstery and matching trim instead of the Bronze Check with brown trim that was introduced for other models.

The seats on all 1985 Range Rovers have a new upholstery pattern, with four narrow pleats on either side of a broad central section, and plain side bolsters. The front seats on two-door models have fixed backrests and integral inertia-reel belts, but those on four-doors have reclining backrests while the inertia-reel belts are mounted conventionally and have height-adjustable top mountings on the B/C-pillars. The backrests are adjusted by a release handle, and the angle of the cushion can be adjusted by a plastic turnwheel.

All front seats have adjustable head restraints trimmed in plain velour to match the upholstery. These are the same design as those fitted to contemporary Austin Maestro and Montego cars. The grey Vogue front seats have adjustable inboard armrests, but the standard Bronze Check seats have none. The metal seat bases differ from earlier types, and are painted to match the upholstery colour. In each case, there is a moulded plastic outer finisher for the base, attached rather insecurely by double-sided sticky pads.

Standard four-door and two-door models share the same rear seat, which has no armrests or head restraints. However, the grey Vogue seat has both adjustable head restraints and centre and side armrests. The head restraints have the same shape as those on the front seats, lacking the detachable pads fitted to earlier models.

Both front and rear safety belts are inertia-reel types with pointed tongues. Rear belts are standard on Vogue and other high-line four-doors, and optional on other models; they are always accompanied by 'flower-pot' keeps. All belt webbing is brown or grey to suit the upholstery, but Australian vehicles have black webbing. Vehicles destined for Saudi Arabia are fitted with a front seat safety belt warning buzzer, and the wiring for this is incorporated in the belt buckle.

Footwell trim panels are the same as those on 1984 models, except that grey panels are fitted with the grey Vogue upholstery. The cubby box and transmission tunnel cover are also the same, except that the cubby box is grey instead of brown with the grey Vogue upholstery.

Door trim pads and door furniture on two-door Range Rovers are unchanged, but four-door models have completely different trims in brown or grey, to suit upholstery colour. These are single-piece mouldings, trimmed with leathercloth and

four door tread-plates instead of two, but they have the same specification as the two-door type.

Four-door models fitted with the four-speed manual gearbox have the same tunnel carpet and ashtray as contemporary two-doors. The same material is used on automatic and five-speed manual models, although each has a differently-cut and differently-moulded section. The ashtray is not fitted to these models, which have a centre console finisher.

Four-door models have a carpeted load area from the beginning. There is a single piece of carpet over the PVC floor mat, and the inside of the tailgate has a carpet cover, attached by drive screws with cup washers. The tool curtain is made of carpet, and there are one-piece moulded carpet sections glued to each rear wheelarch. The spare wheel cover is also made of carpet. The wheel itself is secured by the strap-type fixing, although it is possible that some very early four-doors had the cranked handle and plate fixing.

secured by plastic fir-tree clips. The front trims have perforations at their upper front edges for the radio speakers, which are screwed to the inner door behind the trim. Both front and rear trims have a perforated-velour panel at the bottom, coloured to match the upholstery. The plastic door release handles have hook-type pulls within a rectangular surround and are also in grey or brown to suit the upholstery. On models with manually-operated windows, the black winding handles are shared with contemporary two-doors.

Both front and rear door trims have a beaded edge, and the upper end of the beading is trapped under the wooden capping panel, which is standard on all models. These capping panels are secured by metal clips and have no visible screw fixings. Each one carries a plastic tube insert for the sill locking button. The inserts and buttons are in grey or brown to match the upholstery.

The rectangular armrests once again double as door pulls. They are made of soft-feel plastic over a metal armature, and are mounted to the door by two set-screws. The heads of these screws are concealed behind a finisher panel which presses into place and is retained by a moulded rim on the armrest. The finisher is in plastic to match the upholstery on low-line models, or in wood veneer to match the door cappings on Vogue and equivalent models. Front and rear armrests differ, the rears being shorter, but neither type is handed. Rear armrests on models with electric windows incorporate a black plastic control switch with white arrow markings. This switch is fitted at the leading edge of the armrest, and the finisher panel is correspondingly shorter than the one used on Range Rovers with manual windows.

The headlining is again a two-piece type with a brushed nylon covering, this time in beige or grey to match the upholstery. There is provision for rear speakers on both two-door and four-door models; the nylon covering remains unpierced when speakers are not fitted. Two-door models again have just two grab handles, but four-doors have three – one above each rear door and one above the front passenger door.

The windscreen pillars once again have moulded plastic trims, but these are in lighter grey than the two earlier types.

The B/C-pillar on two-door Range Rovers has separate upper and lower trim pads, as before, and a Bronze velvet facing panel which extends onto the rear side trim panels covers the bottom section. On four-door models, the B/C-pillar trim is also in separate upper and lower sections, in brown or grey as appropriate. The upper section is simply grained leathercloth, glued to the metalwork and trapped under the door seals. The lower section is moulded from ABS plastic, and conceals the reel of the safety belt and the lower section of

the webbing. At waist height, the belt emerges through a moulded plastic guide, which is attached to the door pillar by two self-tapping screws. This guide slips over the top of the lower trim moulding, and is not always a good fit. The upper B/C-pillars also carry adjustable top mountings for the safety belts; the visible sections of these are made of plastic.

The upper D-pillar is trimmed with grained Palomino or Grey leathercloth, to match the upholstery. The lower section, alongside the seat and above the leading edge of the wheelarch, is trimmed separately in the same material.

The rear quarter pillar trims are the same as on 1984 models, except that grey ones are used with grey upholstery.

Floor mats on models with Bronze Check upholstery are in three sections of Palomino PVC. Carpets are in Nutmeg, as in 1984, and the front ones are secured by brown plastic pegs. On models with grey upholstery, the floor mats are black and

With the 1985 models came redesigned front seats and head restraints, and new Bronze Check upholstery. These are seen on a four-door model dating from that year, fitted with optional wood trim. These were the first Range Rover seats not to have integral safety belts and to have fully reclining backrests.

In contrast to other models, the top-of-the-range Vogue four-door, launched with the BA-series, has special Silver Grey upholstery.

the carpets are grey with black fixing pegs. Manual and automatic Range Rovers have the same moulded black sound insulation panel over the transmission tunnel.

There is a bound floor carpet in the rear, and a separate heelboard carpet gripped by a metal plate under the front edge of the seat. This plate is painted brown or grey to match the upholstery and is fixed to the floor by four plastic studs, as on earlier models.

Two-door and standard four-door models have the same load area floor mat as before. Four-doors have a Nutmeg carpet on top of this, and the tool curtain is once again Nutmeg carpet. Vogue and other models with grey upholstery, however, have a black floor mat and grey carpet. Vogues came as standard with a removable, rigid parcels shelf. This is supported on the right by a small shelf which replaces the tool curtain support, and on the left by a box-like structure which fits around the spare wheel. From BA 157142, a small rubber

block is fitted in the rear of the spare wheel recess to provide more clearance between wheel and lower tailgate. Later on, the floor pan was modified to provide this clearance.

On standard two-door and four-door models, the spare wheel cover is Nutmeg carpet, as in 1984. A grey carpet cover is used on models with grey upholstery.

All vehicles now came with an L-shaped drain plug spanner in the tool kit, and a single type of foot pump now seems to have been used. Slip-grip pliers replaced the adjustable King Dick wrench, and the two-pin plug was no longer supplied. The screw jack could be replaced optionally by a hydraulic type with a two-piece operating handle; the new jack and handle were painted brick red.

CA-series (1986 models)

Although Vogue models still topped the range for the 1986 model year, they had moved on to fuel-injected engines and are therefore not covered by this book. Turbo D models with diesel engines were introduced in April 1986 during the lifetime of the CA-series vehicles, and are also not covered here. However, the two-door and standard four-door models were available with carburettor engines throughout the 1986 model year.

The 1986 seats are unchanged in essentials from the 1985 Bronze Check types, but at CA 268571 two screws were added to the upper sides of the front seats to improve retention of the back panels. Longer belt webbing was specified for the safety belts at CA 171460.

There was a new, much neater centre console arrangement, with the transmission cover panel slotting under the edge of the radio surround panel and stretching back to a new cubby box. The whole assembly is covered in grained grey vinyl.

The transmission tunnel cover is bolted to the transmission tunnel through metal brackets. On the right of the transfer gearbox lever, it incorporates a coin tray with anti-slip mat, and behind that is a removable panel with a cut-out for the black plastic ashtray. This panel is secured by four plastic pegs which fit into orange plastic bushes in the main assembly. On automatic models, the panel is positioned so that the ashtray is ahead of the selector lever. On manual models, the gear selector lever is positioned further forwards, and so the cover panel is simply turned round so that the ashtray is behind the gear lever.

The cubby box is moulded separately from the transmission tunnel cover panel, but is permanently attached to it by plastic welds. Its sloping front face has a detachable cover, held in place by plastic pegs and the same orange plastic bushes as the removable plate on the transmission tunnel cover. This cover is located to the left or right of the assembly, to leave room on the appropriate side for the handbrake. It contains the electric window switches on models so equipped; the switches are unchanged from earlier vehicles.

The cubby box lid is hinged at the rear, and has a keylock on early vehicles. From CA 262500 in approximately January 1986, the keylock was deleted and the structure of the cubby box was strengthened. The later cubby boxes have a simple black nylon peg catch to secure the lid when closed. Subsequently it became possible to order a lid with a shaped cut-out to accommodate a cellular telephone.

The cubby box has a black plastic liner, held in place by four screws. This has a sprayed-on black felt-like finish. The fit of this liner was improved at CA 262500, when the cubby box was strengthened. On early 1986 models only, a removable tray for five cassette tapes is fitted in the bottom of the liner. The rear face of the cubby box contains a swivelling black plastic ashtray for

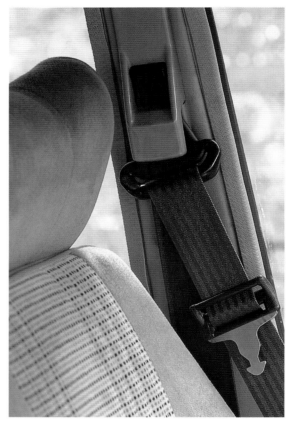

From the start of the 1985 model year, four-door models had conventionally mounted front safety belts with height-adjustable top mountings. Distinctive pattern of Bronze Check upholstery can be seen.

The 1985 models could also be fitted with adjustable rear head restraints and, optionally, the new rigid parcels shelf, just visible in the foreground. Both items were standard on 1985 Vogue models, but they were then coloured grey.

rear occupants, with a cigarette lighter alongside. This lighter matches the one on the radio surround panel. Below the ashtray and lighter are outlets for the rear heater ducts.

The headlining is the same as the 1985 type, but at CA 170612 an additional clip was added at the centre join. All body pillar trims were also unchanged, but a new method of A-pillar trim retention was introduced at CA 168063.

With the 1985 models came new door trims for the four-door Range Rovers. This is the rear left-hand door on an example fitted with optional wood trim and electric windows; standard trims had matching beige panels in place of the wood.

New carpets and noise insulation material were introduced on the 1986 models. Carpet fit and appearance was improved at CA 267439.

DA-series (1987 models)

The 1987 models were introduced in November 1986 at DA 273923 (four-door) and 274121 (two-door). All four-door models have fuel-injected or diesel engines, and therefore only the two-door versions are considered here.

From the start of the 1987 model year, two-door models have Bracken velour upholstery. This has the same pleating pattern as the earlier grey Vogue type. Seat frames are spray-painted in Palomino, and have new side finishers and a front finisher as well, all moulded in Palomino ABS plastic. The front seats on these models are mounted nearer to the centre of the vehicle than before, in order to give clearance for map pockets on the doors. The backrest rake can be adjusted by a turnwheel, and the cushion tilt can be varied by a lever alongside the seat. Both controls are made of black plastic.

Two-door models continue to have a bench rear seat, not the seat with integral head restraints and 60%/40% split fitted to some contemporary four-door models.

Safety belts are inertia-reel with brown webbing, except for Australia, where black webbing is used. The reels of the rear belts are mounted to the rear quarter pillars at an angle and have black covers in soft plastic; these covers are a push-fit over the reels. The rear belts also have brown plastic clip-type keeps for the webbing, mounted on the body sides where earlier models have the 'flower-pot' keeps.

The footwell side trim panels are retained by plastic clips instead of the drive screws used on earlier models. LHD models normally have a footrest bolted to the side of the driver's footwell, and the trim panel has a cut-out section to suit. On models without a footrest, the trim panel cut-out is filled with a rectangular blanking plug.

Modified door trims have a moulded plastic map pocket, which is held in place by self-tapping screws. The wood trim, where fitted, has a dark matt finish instead of the light, shiny finish on earlier vehicles. From DA 285904, the black nylon wood capping retainers were replaced by grey thermo-plastic rubber types. The door speakers are uprated to go with the new audio system.

The first DA-series Range Rovers have a slightly modified version of the 1986 headlining, again in two pieces and trimmed in brushed nylon to match the upholstery. The two sections are held more firmly where they meet in the centre of the vehicle by two clips, coloured to match the covering fabric. The rear section is held to brackets on the tailgate frame by a plastic fir-tree clip on each side. These clips are coloured to match the headlining, and on later models their heads are flock-covered to make them blend in better. The DA-series models have a new type of grab handle, fixed as before.

The later DA-series two-door models, starting with DA 281665, have a one-piece headlining in Savannah (brown). The speakers mounted above the tailgate aperture are uprated to suit the new audio system.

In the load area there is an additional rubber mounting block on the body side to protect the spare wheel. The tool kit includes two black metal wheel chocks, and there is a seventh spanner, this time a ⁵⁄₁₆in x ³⁄₈in AF type.

EA-series (1988 models)

The 1988 models were introduced in October 1987 and had the identifying letters EA. Once again only the two-door versions are considered here because all four-door models have fuel-injected or diesel engines.

There were just two detail changes to the interior trim. From the start of the EA-series, the A-pillar trim fixings include a screw near the bottom of each finisher; the head of this screw is covered by a circular blanking plug. The backs of the front seats were modified at EA 328169 to prevent the lower corners flaring.

Chapter 6

Facia & Controls

As with the previous chapter about the interior trim, changes to the facia, instruments and controls are extremely complicated to follow. To avoid confusion, the original Suffix A specification is set out in detail, followed by the changes made for each successive variant.

Suffix A

Instrument binnacle

The original instrument binnacle was designed so that the same unit could be used for both LHD and RHD vehicles. It is a compact design that does not fill the cut-out in the facia top and thus leaves

plenty of space for oddments stowage.

The core of the instrument binnacle is a white plastic moulding that is invisible when the binnacle is in place. The instruments and warning lamps are located within this moulding, and a printed circuit (on a clear plastic backing) is attached to the back of it. The core moulding is screwed to a metal bracket, which in turn is bolted through the top of the facia rail. The whole assembly then has a front cover, which incorporates the cut-outs for the instruments and warning lamps; the two circular instruments have clear plastic lenses screwed to the rear of the front cover, and there is a T-shaped celluloid strip, coloured and

This general view shows the facia and controls of a LHD Suffix B Range Rover dating from 1973.

All the features of the early instrument binnacle are clear in this view of Range Rover number 1. This three-spoke steering wheel was used to the end of the 1979 model year.

The original speaker panel cover in the facia top was later replaced by a practical trinket tray.

marked for the warning lamps, which clips in place between them.

A back cover conceals the top and sides. This clips under the lip of the front cover, and is held in place by two spring clips on the back of the metal bracket that secures the main moulding. These clips, notoriously, rust and break off, leaving the back cover of the binnacle loose.

The speedometer occupies the right-hand window in the binnacle. It has a trip counter and may be marked in miles per hour or kilometres per hour, depending on market. The re-set knob for the trip counter is on the end of a short cable plugged into the back of the instrument, and the black plastic knob itself emerges on the left of the binnacle through a hole in the side of the rear cover. The speedometer has a right-angle drive screwed to its rear, and the main speedometer drive cable – different for RHD and LHD – is screwed into this adapter.

The left-hand window contains two segment-type gauges, for fuel at the top and water temperature at the bottom. The rest of the aperture is filled by a black-faced masking plate with a bare metal button-type finisher in the centre which matches the base of the speedometer needle. A voltage stabiliser for these instruments is screwed to the back of the core moulding.

There are seven rectangular warning lamp segments in a column between the two instrument dials, plus, on either side at the top, two triangular segments with green lenses for the indicators. Working downwards, the rectangular segments are for headlamp main beam (blue lens, marked BEAM), trailer lamps (red, marked TRAILER), choke (amber, marked CHOKE), oil pressure (red, marked OIL), charging circuit (red, marked IGN), brakes (red, marked BRAKE) and low fuel (green, marked FUEL). The brake warning light is illuminated when the handbrake is on, and is linked to a float in the brake fluid reservoir to give warning of low brake fluid. All the warning lamps – and the

instrument illumination – depend on the same 12-volt, 2.2-watt capless bulbs, which push-fit into plastic holders. These early vehicles were built with Smiths bulbs (part number 4062110974). The instrument lighting incorporates green filters.

To meet local regulations, the Range Rovers introduced to Australia in 1972 had a separate handbrake-on warning lamp. The red brake warning lamp in the binnacle warned of low fluid level and – through a separate and unique system – loss of pressure in the vacuum servo.

Upper facia

The facia top is a universal ABS plastic moulding, designed to suit both LHD and RHD. It has four circular apertures on its top surface to accommodate fixed air vents, and two more in its front face to take adjustable eyeball air vents. An indentation in the centre was designed for a radio speaker but later adapted to take a coin tray. Towards each end is a further large indentation; these are identical and double as the mounting platform for the instrument binnacle and as a parcels tray.

The top rail is reinforced with metal strips at the windscreen side, one long central strip being flanked by identical shorter end strips. Each of the front corners visible inside the car is also reinforced with a plastic finisher which is located by two pegs and held by a screw passing through from the lower facia component beneath it.

The centre aperture on the top of the facia rail contains a perforated plastic radio speaker cover plate, which is secured by two Philips-head screws and has a gauze backing to prevent particles falling through it. Normally, the single speaker for the radio was held underneath this with small bolts which passed through the top rail itself.

The parcels tray is formed out of the indentation at the opposite end to the one used as the platform for the instrument binnacle. A metal plate forms its base and covers the apertures underneath, being held in place by four nuts and washers. At the front end is a vertical finisher which doubles as a grab rail; three studs are moulded into the armature of this and pass through the facia top to be secured by nuts and washers. An anti-slip mat in grey rubber completes the shelf and conceals the fixings. The baseplate, grab rail finisher and anti-slip mat are all handed to suit LHD or RHD.

Underneath the parcels tray is a large L-shaped plastic finisher. This is held to the top rail by three set-screws on the passenger compartment side, and by a longer set-screw on the outboard edge. This long set-screw passes through the end finisher already mentioned.

The four circular demister vents in the top surface of the facia rail are held in place by clips moulded to their undersides and by pop rivets which secure them to the demister funnels under the facia. The demister vents on these models have raised and shaped main cross vanes. The two eyeball vents are made of black plastic and are connected to a plastic manifold under the top rail which also feeds the central fresh air vent in the lower centre section of the facia. Each eyeball vent is held in place by two screws.

When the optional rear wash-wipe is fitted, the rocker switch which controls it is fitted in the dash top, outboard of the steering column.

Australian-market vehicles have a unique handbrake-on telltale lamp in the facia top rail, below the instrument binnacle. This has a black plastic body of the same type as that used later for the differential lock warning lamp. Its red lens is overprinted PARK BRAKE in black.

Lower facia

The lower facia panel on the driver's side conceals the underside of the steering column and is held in place by screws into the facia top rail and bulkhead. The panel has provision for a radio outboard of the driver; when no radio is fitted, the vacant location is filled by a moulded plastic map pocket which simply clips into place.

A hazard warning light switch is fitted in a recess on the upper inboard edge of the panel. The switch is a push-pull-type with a red plastic body. It has a black plastic knurled grip around the standard triangle symbol, which is printed on the top of the lens. The bulb is a 2-watt Lucas 281 or Unipart GLB 281. In August 1971, the original hazard flasher unit was replaced by a UK-made type, shared with Rover cars.

Underneath the radio housing is a grey plastic box-like structure which conceals the choke knob and is screwed to the side of the footwell. The choke knob has a curved grip; very early types are marked with the word 'CHOKE', and later ones carry the international choke symbol.

The lower facia on the passenger's side is occupied by a lockable, drop-down glove-box. The same moulded plastic glove-box is used on both LHD and RHD models, and is riveted at its lower edge to a metal bracket which is in turn screwed to the bulkhead. A black fabric strap is looped over two metal tags riveted to the sides of the glove-box, and through a retainer screwed to the bulkhead. A release catch with keylock is held to the top centre of the glove-box by four screws. The operating handle for the catch is made of bright metal, and the catch itself engages with a metal striker which is screwed to the underside of the facia top rail. The key for the glove-box should be the same small, square-headed one used for the tailgate and petrol filler cap.

Each front footwell has on its outboard side a trim panel made of Palomino ABS plastic. This is attached to the metal of the bulkhead, which wraps around at this point, by two self-tapping screws. The panels are handed, and the one on the driver's side is shorter to make room for the choke control cover.

The handle for the bonnet release cable is located in the passenger's footwell, and uses the bracket on the body which corresponds to the one on the driver's side used for the choke cable. The grip is a black plastic T-handle, oriented vertically.

Central lower facia panel

The central lower facia panel is an ABS plastic moulding and is not handed. It is held to the upper facia by two set-screws and to locations on the bulkhead by two further screws. The panel contains four circular cut-outs for minor instruments in its top edge, two on either side of an adjustable fresh air vent. Directly below this is the heater control panel, and underneath that is a printed plate which gives instructions about correct use of the transmission. When a cigarette lighter is fitted, it is mounted in the driver's side of the facia panel alongside the heater controls. The control for the heated rear window, when fitted, is below this, beside the transmission instruction plate, which is attached by four pop rivets.

Although there is provision for four instruments, only one – a clock – was standard on Suffix A models. The three redundant holes were plugged with black plastic blanking discs, which have been unavailable for many years. The clock was usually fitted in the hole furthest from the driver on both LHD and RHD vehicles, but sometimes in the hole next to it. This clock is a Kienzle electrically-wound mechanical type, with a metal casing and a black plastic adjuster knob in the middle of the face. It is held to the facia panel by a U-bracket with a single knurled nut fixing, and is illuminated by a Lucas 281 2-watt bulb.

Three instruments were available as options for Suffix A models, and could be fitted individually and in whichever position or positions the owner chose – but they were rarely ordered. They were an oil pressure gauge, an oil temperature gauge and an ammeter, each illuminated by a

The choke control – this one is on a 1973 Suffix A model – was mounted below the facia on the driver's side.

Redundant instrument locations were filled by blanking plugs on Suffix A models.

single GLB 987 bulb. The oil pressure gauge (part number 589028) is a Smiths bi-thermal unit with a hanging needle, calibrated from 0 to 60lb/sq ft. It is labelled OIL and is attached to the facia panel by a U-bracket with a single knurled nut.

The oil temperature gauge (part number 545152) is a Lucas unit with a hanging needle, calibrated from 30 to 110°C. The label on its face reads OIL TEMP, and the gauge is held in place by a U-bracket with two knurled fixing nuts.

Two types of ammeter were available. On vehicles with the 16 ACR, 17 ACR and 18 ACR alternators, the gauge is a Lucas type with a hanging needle and a 50-0-50 scale. The face-plate label reads AMPS, and the instrument is secured by a U-bracket with two knurled nuts and a detachable insulating plate. This instrument has been unavailable for many years. On vehicles fitted with a 20 ACR alternator, the gauge is part number 589297 and has 80-0-80 calibration with a needle pointing upwards, and a face-plate label that reads AMPERES.

The fresh-air vent is made of glossy black plastic, and has two knurled adjusting knobs in bright metal. It is a simple push-fit into the facia panel, and engages with an air distribution box behind the facia. The heater control panel is a printed metal plate, which is held to the front of the heater itself by two set-screws, and stands proud of the facia panel. The heater knobs are black plastic, push-fitted onto the ends of the four heater control rods. There is no illumination for the heater controls.

The heater itself is contained in a metal casing concealed behind the centre section of the facia. Around April 1972 (at 355-01237A, 356-00014A and 358-00178A), the heater hoses were changed to provide a reverse flow of water through the matrix for greater efficiency. Early hoses were both S-shaped. With the later arrangement, the lower hose (now the inlet) remains an S-shape but the upper hose (now the outlet) is almost straight.

The cigarette lighter, which was optional on Suffix A vehicles, has a hard black plastic knob without any identifying symbol. A dished washer was fitted between the front face of the lighter and

the front of the facia panel. Illumination is by a single GLB 643 bulb, in a clip on the lighter casing behind the facia panel.

The heated rear window switch is a push-pull type, identical to the one used in Rover cars before 1975, with a hard black plastic knob containing a telltale lens. This lens was probably coloured white on all Suffix A models. The switch has a threaded shank which passes through a hole drilled in the facia panel; the switch is then secured by a bright metal threaded ring which is tightened over it. A black plastic ring is trapped between the screwed ring and the facia panel, and is printed with the words REAR WINDOW. This label is identical to the one used in Rover P6 saloons before 1970.

Steering wheel & column

The steering wheel has three spokes in a T-shape and is made of dark grey plastic over a metal armature. A finisher covers the spokes and is secured by six screws. An alloy cap fits into the centre of the finisher, and this carries the Range Rover name printed in black capital letters. Parts catalogues also list a special export steering wheel, although it is not clear whether this ever existed.

The steering column shroud is made of grey plastic with a grained finish to match the rest of the dashboard. It is in two halves, top and bottom, the lower half incorporating a metal bracket which holds the minor stalk switches. The top half is held to the bracket for the two main stalks by one screw, and four screws pass from the bottom half into the top to keep the assembly rigid.

The lower half of the shroud has a circular cutout for the ignition switch on the right. On the left, it has two sliding switches, the one nearer the driver controlling panel illumination (on or off) and the further one controlling the interior light. Beneath these are red and black sockets for an inspection lamp. Early Range Rovers destined for Italy had no panel light switch, and the redundant position was covered by a small blanking plate; it is not clear if any Suffix A models were affected. The original steering column lock assembly had a Lucar connector to suit an audible warning switch system. However, this system was never fitted in production, so this connector was deleted in approximately April 1972, at 355-02560A, 356-00043A and 358-00378A.

The four stalk switches on the steering column are all moulded in black plastic and the main ones carry white printed symbols. The main stalk on the left operates the two-speed windscreen wipers (up and down) and washers (press), while the main stalk on the right is for horn (press), main beam (push away), headlamp flash (pull) and indicators (up and down). LHD models use different stalks, but their positions are unchanged.

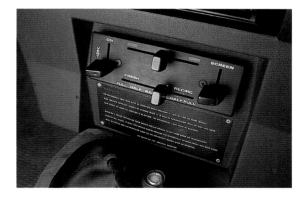

The early heater control panel and differential lock control with integral warning lamp, seen on a Suffix A model.

Early indicator switches sometimes suffered from melting near the contacts and had high cancelling torques, so a modified type was used from November 1972. This is identifiable from the date stamp on the body of the unit; the earliest ones carry a stamp of 45/72 (week 45, 1972).

The shorter stalks behind these two main stalks are for the auxiliary lamps when fitted (left) and vehicle lighting (right), the latter with one position for sidelights and another for headlights. The auxiliary lights switch and associated wiring are present regardless of whether any additional lights are actually fitted to the vehicle.

Other controls

The accelerator, brake and clutch pedals are all handed to suit LHD or RHD, but in each case the same pedal pads, of ribbed black rubber, are used. The accelerator has a simple pad, while the brake and clutch pedals share a different pad design with an R moulded into the centre. The shaft of the brake pedal operates a plunger switch connected to the brake lights.

The handbrake is mounted on the driver's side of the transmission tunnel. On LHD vehicles it operates the transmission brake through a relay lever. Both LHD and RHD types have the same lever with a smooth black plastic grip, although the mounting brackets differ. The handbrake lever is held to its mounting bracket by ⅜in bolts, and a plunger switch underneath the lever operates the handbrake-on warning light.

The main gear lever is handed (cranked towards the driver) to suit LHD or RHD, and has a black shank with a round black hard plastic knob with gearchange positions etched in white. It has a round rubber gaiter at its base, and a rubber sleeve at its lower ends.

The transfer box selector lever is located on the right of the transmission tunnel, looking forwards, regardless of whether the vehicle has LHD or RHD. It has a black shaft and a hard black plastic knob, with the positions L-N-H etched into it in white. Also on the transmission tunnel – to the right of the main gear lever – is the differential lock control, a black pull-up switch that operates a vacuum control; the top of it incorporates a clear-lens warning lamp. On very early models the differential lock control is mounted directly to the gearbox, but this was soon changed for a remote mounting on a bracket fixed to the tunnel inspection cover.

Suffix B (from Jan 1973)

Four auxiliary instruments became standard on Suffix B models, but were lined up in a different order for RHD and LHD. For RHD they cover (from the left) oil pressure, clock, ammeter and oil

temperature, whereas for LHD the order is (from the left again) ammeter, oil temperature, clock and oil pressure.

The clock is the same as the Suffix A type, but the oil pressure gauge differs – and there were two different types. Vehicles for most markets were fitted with part number 589262, which has a hanging needle and is calibrated from 0 to 60lb/sq ft, with kg/sq cm markings below the scale.

Early Range Rovers had black plastic gear lever gaiters. Note also the controls for the optional rear wash-wipe and heated rear window, the latter with red warning lamp lens.

The early type of indicator stalk is seen here on the right-hand side of the steering column. Not visible on the shorter stalk is the white graphic which marks it as operating the sidelights and headlamps.

The very early 'long' transfer box selector (left), seen on YVB 158H, a pre-production model. Note also the early type of ashtray, with ribbed chrome lid, used only on Suffix A models; and the

early type of choke control. The rubbers of the brake and clutch pedals (above) carry an 'R' symbol and horizontal ribbing, while the accelerator rubber has vertical ribbing and no symbol.

The warning lamp for the centre differential lock moved to the facia top rail for Suffix C models.

In these views of a 1977 model, note the carpet gaiter for the main gear lever, and the centre differential lock control without warning lamp. Later type of ashtray has a smooth, satin-finish lid.

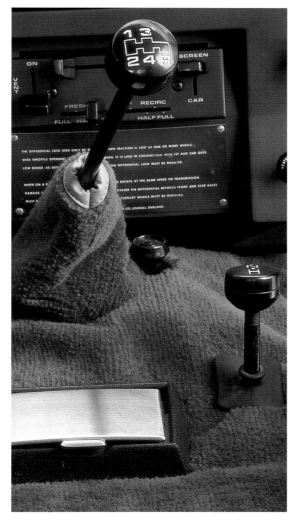

However, vehicles for Australia and New Zealand always had part number PRC 1055, which has only metric markings. Both types have bi-thermal operation. The standard 50-0-50 ammeter was part number 589242, which was visually similar to the earlier type. If a 20 ACR alternator was fitted, the optional ammeter was always the same 80-0-80 type as found on Suffix A models.

The cigarette lighter became standard on Suffix B and later vehicles. It is the same as the Suffix A type, but does not have the additional dished washer between the front face of the lighter and the front of the facia panel.

The two main stalk switches differ, although their functions are unchanged. These switches have a different clamp bracket holding them to the steering column. New Lucas part numbers are 30425 (RHD) or 30426 (LHD) for the left-hand wash/wipe stalk, and 30423 (RHD) or 30424 (LHD) for the right-hand stalk.

Suffix C (from Oct 1973)

The switch for the centre differential lock control no longer has an integral warning lamp. The lamp, instead, is now in the facia top rail below the instrument panel, directly beneath the vertical strip of warning lamps in the instrument binnacle. It is made of black plastic and has a cylindrical bulb-holder on the back of a rectangular lens unit. The bulb-holder is inserted through a hole drilled in the top rail, and two guide pegs on the back of the lens unit then locate in smaller holes to keep the whole assembly in place. The amber lens is a plastic snap-fit type, overprinted with the

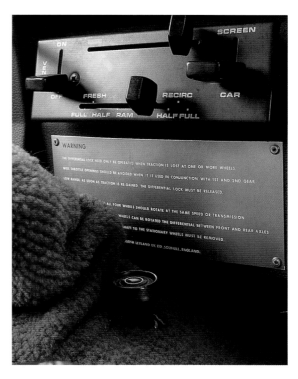

words DIFF LOCK in black.

From June 1974, the heater flap was modified to improve the clearance between heater deflector and transmission tunnel carpet.

Early handbrake levers are held to the mounting bracket by ⅜in bolts, later levers by ⁵⁄₁₆in bolts.

Suffix D (from Apr 1975)

Instruments were unchanged until chassis numbers 355-38132D (RHD) and 358-38134D (LHD), when an air-cored oil pressure gauge replaced the bi-thermal type. This came in two varieties, as PRC 1732 with both Imperial and metric markings, or as PRC 1733 with metric markings only for Australia and New Zealand.

The heated rear window switch normally has a red lens by this stage, in place of the earlier white one. Green lenses have also been seen, although it is not clear whether these are original.

Suffix E (from Oct 1975)

The ammeter was replaced by a voltmeter (part number PRC 1111). The face plate is labelled VOLTAGE and the hanging needle runs in a crudely-calibrated scale with three segments, the middle one being marked NORMAL.

Suffix F (from c. May 1977)

At chassis serial number 55137F, the original mechanical clock was replaced by a quartz one. Two types – manufactured by Borg or Kienzle – were used in production, and seem to have been alternatives. The Borg clock uses a GLB 281 bulb for illumination, the Kienzle a GLB 288 bulb.

Suffix G (from c. Sep 1978)

The most important development was the introduction of an optional factory-installed in-dash air conditioning system, made by ARA of Texas. At this stage it was available only on LHD vehicles. When air conditioning was fitted, the passenger's side glove-box was deleted, a vent rail was fitted under the facia top rail, and a shorter central lower facia panel was used. In addition, a fifth louvre was fitted in a box on the underside of the driver's lower facia panel.

The evaporator unit for the air conditioning is fitted under the facia on the passenger's side in the place where the drop-down glove-box would otherwise be. It is concealed by a grey plastic cover panel which extends across the top of the central lower facia panel and is screwed to the underside of the vent rail. The vent rail is moulded of grey ABS plastic to match the rest of the facia, and carries four black plastic louvres with adjustable

Eyeball vent, oil pressure gauge and clock are seen in this detail of a 1979 model. Poor fit of facia components was normal.

vertical vanes. These louvres are a snap-fit into the vent rail. At the driver's end of the vent rail is a panel – made of metal and finished in black with printed settings – containing two sliding switches with black plastic knobs: the upper switch controls the blower fan and the lower one the air temperature.

The central lower facia panel is pre-drilled with holes to take the cigarette lighter and heated rear window switch on the driver's side. It is secured by four screws which locate on bulkhead mountings, and by three more which screw into the underside of the vent rail. The four minor instruments in the central lower facia panel occupy the same relative positions as on Range Rovers without air conditioning. The box for the fifth louvre is held to the underside of the driver's side lower facia panel by four screws; the louvre itself is the same as the four in the main vent rail.

From January 1979 approximately, a recalibrated oil temperature gauge was fitted. This is distinguished by a scale with MAX marked vertically on the right. It registers no increase until the oil is nearly at normal operating temperature – which caused many Range Rover owners to complain that it was not working properly when the vehicles were new!

In May 1979, at chassis serial number 52289, a modified handbrake lever (part number NRC 3398) was fitted, in order to reduce the effort needed to apply the transmission brake.

At gearbox number 355-75524C in summer 1979, the gearbox end of the main gear lever was modified to improve the gearchange quality.

General layout of the facia and controls was unchanged by the time of this 1983 model, an In Vogue special edition. Note, however, the trinket tray in the facia top, the four-spoke steering wheel and the five-speed gear lever with its grey gaiter in a special centre console panel. A ribbed handbrake grip has also replaced the earlier smooth type, and there are clearer graphics on the heater control panel.

The four-spoke steering wheel has the Range Rover logo on its central pad, and in this case is leather-bound as well. By the time of this 1983 vehicle, the stalk controls have swapped sides, placing the indicator stalk on the left.

AA-series (from Sep 1979)

The handbrake-on warning function was deleted from the brake warning lamp at AA 103441 in March 1980, so that the lamp now served only to warn of low fluid level. Australian-market Range Rovers were unaffected, continuing to have a second function for this lamp (warning of vacuum loss in the brake servo) and a separate handbrake-on warning lamp.

The original instrument voltage stabiliser was found to absorb ambient heat on air conditioned models and to cause high oil and water temperature readings, so a new type (part number PRC 4034) incorporating a heat sink was introduced at AA 126489 in approximately July 1983.

The speedometer cable was re-routed at AA

135661 in October 1983, to prevent kinking and the resultant wavering needle.

From about November 1980, the choke was relocated to the facia top, just outboard of the rear wash-wipe switch. The control itself has a round black knob with the international choke symbol in its centre. When door-mounted radio speakers became standard equipment in August 1982, the redundant speaker aperture in the facia top was fitted with a moulded coin tray. This is secured by four set-screws passing into captive nuts in a pair of metal brackets which fit underneath the facia top; the screw heads are concealed by a grey rubber anti-slip mat with moulded edges.

From AA 100783 in 1979, two telltale lamps were added to the facia top rail (below the instrument binnacle) either side of the differential lock light, informing of the use of rear fog guard lights (left) and sidelights (right). Fitted with GLB 281 bulbs, both have the same design of body and lens, with standard international pictorial symbols printed on their lenses. Their positions were reversed at AA 123531, in spring 1982, so that each lamp was more logically adjacent to the column stalk which operated it. Heat from the bulb of the sidelight telltale sometimes caused the holder to melt, resulting in a Service modification that advised use of a 24-volt bulb (part number 575221) to reduce heat. Eventually the sidelight telltale was deleted, at AA 146000.

When automatic transmission became optional in 1982, Range Rovers fitted with it had a fourth warning lamp below the instrument binnacle. This warns of high temperatures in the transmission oil, and is always fitted outboard of the other three lamps. The lens is printed with the words TRANS OIL TEMP. Note that a redundant three-way electrical connector for the oil cooler is fitted behind the grille on manual vehicles. It should be protected by a waterproof cover; if this is not fitted, water may cause a short that will illuminate the oil temperature warning light.

On all models from AA 103441 in February 1980 (but sold from June), the bonnet release was relocated from the passenger footwell to the driver's footwell, but was still mounted on a bracket on the outboard side. During this period, the early type of release handle was changed for one with a symbol of a car with its bonnet open.

An illuminated heater control panel with revised graphics is a feature of 1984 models, built from June 1983 approximately. Two capless 1.2-watt bulbs are fitted into a holder behind the facia, and shine onto the control panel from above. In September 1980 there came a revised heater box that is broadly similar to the earlier type but with different mounting brackets.

The in-dash air conditioning already available on LHD models became optional on RHD models for the 1981 model year, beginning in June 1980. The installation was the same, but handed to suit the right-hand steering.

The support rods on the air conditioning condenser cooling fan motor tended to break when the vehicle was used in rough terrain, so extra clamping brackets were added to support the rear of the motor at AA 109104 in March 1981. The wiring to the condenser cooling fans was also changed on 1983 models with automatic transmission. The initial launch stock of these vehicles was wired so that only one of the fans operated constantly with the air conditioning, but from AA 127442, in October 1982, both fans were wired together. An appropriate modification could be made in service if required.

The shorter central lower facia panel on RHD models is a mirror-image of the LHD type, with cigarette lighter and heated rear window switch on the driver's side.

On 1980-model AA-series Range Rovers, the footwell side trim panels are handed, the one on the driver's side being shorter to make room for the choke control cover. On 1981 models, with the relocated choke control, tall panels are used in both footwells. New panels were introduced in June 1981 for 1982 models, coinciding with the introduction of four-door versions. These are distinctively moulded, with a recessed section at pedal level, and have a channel-like moulding at the top to conceal some of the under-dash wiring. They are retained by drive screws.

From September 1979, a four-spoke steering wheel with a thicker rim replaced the three-spoke

This arrangement, with three warning lamps under the instrument panel, was introduced for the AA-series. Unlike the earlier single lamp for the differential lock, these lamps are hooded.

This type of facia was used on air conditioned models. Note how the air distribution rail contains not only directional vents but also the air conditioning control panel itself (next to the steering column). The minor instruments are displaced to a position alongside the heater control panel. This is a 1981 In Vogue two-door.

type. In theory, this was fitted from AA 100783, although in practice it almost certainly arrived rather later. This wheel has a cover panel in the centre with the Range Rover name moulded into it; the cover panel is secured by a single screw. The original four-spoke wheel has a plain moulded rim, but the 1981 and later models (from AA 103441) have a leather-trimmed version.

Beginning with AA 100783, 1980 models have a stalk control for the rear fog guard lights in place of the earlier auxiliary lighting stalk. The wiring is arranged so that these lamps are automatically cancelled if the headlights are switched to main beam.

For 1982 models, all stalk switches changed sides to meet internationally-agreed standards.

The change actually took place at AA 111959 in June 1981, and did not coincide exactly with the start of 1982-model production. The switches on these models are therefore different from previous types, whose symbols would be upside down if they were used in the revised positions. The main left-hand stalk now controls the indicators, horn and main beam, while the main right-hand stalk is for wash/wipe functions. This has the additional option of a pre-set delay for the wipers, and the switch is plugged into a Lucas wiper delay unit that is screwed in position under the facia. The shorter left-hand stalk is now the main lighting switch, and the shorter right-hand stalk operates the rear fog guard lamps.

From approximately AA 139720 in November 1983, the ignition switch incorporates a key centralising barrel with an additional tumbler, which makes insertion of the key easier.

There are some differences in the accelerator countershaft and lever from engine suffix D, on automatics and on Australian-market vehicles, which also have a different accelerator cable. The brake pedal on the automatic models built in the 1983 and 1984 model years is much wider than the manual type. LHD and RHD brake pedals differ, but share the same ribbed rubber pad. Unlike the manual type, this does not have the letter R moulded into it. The brake pedal bracket, bolted to the bulkhead, is the same as the one used on manual models.

As the handbrake lever no longer operated a warning lamp on non-Australian vehicles from AA 100783, the plunger switch under the lever was deleted. The handbrake has a ribbed car-type grip from AA 130854 in July 1983 (for the 1984 model year).

The gear selector on automatic Range Rovers of this period is handed to suit LHD or RHD. It is a metal assembly with the selector positions visible through a window on the driver's side of the lever. A large rubber boot is fitted underneath it, to reduce noise and protect the shift linkage. The knob is a flat, square type made of black rubberised plastic, with the gearchange pattern marked in white. The gate is a reversed E, with L (Low), N (Neutral) and H (High) on the right, and three positions marked 'Diff Lock' on the left.

Unlike the earlier four-speed manual gear lever, the five-speed lever on 1984 models is not handed, but angled towards the driver by adjustment. It has a black plastic knob similar to the four-speed type, but etched with the appropriate gear positions in white.

On automatic and five-speed models, the lever for the transfer gearbox is located further forward than on four-speed types. It is centralised on the transmission tunnel rather than offset, and operates the differential lock as well as the transfer

gearbox itself. Five-speed models have a round knob with selector positions in two planes etched into it in white. The knob on automatics has similar markings, but is a black rubberised plastic item shaped to match the main gear selector knob.

BA-series (1985 models)

The facia was completely redesigned for the 1985 model year, and Land Rover made a real attempt to get the colours of all the different components to match. As a result, almost every component differed, even though many looked the same. The chosen colour was light grey.

The instrument binnacle is much larger than the earlier type, completely fills the indentation in the top of the facia rail, and is offset slightly from the steering column. The binnacle, which is the same for both LHD and RHD vehicles, has a plastic core moulding with a printed circuit attached to the back. A metal bracket bolted through the top of the facia rail holds this core moulding in position, and has two spring clips which press the back panel of the binnacle against the front. The front cover assembly consists of the visible grey plastic shroud, a shaped casing screwed to the back of it, and a clear plastic lens which clips into this casing.

The two main instruments have quadrant-style faces and are broadly similar to those used in the contemporary Austin Maestro saloon car. The speedometer is always on the right-hand side, and is marked in miles per hour or kilometres per hour as required. It has a trip counter as well as a distance recorder, and the re-set button for the trip counter protrudes from the face of the instrument. Illumination for the speedometer is by fibre-optic cable and is concealed behind a shroud which projects from its front face. This shroud also conceals the base of the needle and is marked in white letters with MPH or KPH, as appropriate.

A right-angle drive is screwed to the back of the speedometer. This is different from the type used with the earlier small binnacle, and has its own gasket. The speedometer drive cable is in two parts, a short upper cable which runs from the angle drive at the speedometer end, and a longer lower cable which leads to the gearbox. The upper cable is the same for both LHD and RHD models, but there is a special variant for Saudi Arabian export models. The lower cable comes in three different versions, for LHD, RHD and Saudi Arabia respectively. Problems with noise from the speedometer and with wavering needles prompted a change to the cables; a shorter cable was fitted to RHD models from BA 150504, and a longer cable to LHD models from BA 157668.

The left-hand position is occupied by a rev counter, with a fuel gauge at its bottom left and a

From the start of the 1981 model year, the choke control was re-located alongside the switch for the rear wash-wipe, on the facia top panel.

water temperature gauge at bottom right. Illumination for the rev counter, and its needle, are concealed behind a shroud which matches that on the speedometer. This shroud is marked in white with the letters RPM. The fuel and temperature gauges are actually part of a single assembly which fits behind the face of the rev counter. They are governed by a PRC 4350 voltage stabiliser screwed to the back of the instrument core moulding.

Between the main instruments is a bank of 15 warning lamp locations, and as a result there is no need for the earlier additional lights on the top rail below the instrument binnacle. Not every location is used. The ignition warning lamp has a unique bulb and holder, but all the others have the same capless bulbs in plastic holders. The same type of bulb and holder is used as the light source of the fibre-optic instrument illumination.

The same facia top moulding is used for both LHD and RHD Range Rovers. It looks similar to the earlier facia top, but is a lighter shade of grey, has no apertures for eyeball vents, and has side window demister vents at its outer edges. The four windscreen demister vents are not the same as those used on earlier models, but have flat top surfaces. The choke control is in the same place as before, and has the same black control knob, but there is no rear wash-wipe switch as the control for this is now among the steering column stalks.

Three stiffeners remain along the windscreen side of the facia top, but are supplemented by a stiffener running across the lower front edge on the passenger's side and in the centre (LHD and RHD types differ). The parcels tray and its anti-slip mat are unchanged, as are the central coin tray, its supporting brackets and anti-slip mat. The outer edge finishers have the same shape as before but are a different colour. In addition, there is a substantial moulded grab handle – without the leather cover found on later types – on the front of the passenger's side parcels tray finisher.

The windscreen demister vents were found not to be fully effective in some cases, and so a Service modification was introduced in January 1985 to cure problem cases. This consisted of rotating the outer vents clockwise by 60° in their housings.

An air vent rail runs across the passenger's side and centre of the facia and is screwed to the underside of the top rail. It is handed to suit LHD or RHD and contains four louvres on air conditioned vehicles, or two on those without air conditioning. These louvres have large vertical vanes, as on earlier air conditioned Range Rovers.

In the centre of the vehicle, the air vent rail carries a rectangular clock. This has a black plastic bezel and an adjusting knob at the lower right of the face. At the steering column end of the air vent rail on air conditioned models, a cut-out contains the switch-plate for the air conditioning.

This contains two sliding controls, the upper one for the four-speed blower fan and the lower a thermostat. The early temperature control was prone to turn itself off when its washer lost tension and allowed the lever to slip, so from BA 153840 a modified switch and a new washer were fitted.

The lower facia panel on the driver's side is similar to earlier types, but incorporates the instrument panel lighting rheostat at its inboard top corner. The rheostat control is a black thumbwheel, and the whole assembly is held to the back of the panel by two screws. Outboard of the driver is an aperture which holds either a radio or the map pocket seen on earlier models.

Four screws hold the central lower facia panel to the bulkhead, and a further four attach it to the

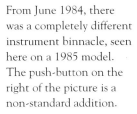

From June 1984, there was a completely different instrument binnacle, seen here on a 1985 model. The push-button on the right of the picture is a non-standard addition.

The 1985 models also brought new minor switchgear. Note, too, the different graphics on the heater control panel and the new type of cigarette lighter.

The late type of transfer box control is seen here on a 1985 model; the differential lock control is integral with it.

underside of the facia top panel. LHD and RHD types differ. The metal face-plate for the heater controls is the same as the 1984 type, and again screwed to the heater itself rather than to the facia panel. As before, it is illuminated from above.

Underneath the heater control panel, a printed instruction plate is held in place by four pop rivets. This plate displays instructions for correct use of the transmission controls, and carries its part number of MRC 9563. Alongside it, on the driver's side in every case, is the cigarette lighter. This differs from the earlier type, and its knob has a smoking cigarette symbol printed on it in white.

On the passenger's side of the centre facia panel is the detachable fuse box cover. This is moulded in grey ABS plastic with a raised edge, and is the same for LHD and RHD. Matching it on the driver's side is a switch panel. The panel and its four switches are all made of black plastic, and the switches incorporate warning lamps with coloured lenses and identifying symbols printed in white. These symbols are back-lit from a fibre-optic source under the facia when the sidelights are on. The fibre-optic cables are plugged into the frame clips which retain each switch behind the panel. From the left, the four switches are for hazard warning lamps, interior lights, rear fog guard lamps and heated rear window.

Range Rovers without air conditioning have a parcels shelf under the passenger's side of the facia, held in place by set-screws. Both LHD and RHD versions are folded up from black-faced cardboard, and have the same grey plastic finisher along their top edge. From BA 170458, the shelf is reinforced by an upper moulding or roof section. On Range Rovers with air conditioning, a grey plastic panel conceals the air conditioning evaporator unit mounted above the passenger's footwell. This panel extends under the air vent rail across the centre of the car, and is held in place with screws into this rail and into bulkhead mountings.

The leather-rim, four-spoke steering wheel introduced on 1981 models continued to be used, but the centre boss has minor differences. The steering column shroud has the same top half, but the bottom half is a different moulding available in two versions. One version has a cut-out on each side for a joystick switch which adjusts the electrically-operated mirrors on models so equipped. The other is for vehicles without electric mirrors. The joystick controls are made of black plastic and have a pyramid-shaped head.

The two main stalk switches on the steering column have the same functions as before, and the shorter left-hand stalk is once again the main lighting switch. However, the shorter right-hand stalk now operates the rear wash-wipe, and is attached to the steering column by a special bracket. Although all the switches are visually similar to those used earlier, they are all pre-wired with the multi-pin connectors characteristic of the BA-series and later Range Rovers.

CA-series (1986 models)

Despite appearing broadly unchanged, the 1986 facia has some significant differences.

From CA 264660, the front shroud of the binnacle overlaps the rear casing to give a more positive fit, and there are additional retaining clips. Early automatics in this model year have a warning lamp for high gearbox oil temperature that carries the symbol of a thermometer inside a gear ring, but on later vehicles the symbol is a simple exclamation mark.

A one-piece speedometer cable is fitted from CA 262629, and an improved right-angle drive from CA 270321.

The facia top panel has remodelled front outer corners from CA 271170. This allows deletion of the filler pieces between upper and lower sections.

The louvres in the air vent rail are quite different from the earlier type. They are once again made of black plastic but their vanes are predominantly horizontal, and they have a rectangular adjuster in the centre to control the sideways deflection of air. Each louvre unit has a restrictor on the back, with a 12mm wide letter-box opening. Later examples had a wider opening, and a Service modification specified an increase the early 12mm opening to 25mm on the inboard passenger's side air vent if the customer complained of poor air flow.

From CA 265469, the lower edge of the clock's perspex rim is finished in matt black to prevent reflections in the windscreen.

The radio is located centrally on 1986 models, which have a completely different lower facia moulding, and, in front of it, is a smaller moulding containing the radio. This radio surround panel is trimmed in grained grey vinyl, and carries the cigarette lighter on the driver's side. When no radio is fitted, the radio aperture is filled by a moulded black plastic oddments box with a sprayed-on felt-like lining. The redundant radio aperture outboard of the driver is filled with the 1985 type of map pocket or, when air conditioning is fitted, a bezel and louvre.

The heater face-plate is also differs, being moulded from black plastic and back-lit by several small bulbs linked by fibre-optic cables to a single larger bulb under the facia.

The fuse box cover on the passenger's side has an angled outer edge and carries a label with instructions for the transmission controls; labels for manual and automatic models differ. The cover was modified to give a better fit at CA

166800. The driver's side switch panel on 1986 models is a new black plastic moulding, containing six switch locations. The switches are back-lit push-push types. The normal complement is four switches, with black blanking plugs in the two unused locations on the right-hand side. Locations are the same on LHD and RHD models: at top left is the interior light switch, and below it the rear fog guard light switch; top centre is the heated rear window switch, and below that is the hazard warning lights switch. When driving lights are fitted, their switch occupies the top right-hand position. From CA 267805, in July 1986, the rear fog guard lamps are wired to operate with main or dipped headlamp beams, whereas on earlier vehicles they are automatically extinguished when main beam is selected. From CA 153746, a modified indicator and lights stalk is fitted, with an improved Lucar connector position.

The handbrake was relocated on top of the transmission tunnel, on the driver's side of the new cubby box (see Chapter 5). The same type of ribbed grip was used, but a new linkage (designed to suit the new ZF automatic transmission option) further improved the feel. The gaiter is still made of leathercloth, and attached to the inside of the cubby box by Velcro patches. The fit of this gaiter was improved at CA 267805.

The 1986 models were the first to dispense with the traditional wand-like gear lever, in favour of a short, remote shift lever. This has a black plastic knob with the gear positions moulded into it. There was also a new automatic selector lever to go with the ZF gearbox, which replaced the Chrysler type on 1986 models. The ZF selector has a black handle with a snap-fit top cover and a detent release underneath. Gear positions are shown on both sides of the black plastic indicator plate, which is illuminated (in green) when the ignition is switched on. The selector assembly incorporates a roller slide which indicates (by a red lens) the selector position. The roller slide band tended to tear on early examples, so its tension was modified at CA 164000.

Both the manual gear lever and the transfer box lever have grey leathercloth gaiters. On both manual and automatic models, the round knob of the transfer box lever is made of black plastic and has the gear positions moulded into its top surface.

DA-series (1987 models)

The instrument core differs, having a different printed circuit to suit the revised arrangement of warning lamps. The instrument lighting on these models is green, and the green filter is mounted on the front face of the instrument core. The fuel/temperature gauge unit differs, being the same as that fitted to diesel models introduced in April 1986. From DA 279045, a different temperature transmitter was fitted on Range Rovers destined for the Middle East, in order to keep the needle of the gauge on Normal!

The warning lamp lens block incorporates two additional lamps, for low engine coolant (also used on diesel models from April 1986) and low fluid in the windscreen washer reservoir. The lamp for the centre differential lock is now on the radio surround panel.

The grab handle on the passenger's side parcels tray is now covered in grey leather, and there are different mounting brackets for the coin tray. The choke control is in the same place as before, but a different type is used to suit the SU carburettors introduced on 1987 carburettor engines.

The air vent rail differs once again from the 1986 type, in order to suit the new top rail moulding. With air conditioning there are four vents in the rail instead of two; the vents themselves are the same as on 1986 models. At the inboard (driver's) end of both types of air vent rail is a square aperture. If electrically-adjustable mirrors are fitted, this incorporates the adjuster controls, which are made of black plastic in a black plastic bezel. They consist of a changeover switch for the right-hand and left-hand mirrors, with arrows printed in white, and a pyramid-shaped joystick control for vertical and horizontal adjustment. On vehicles with air conditioning but no electric mirrors, this aperture is filled by a black plastic blanking plate with moulded Range Rover logo.

The driver's side lower facia panel differs at the top outer corner as a result of remodelling to eliminate the filler panel. On Range Rovers without air conditioning, a plastic map pocket insert is fitted into the aperture outboard of the steering wheel. On air conditioned vehicles, there is a bezel in front of this (screwed to the underside of the top rail and to the lower panel itself, as before). The bezel contains an adjustable air vent made of black plastic and matching the other vents in the facia. RHD vehicles have a new moulding for this bezel, but LHD vehicles retain the earlier moulding.

The radio surround panel now carries the differential lock warning lamp on the passenger's side, as well as a cigarette lighter on the driver's side. The lamp has an orange lens with a black printed symbol, a black plastic bezel, and a 2-watt bulb. DA-series models all had higher-specification audio units than earlier vehicles, and the speakers were uprated to suit. Different types of audio units were fitted to suit different markets. The position of the radio right beside the heater outlets obviously caused some problems, so in April 1987, at DA 279738, a strip of foam was applied round the tunnel aperture on the centre panel to inhibit the spread of heat.

The first 1987 models have the same fuse box cover as 1986 models, but from DA 274145, in January 1987, a new type with different fixing lugs was used. The early type has two legs and one peg; the later type has one leg and two pegs to make removal easier. The 1986 transmission instruction labels are used on both early and late covers. In addition, the rear of the cover on 1987 models has an additional label, explaining the layout of the fuses. There are different labels for models with and without air conditioning.

The switch panel on the driver's side is the same as on 1986 models, except that the warning lamp for the rear fog guard lamps is now incorporated in the switch (and deleted from the main bank of lamps in the instrument binnacle).

The heater surround panel on 1987 models is marked to suit the three-speed blower which replaced the four-speed type on earlier models, and there are different versions to suit Range Rovers with and without air conditioning. The air conditioned type has an additional 'snowflake' symbol among the lower left-hand group of symbols. Behind the panel, the 1987 models also have a boot-type terminal cover for the heater illumination harness.

On the passenger's side lower facia panel, the J-shaped finisher which screws underneath the top rail is remodelled to suit the new moulding of the top rail which eliminates the filler piece. Otherwise, the cover panel on air conditioned models and the parcels shelf on others are unchanged.

The heater is fitted with a solenoid-operated vacuum unit behind the lower facia panel. This controls the flap which admits fresh air or turns it off to allow the air inside the cabin to recirculate. The vacuum reservoir is located on the left-hand inner wing, and is a black plastic ball-shaped unit with two small-diameter flexible black air hoses.

The 1987 models have a new two-spoke steering wheel of smaller diameter. It has an untrimmed plastic rim, and the central finisher is a push-fit over the hub and spokes.

The steering column shroud is also completely different. It has a different shape and consists of right and left halves, held together by screws which pass through the plastic into long threaded tubes. Two screws passing through from underneath hold it to the facia panel. A red hazard warning light switch projects from the top; this does not align with the centre of the instrument panel, which is slightly offset.

The shroud carries two paddle switches. On the left is the main lighting switch with three positions (off, sidelights and headlights), and on the right is the rear wipe/wash control, giving intermittent wipe (pull towards driver) or a linked wash/wipe cycle (push away). There is no longer any provision for an inspection lamp.

The 1987 Range Rovers have only two black plastic stalks, which form part of a single assembly attached to the steering column. These stalks were shared with the Austin Maestro and Montego. The left-hand stalk controls indicators, headlamp flasher, horn (press) and main beam, and the right-hand stalk controls the windscreen wipers (two speeds and a fixed delay) and washers (operated by pressing, which also gives five sweeps of the wipers). The symbols printed in white on these stalks are not illuminated internally, unlike later similar types.

The accelerator pedal is the same as the 1986 type, but on LHD models it changes at DA 277451 and has a different rubber pad.

Several changes were made at DA 301158, consequent upon the introduction of the new Girling brake servo just before the start of the 1988 model year. A new, metricated pedal box was fitted for the brake pedal, and the accelerator pedal mounting plate on automatics was changed at the same time. The clutch pedal on manuals also changed, from a Lockheed to a Girling type. The rubber pads on the pedals were unchanged.

At DA 285274 in August 1987, the handbrake was modified to give greater clearance between its grip and the tunnel finisher.

EA-series (1988 models)

A different type of voltage stabiliser is fitted from EA 330904, late in the 1988 model year.

The air vent rail on RHD vehicles was remoulded in 1988 at EA 303698 to improve the fit of the left-hand vent. At EA 327092, a self-adhesive plastic clip was added inside the facia airbox of air conditioned Range Rovers. This was used to secure the thermostat capillary tube and prevent it from rattling. From EA 336301, in approximately May 1988, plastic spacers were added to prevent distortion of the air vent rail at the points where it screws to the facia top panel. At the same time, the end finisher on the passenger's side was modified with a third locating lug to improve its fit. The nozzle of the side-window demister was notched to suit, and the modified area sealed with a black rubberised solution.

The label on the inside of the fuse box cover changes at EA 320304 to reflect the use of a 20-amp fuse (instead of 15-amp) for the heater circuit. As before, there are different labels for vehicles with and without air conditioning.

A different detent button is used on the automatic gear selector from EA 331996 in approximately November 1987. This has an L-shaped profile rather than the square shape of the earlier type. Further trouble with the roller slide indicator in the automatic transmission selector led to another modification, at EA 325406.

Chapter 7

Engine

All Range Rovers covered in this book have a version of the 3528cc V8 engine which was bought from General Motors in America during 1965. First used in Buick, Oldsmobile and Pontiac cars between 1961 and 1963, it was adapted for British manufacture and use in the mid-1960s, and introduced as a power unit for Rover saloon cars in 1967. More than 30 years later, larger-capacity descendants of the engine are still used in Land Rover products.

The engine is an all-alloy lightweight type with dry cylinder liners. Its overhead valves are operated by pushrods and rockers from a single chain-driven camshaft in the centre of the vee. Hydraulic tappets automatically maintain correct valve clearances. The crankshaft runs in five bearings and the pistons are made of aluminium alloy, with two compression rings and one scraper ring each. The pent-roof inlet manifold carries two carburettors and is water-heated.

Cylinder block and heads, timing cover, rocker covers and inlet manifold are all unpainted. Brackets bolted to the engine were always painted black, as was the pressed steel sump. Details of

Representative of the earliest engine bays is that of YVB 151H (chassis number 1). Red washer tubing clips are incorrect.

other painted elements are given later.

There were several different variants of the engine to suit different markets and specifications, each one identified by its own prefix code. A table listing these codes and their market applications can be found in Chapter 14. The text which follows here gives details of the specification of each engine variant. The early engines (with all-numerical identifying prefixes) are listed first, and the later types (with alpha-numerical identifying prefixes) after them. Note, however, that the numerical order of the earlier engines does not correspond exactly to the order of their introduction. Thus, the 341 series engines, which head the list, were actually introduced later than the 355 series types that were the 'standard' engine throughout the 1970s. As with the pre-VIN Range Rover chassis, a suffix letter was used to indicate changes of specification which were important when servicing the vehicle.

Certain series codes were allocated specifically for Service exchange engines. The 342 series was the Service equivalent of the 359 series production engines, the 357 series equated to the 355 series, and the 399 series equated to the 398 series. In addition, the 344 series was allocated for CKD vehicles built in Pakistan, but it is not clear whether this was actually used. No special series were allocated for Service engines under the later alpha-numerical identification system.

Fuel-injected engines were introduced in October 1985 on high-line four-door CA-series Range Rovers, such as the UK-market Vogue. At this date, sales of carburettor Range Rovers ceased altogether in Australia and South Africa. Fuel-injected engines were standardised on all petrol four-door models from December 1986, but carburettor engines remained available in two-door vehicles until the summer of 1988.

The earliest Range Rover engines had Champion L87Y spark plugs as original equipment. However, these were prone to sooting under constant light load, so Champion L92Y became the standard fit from engine numbers 355-10932B and 355-00087B in April 1973. These hotter-running plugs were used on all subsequent engines up to the introduction of the high-compression types in 1981, when Unipart GSP 131 or Champion N12Y became the recommended fit.

341 engines

The earliest 341-series engines are to Suffix C specification. They were introduced in March 1971 for Germany, Norway and Sweden with an 8.25:1 compression ratio. From the start of Suffix F production in 1977, they had Pulsair air injection and an 8.13:1 compression ratio. Parts catalogues suggest that the earliest Suffix F engine was

341-38127F, although this number is sometimes given as 341-83127F; it has not been possible to resolve the contradiction.

The Pulsair system draws air through non-return valves into the exhaust ports during the negative pulse of the combustion cycle, to burn off any residual hydrocarbons and reduce noxious emissions. It consists of air rails, valves and hoses running alongside each cylinder head, connected to the inlet manifold and to the cylinder heads. On the 341-series engines, the system draws air from the air intake elbows and injects it into all

This is YVB 151H again. Note angled mounting of the ignition coil and, visible to its left here, the early mechanical fuel pump.

eight exhaust ports. Pulsair engines have different cylinder heads from those used on other types.

These engines were the first Range Rover types to be fitted with the thermostatically controlled air intake. The air intake tube is shorter than the type fitted to early 355 engines, and the air cleaner body is painted black. A hose attached to the intake leads to a rectangular-section metal intake with a circular air temperature control valve mounted on top of it. A small hose runs from this to a sensor on the air cleaner box and a second hose runs from the sensor to a non-return valve on the inlet manifold. A large-diameter hose is attached to the underside of the air intake, and leads down to a hot air chamber on the right-hand exhaust manifold.

The system works by drawing in warm air from around the exhaust manifold while the engine warms, so that operating temperature is reached as quickly as possible. At this point, a flap valve in the intake opens and allows ambient air to be drawn in through the nose of the intake and to mix with the heated air. The thermostatic control valve then keeps the air at a controlled temperature in all conditions, so stabilising fuel usage and emissions. At full throttle, the valve opens fully to cold air, so that peak performance is unaffected.

Vapour formed in the induction system under 'hot soak' conditions is vented to a charcoal canister mounted in a bracket on the right-hand inner wing. The canister has a single outlet at the top and another at the bottom, and is connected by pipes to the carburettors and inlet manifold. The breather system also incorporates a pipe between air cleaner and inlet manifold, and there is a vacuum switch linked by hoses to the inlet manifold and to the distributor.

Carburettors are vented Zenith-Stromberg 175 CD2S constant-depression types, and have a hose connection in their adapter plates for the vent pipe. They have a temperature compensator – which looks like a closed penknife – on the outside of their bodies. A modified carburettor is used on Suffix E and all later engines, and the carburettor linkages are different again on Suffix F engines. Suffix D and later engines were fitted with a modified inlet manifold, which can be identified by the casting number ERC 2159 R/R on top of the pent-roof feature.

The original water pump and cover assembly were changed in January 1976 for a type with improved seals. There is no visible difference between the two types. December 1978 brought new hydraulic tappets with an 8lb plunger spring instead of the 2lb type used from the beginning. From engine number 341-29504F in November 1979, there were minor internal modifications to improve the security of the main bearing cap bolts. At 341-40401F in May 1981, an improved

Twin Zenith-Stromberg carburettors were fitted to all Range Rovers before the introduction of SUs in the mid-1980s. Air cleaner is finished correctly in aluminium paint. It is a Rover P5B car type, and the two holes in its intake trumpet are for the choke cable mounting on that model. The extra clip on the intake trumpet was not standard and its purpose is unclear. The early oil filler cap is grey rather than orange.

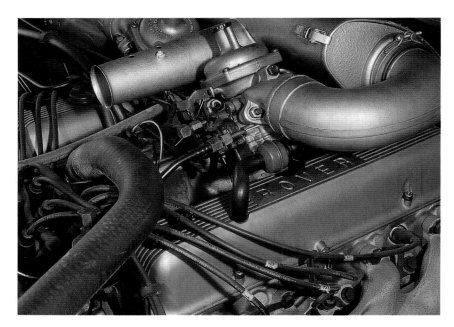

timing chain was fitted, identifiable by a single copper-coloured link. An oil seal was added to the inlet valves at 341-41021F in September 1981.

355 engines, Suffix A

These were the only Range Rover engines built with an 8.5:1 compression ratio. The rear main bearing oil seal is in two halves, and the oil seal packing piece is straight (vertical) on early examples but cruciform from engine number 355-00518A; this change was introduced because the

These are the correct black ignition leads, each labelled with the number of its cylinder. Note the flame trap on top of the rocker box; like the air cleaner elbow, the rocker box has a dull metal finish.

This view of YVB 151H shows the early alternator, exhaust manifold and steering box.

early packing piece tended to slip. The front cover has an aperture on the left-hand side to accommodate a mechanical fuel pump, and a blanking plate is fitted over this on vehicles with an electric fuel pump. When stocks of this front cover ran out in March 1977, the Service recommendation was to fit the later type with its associated vibration damper. From engine number 355-04787A in about August 1972, a mud excluder ring was fitted around the crankshaft aperture in the front cover.

These engines all have a fixed cooling fan with five metal blades riveted to a central hub. The dipstick handle is a metal loop, and there are two different dipstick tubes. The shorter of these is just 2 $^{11}/_{16}$in long, and the longer type is 11in long; neither type has a support bracket. The rocker covers have the word 'Rover' stamped into them and the right-hand cover has a grey plastic oil filler cap on a short extension which is painted to match the grey enamel of the rocker cover.

The pent-roof manifold carries two Zenith-Stromberg 175 CD2S carburettors; these are non-vented types. Each has a separate flame trap, mounted horizontally in a bracket on top of the rocker cover on the same side of the engine; a black hose leads from carburettor to flame trap, and a second one from flame trap to rocker cover.

The air cleaners on these engines have an oval-section body with a long trumpet-type intake, and are stove-enamelled in silver. The top surface of the intake contains two redundant holes, which were occupied by choke cable clips when this air cleaner was used in Rover P5B cars. A rubber, ball-shaped dust valve is fitted into the underside of the air cleaner box, and a hose leads from the air cleaner to a crankcase vent air filter mounted horizontally at the back of the engine, while a second hose leads from this to the cylinder block. At each end of the air cleaner is a U-shaped metal elbow, which has a rubber gasket where it enters the air cleaner and is secured by a large screw-adjustable wire clip. These pipes are painted grey to match the rocker covers, and at their other ends fit over similarly-painted adapter plates which are bolted to the carburettors.

355 engines, Suffixes B to E

The Suffix B version of the 355 engine was introduced in approximately April 1972, and the Suffix E version ceased production during 1977. Among the changes introduced for Suffix B were pistons with a new W-slot design to improve control of piston expansion, and more flexible top compression rings to resist fracture. A new crankshaft was fitted at the same time to compensate for the greater weight of the new pistons.

These engines were once again the 'standard' type, but were not fitted to Range Rovers for Germany, Norway or Sweden, which continued to have the special 341 engines with Pulsair air injection. From 1975 and the end of 355 Suffix D engine production, Australian Range Rovers also had their own engines, in the 398 series.

All these engines have an 8.25:1 compression ratio and a single-piece rear main bearing oil seal with a cruciform packing piece. The dipstick tube has a support bracket, but the dipstick itself is the same as on 355-series Suffix A engines. The inlet manifold is the same as the Suffix A type on Suffix B and Suffix C engines; Suffix D and Suffix E engines have a different type. When a choke warning light is fitted, the inlet manifold has an Otter thermostatic switch near its front end and connected to the dashboard lamp.

The front cover has a mud excluder ring bolted around the crankshaft aperture, and again has an aperture for the mechanical fuel pump which is covered with a blanking plate on vehicles with an electric fuel pump. The oil pump cover contains an oil pressure transmitter and oil temperature transmitter. Three different types of crankshaft pulley are fitted: a single pulley for vehicles with neither power-assisted steering nor air conditioning, a twin pulley for those with power-assisted steering but no air conditioning and for those with air conditioning and either non-powered or power-assisted steering, and a triple pulley on Australian engines.

The camshaft on these engines is the same as that on the earlier variant with the 8.5:1 compression ratio. Rocker covers have the Rover name cast into them, and a special right-hand rocker cover is used on detoxed engines in vehicles with both power-assisted steering and air conditioning. This has a taller oil filler neck with a metal 'eared' filler cap.

All these engines have nylon cooling fans with

a viscous coupling. On Suffix B engines, the fan has 13 blades and is mounted ahead of the viscous coupling. On engines with Suffixes C to E, the fan has seven blades and the viscous coupling is in front of it. Engines on Range Rovers equipped with air conditioning have twin pulleys on the nose of the water pump behind the fan, whereas engines on non-air conditioned vehicles have a single pulley. During production of Suffix E engines in January 1976, a new water pump and cover assembly with improved seals were fitted; there is no external difference between the old and new types.

Suffix B and C engines have the same carburettors, air cleaner and breather system as Suffix A units. However, 355-series units were 'detoxed' to meet new European ECE 15 emissions control regulations for the 1974 model year. Suffix D and E engines therefore have the modified inlet manifold already described for the 341 engines, and a thermostatically controlled air intake.

Non-vented carburettors are used on Suffix B engines, and vented types on Suffix C and D types A third variety of carburettor is used for Suffix E units, and mixture adjustment on these is carried out by moving the jet assembly; they were fitted to vehicles from chassis numbers 355-09864C, 356-02859D and 358-08621D, in October 1974. All carburettors have a temperature compensator, and the adapter plates of the vented types have a hose connection for the vent pipe.

355 engines, Suffix F

These engines were introduced in 1977 and remained available until approximately 1983. Like other Suffix F engines, they have an 8.13:1 compression ratio. They were the 'standard' Range Rover engine until the 11D high-compression type took over in 1981. Thereafter, the 355 engines were used in markets where conditions demanded their lower compression ratio. These engines were not used in Australia, where new emissions control regulations demanded the special 398 engine, and they were not used in Germany, Norway or Sweden, where the 341 engines with Pulsair air injection were specified.

The rear main bearing oil seal is a single-piece type and has a cruciform packing piece. The cylinder block is fitted with drain plugs instead of drain taps. The dipstick tube is supported on all engines, and the dipstick again has a looped metal handle.

The front cover on these engines has no provision for a mechanical fuel pump. Two different types of oil pressure transmitter were used, both screwed into the same location on the oil pump housing. The earlier type is found on chassis up to 355-38132D and 358-38134D. It is a bi-thermal type, and is shallower than the later air-cored

transmitter. On these engines, the Rover name is no longer cast into the rocker covers. The cooling fan once again has seven blades, but the viscous coupling is mounted behind it.

These engines are detoxed types, with the thermostatically controlled air intake. Air from the cooling fan could be forced into the intake pick-up and cause backfiring, so a Service modification of a baffle on the open end of the intake was introduced in September 1979. A different version of the Zenith-Stromberg carburettor was introduced on the first Suffix F engines, and from engine number 355-42953F yet another variety was used. There is a cylindrical fuel trap, mounted vertically in a bracket at the front of the engine. The fuel trap is connected by one hose to the left-hand carburettor and by a second to the distributor vacuum advance mechanism.

As on contemporary 341-series engines, the original hydraulic tappets were replaced by tappets with uprated plunger springs in December 1978. The security of the main bearing cap bolts was improved in November 1979, at engine number 355-36584F, and the same change was made on 357-series Service exchange engines at 357-01223F. The improved timing chain with identifying copper link arrived in May 1981 at 355-42559F, and oil seals were added to the inlet valves at 355-43727F and Service exchange engine 357-02367F in September 1981.

This is the engine of a 1979 model. Note particularly the black-painted air cleaner with its rectangular intake trumpet. Thermostatic intake control is in the circular box on top of the trumpet, and hot air is fed from the hot box on the right-hand exhaust manifold through trunking to the underside of the air intake.

359 engines

The 359-series engines were introduced in approximately May 1973 for Range Rovers exported to continental Europe. They have an 8.25:1 compression ratio and are generally similar to the contemporary 355 types, but are 'detoxed' with a limited amount of emissions control equipment to meet European regulations. They were not sold in Germany, Norway or Sweden, where tighter exhaust emissions regulations demanded the special 341 engines.

These engines have carburettors with temperature compensators, and have the thermostatically controlled air intake and exhaust 'hot box' used with the 341-series engines. They also have a charcoal canister for vapour absorption, fitted to the right-hand inner wing.

398 engines

For the 1975 model year, Australia introduced new standards on exhaust emissions. These were known as the ADR 27A regulations, and the 398-series V8 engines were developed specially to meet them. They were generally similar to contemporary 355-series types, but with features unique to Australia. The first 398-series engines have an E suffix and an 8.25:1 compression ratio. Tighter regulations (still under ADR 27A) introduced in 1977 demanded the introduction of a pumped-air injection system, and these later engines to Suffix F specification have the 8.13:1 compression ratio used on all other engines with that suffix. They went out of production in 1982.

Unlike contemporary 355 cylinder blocks, those of 398 engines retain the earlier type of drain taps. Suffix F engines also have a special dipstick, tube and support. All 398 engines have special rocker covers, which are ribbed but do not have the Rover name cast into them. There is a breather filter at the front of the right-hand cover, and the oil filler neck is at the front of the left-hand cover. These engines have the standard water pump, but there is a bolt rather than a stud fixing at the top left (ie, right-hand side of the engine). The later pump with improved seals was fitted in January 1976, during Suffix E production.

The Suffix F engines have a belt-driven air pump on a bracket attached to the right-hand side of the engine, and an additional belt tensioner pulley on a bracket attached to the front cover. Early pumps have Imperial fixings, and later examples have metric fixings. From April 1978, the air pump pulley is stamped FRONT, to ease the assembly operation. The air pump supplies a system of hoses and air rails running alongside the cylinder heads, which is generally similar to the Pulsair system. Engines up to 398-00643F have a

check valve at the front, but later engines have a diverter valve instead, with a slightly more complicated arrangement of hoses at the front. A special inlet manifold is fitted with the diverter-valve air injection system.

Suffix F engines for Australia have Stromberg carburettors with an automatic choke, and special air cleaner arrangements. The right-hand carburettor has a temperature compensator while the left-hand carburettor has a heat mass at the front and some additional hoses. Each carburettor has a separate air cleaner box mounted on a special adapter plate. Each air cleaner has its own temperature control valve in the intake (identical to the one used on detoxed engines for other countries), and, of course, there is a profusion of extra hoses to suit.

Matching specification changes on contemporary engines for other markets, these units were modified to improve main bearing cap security at 398-02094F in November 1979, and gained inlet valve oil seals at 398-03427F in November 1981.

11D engines

The 11D engines were the first ones to have a higher 9.35:1 compression ratio. They were introduced in February 1981 on the UK-model In Vogue limited edition, and then on both four-door and two-door Range Rovers for most markets from July 1981. The camshaft has a lower valve lift and different timing from that used on the low-compression engines. The 11D engines are emissions-controlled to meet ECE 1503 regulations, and require 97-octane petrol.

These engines were always used with the 12C-series four-speed LT95 gearbox with its taller high-ratio gearing. Quoted power output of 125bhp is lower than the 132bhp of the contemporary low-compression (8.13:1) engines, but it is developed 1000rpm lower, at 4000rpm – with the result that engine noise at speed is considerably reduced. The quoted torque of 185lb ft at 2500rpm is almost identical to that of the low-compression engines.

The 11D engines have Zenith-Stromberg 175 CDSE carburettors with BIFH needles, and the idle mixture and idle speed settings are tamper-proofed with seals to suit ECE 1503 regulations. The air cleaner has a black body with a thermostatically controlled air intake, and Pulsair air injection is fitted. The distributor is a Lucas 35D8 number 41872, with sliding contacts and a blue plastic anti-tracking cap. The vacuum unit also carries a spot of blue paint.

Like the rocker covers on other V8 Range Rover engines built after the beginning of 1981, those on the 11D engines do not have the Rover name cast into them. The 11D cylinder blocks are more rigid than those on low-compression types,

and are fitted with drain plugs rather than drain taps. The rear main bearing oil seal is a single-piece type and has a cruciform packing piece. The dipstick tube is supported, and the dipstick has a looped metal handle. Pistons are shared with the contemporary Rover SD1 car version of the V8. A cylindrical fuel trap is mounted vertically in a bracket at the front of the engine, connected by one hose to the left-hand carburettor and by a second to the distributor advance mechanism.

Running changes included the introduction of lower-stressed valve springs in October 1981 and the addition of an oil seal to the inlet valves a month later. The valve spring change probably took place at engine number 11D-00440 (the number given in Service literature is 116440), and the oil seals were added at 11D-02550.

13D engines

The 13D engines were introduced in 1982 and were built with an 8.13:1 compression ratio for export markets. They were intended for use with the three-speed automatic gearbox and are non-detoxed types with 175 CD3 carburettors. The Suffix A engines have sliding contact ignition; Suffix B engines introduced in 1984 have electronic ignition. Softer engine mounting rubbers

are used on these, as on all engines intended for use with automatic transmission.

The carburettors are the same as those on Suffix F engines from 355-42953F, and the air cleaner has a black body and the thermostatically controlled air intake. The cylinder block is the same as the 11D type on Suffix A engines, but minor differences were introduced for Suffix B. The dipstick tube and handle, and the cylindrical fuel trap, are also the same as on 11D engines. Pulsair air injection is fitted, and the connecting hoses used on Suffix B engines have minor differences from those on Suffix A types.

Several running changes affected the specification of these engines. From chassis number BA 154210 in April 1985, the cylinder head bolts were coated with Loctite 572 sealant. The original paper gasket between sump and cylinder block was replaced at chassis number BA 158988 by Hylosill RTV liquid sealant, and then at CA 264072 the sump flange was redesigned to improve the seal further. From CA 268576, a new camshaft was introduced: colour-coded grey and stamped with the number 6, it is made of the same material as the type introduced earlier on the fuel-injected engines. In May 1986, the introduction of a new type of oil filter extended oil-change intervals from 6000 miles to 12,000.

This later carburettor engine is fitted to a driveable demonstration chassis which now belongs to the Heritage Collection. Its precise date is unknown but it has an early-1980s specification. The air cleaner has been removed for clarity. Note the orange oil filler cap, the air rails of the Pulsair air injection system, the emissions-controlled carburettors, and the chimney for the hot box on the right-hand exhaust manifold. The alternator has been displaced to the left-hand side of the engine by an air conditioning compressor.

A 1983 In Vogue model: note the blue distributor cap, the deflector on the nose of the air intake, and the hot air chimney in the background. The air rail for the Pulsair air injection system can be seen clearly alongside the rocker cover.

15D engines

The 15D engines, introduced in 1982 for use with the three-speed automatic gearbox, are the high-compression equivalents of the 13D types, with 9.35:1 compression and Pulsair air injection. Suffix A engines have sliding-contact ignition with the Lucas 35D8 distributor, while Suffix B types introduced in 1984 have electronic ignition.

These engines have 175 CDSE carburettors, with additional vacuum pipes between carburettors and distributor, and an orange delay valve. From the start of the CA-series chassis in October 1985, the Pulsair injection is a six-port type, drawing air from the air cleaner (rather than the elbows) and injecting it into three of the four exhaust ports on each side (rather than all four).

The running changes which affected these engines took place at the same time as those for the 13D engines. They were the addition of Loctite sealant to the cylinder head bolts; the use of Hylosill instead of a paper sump gasket and the subsequent modification of the sump flange; and the introduction of the new oil filter giving extended oil-change intervals. The new camshaft introduced towards the end of CA-series chassis production was colour-coded light green and stamped with the number 7. A further change in October 1985, at the beginning of CA-series production, did not affect the low-compression engines. This was the standardisation of a Thermac air deflector plate at the air intake opening, to prevent fan-driven air being forced into the air cleaner and causing misfires.

16D engines

These engines have a 9.35:1 compression ratio and were introduced in 1982 for Range Rovers with the three-speed gearbox destined for Australia. They have 175 CDSE carburettors, Pulsair air injection and Evaporative Loss Control to meet Australian ADR 36 rules. There is sliding-contact ignition on Suffix A types, and electronic ignition on Suffix B types introduced in 1984.

The additional vacuum pipes and orange delay valve are the same as those on the 15D engines.

The Evaporative Loss Control system has more complicated breather arrangements. Hoses from the carburettor elbows run to a Y-piece and from there a single hose runs to the breather at the front of the right-hand rocker box. The engine breather filter is mounted horizontally, behind the carburettors. There is a vacuum switch between distributor and inlet manifold, but this uses a different bracket to that on non-Australian engines.

A charcoal canister is also used with these engines, but it differs from other types by having three outlets at the top. The system also incorporates a petrol catch tank, mounted on the right-hand side of the load bay behind the wheelarch.

Running changes were otherwise the same as those for the 15D engines. Loctite sealant was added to the cylinder head bolts; Hylosill sealant replaced the paper sump gasket and the sump flange was subsequently modified; and the new oil filter extended oil-change intervals. The new camshaft was colour-coded light green and stamped with the number 7, and the Thermac air deflector plate was fitted.

17D engines

These are the manual-transmission equivalents of the 15D types. They have 175 CDSE carburettors, a 9.35:1 compression ratio and Pulsair air injection, and were introduced in 1983 for use with the five-speed LT77 gearbox. Suffix A types have sliding-contact ignition, and Suffix B types introduced in 1984 have electronic ignition.

The original rear engine mountings, identifiable by a yellow spot, were found to cause some harshness and vibration. Softer mountings with a white spot code were therefore used from chassis number CA 165239. From October 1985, the six-port version of the Pulsair system was fitted.

Other running changes paralleled those made on the 15D engines. Loctite sealant was added to the cylinder head bolts; Hylosill sealant replaced the paper sump gasket and the sump flange was subsequently modified; and the new oil filter extended oil-change intervals. The new camshaft was colour-coded light green and stamped with the number 7, and the Thermac air deflector plate was fitted.

18D engines

These are the low-compression equivalents of the 17D types, destined for export models with the five-speed manual gearbox. They have 175 CDSE carburettors and are detoxed to meet European ECE 1503 regulations. They have Pulsair air injection, which in October 1985 changed to the six-port type. Suffix A engines have sliding-contact ignition while Suffix B types have electronic ignition.

Running changes were the same as those made on other versions of the engine in production at the time. The cylinder head bolts were sealed with Loctite; sealant replaced the paper sump gasket and the sump flange was subsequently modified; and the new oil filter extended oil-change intervals. The new camshaft was colour-coded grey and stamped with the number 6, but the Thermac air

deflector plate was not fitted. Like the 17D engines, the 18D types switched to softer engine mountings during CA-series chassis production.

19D engines

The 19D engines were built for Australian five-speed manual models, beginning in 1983. They went out of production at the end of the 1985 model year, when Australia switched to fuel injection for all 1986-model petrol Range Rovers. They have the 9.35:1 compression ratio and pumped air injection. Suffix A types have sliding-contact ignition, and Suffix B types have electronic ignition.

Once again, running changes were the same as those made on other contemporary versions of the engine. The cylinder head bolts were sealed with Loctite; sealant replaced the paper sump gasket and the sump flange was subsequently modified; and the new oil filter extended oil-change intervals. The new camshaft was colour-coded light green and stamped with the number 7, but the Thermac air deflector plate was not fitted. A change was made to softer rear engine mountings during CA-series chassis production.

20D engines

These engines were introduced in 1983 for five-speed manual vehicles destined for Saudi Arabia. They have 175 CDSE carburettors, an 8.13:1 compression ratio, Pulsair air injection, and Evaporative Loss Control. Ignition is by sliding-contact breaker on Suffix A types and is electronic on the Suffix B versions introduced in 1984.

The 20D engines retained the eight-port Pulsair air injection after other engines switched to the six-port type in 1985. Other changes were the same as those made on contemporary engines for other markets. The cylinder head bolts were sealed with Loctite; sealant replaced the paper sump gasket and the sump flange was subsequently modified; and the new oil filter extended oil-change intervals. The new camshaft was colour-coded grey and stamped with the number 6, and the Thermac air deflector plate was fitted. A change was made to softer rear engine mountings during CA-series chassis production.

21D engines

These are the same as the 20D engines, but intended for use with the three-speed automatic transmission. Built for Saudi Arabia, they entered production as Suffix A types in 1983 with sliding-contact ignition, and switched in 1984 to electronic ignition at Suffix B. They have the 8.13:1 compression and eight-port Pulsair throughout.

ENGINE OUTPUT FIGURES

Dates	Variants	Compression	Power	Torque
1970-71	355 suffix A	8.5:1	135bhp @ 4750rpm	185lb ft @ 2500rpm
1971-77	355 suffix B to E	8.25:1	130bhp @ 5000rpm	185lb ft @ 2500rpm
1977-86	355 suffix F, 13D, 18D	8.13:1	132bhp @ 5000rpm	186lb ft @ 2500rpm
1981-86	11D, 15D, 17D	9.35:1	125bhp @ 4000rpm	185lb ft @ 2500rpm
1986-88	26D, 27D	9.35:1	134bhp @ 5000rpm	187lb ft @ 2500rpm

The power and torque of the carburettor V8 engine varied considerably between versions built for different markets and at different times. The table above is intended to give some indication of the differences, and is not exhaustive.

Early engines had a fixed, red-painted, metal fan (top), whereas the later fan is viscous-coupled and has plastic blades (above).

Like the 15D and 16D high-compression engines destined for use with automatic transmission, the 21D types have additional vacuum pipes and an orange delay valve. Other features were the same as those on the 20D engines, but there was no change to the rear engine mountings.

26D engines

The 26D engines were introduced in 1986 and have a 9.35:1 compression ratio. They are emissions-controlled types to meet the then-new European ECE 1504 regulations, intended for use with the LT77 five-speed gearbox, and have two SU HIF44 carburettors. The change from Strombergs was made on all carburettor V8 engines at this time because manufacture of these carburettors ceased.

Running changes included new hydraulic tappets in the middle of the 1987 model year, and a modified water pump seal at DA 293610. The new tappets were introduced at approximately DA 280143, and have three identifying grooves on their bodies.

27D engines

These are the equivalents of the 26D types, but intended for use with automatic transmission. Running changes were the same.

28D engines

These are low-compression (8.13:1) engines, without emissions control equipment. They have SU HIF44 carburettors and were export-specification engines, intended for use with the LT77 gearbox. Running changes were the same as for contemporary engines with SU carburettors.

29D engines

These are the equivalents of the 28D types, but intended for use with automatic transmission. Running changes were the same.

30D engines

These engines were specific to Range Rovers destined for Saudi Arabia. They have an 8.13:1 compression ratio, SU HIF44 carburettors, and Evaporative Loss Control. They were for use with the LT77 gearbox only. Running changes were the same as for other engines with SU carburettors.

Cooling system

The cooling system is a conventional water-based type, assisted by an impeller pump and a radiator cooling fan. The system operates at 15psi and uses an 88° thermostat, or an 82° type on detoxed engines. The earliest automatic models all had 88° thermostats, but an 82° type was fitted from chassis number AA 127442 in October 1982. The thermostat elbow is normally a simple curved type, but the 398-prefix Australian engines have a more angular fitting, with a water temperature transmitter screwed into its top.

The radiator is a crossflow type with a separate expansion tank. Air conditioned models have a different radiator from the one used on standard Range Rovers. A warning label was always attached to the top surface of the radiator, next to the black plastic filler plug: 'This plug must not be removed when engine is hot.' An air bleed hose runs between the top of the radiator near the filler plug and a connection on the inlet manifold. The expansion tank is made of black metal and is carried in a cradle bracket bolted to the platform behind the battery on the right-hand inner wing. Its filler cap is a conventional eared pressure cap with a bright metal finish.

Radiator modifications were made in November 1980 and January 1983. The earlier change occurred at chassis number AA 109589, when the brazing of the inlet and outlet tubes was improved. The second change was made at AA 128216, and brought improved soldering of the cooling rails to the side tanks, with increased joint areas to prevent leaks. The first of the improved radiators carried the date code 40.

Rubber sealing strips are fitted between the radiator and the front panel. Vehicles of chassis Suffix A to C have flat seals, but from Suffix D hollow-section seals were used. Steel retaining plates secure these seals on all four sides, and were changed to suit the later type of seal. Behind the radiator is bolted a black plastic cowl which also acts as a fan shroud; the cowl on air conditioned vehicles differs from the standard type.

Exhaust system

The left-hand exhaust manifold is the same on all Range Rover carburettor engines, but the right-hand manifold has several variants. A plain four-branch manifold is used only on engines with the prefixes 341, 355, 359, 398, 13D and 18D. On detoxed versions of the Suffix B 355-series engines for Europe (and possibly also Suffix A types), a hot air chamber is mounted around the manifold, and a hose runs from this to a control valve on the air cleaner. On later 355-series detoxed engines, and on 341-series detoxed types, a simpler manifold shroud is used to achieve the same ends, and a slightly different hose runs from it to the control valve. From engines 355-37700F and 341-33523F in late 1979, the left-hand manifold had larger cast webs to resist cracking. Stainless steel nuts were used to secure the exhaust manifolds from AA 100661 in April 1980.

On engines with the prefixes 11D, 15D, 16D, 17D, 19D, 20D and 21D, the right-hand exhaust manifold casting again incorporates a hot air chamber. The lid of this has a hot air chimney, painted light blue, and a second connection for the hose which runs to the control valve. This hose is the same as the one used on 341-series and later 355-series detoxed engines.

A downpipe runs from each exhaust manifold to meet a Y-pipe. These sections have push-fit overlapping ends, and are clamped together; the clamps may have Imperial or metric bolts. From February 1980 and engine number 355-58568F, twin-skinned downpipes were fitted. In March 1982, an optional Service modification was introduced for hot climates where high temperatures were causing heat from the exhaust to melt the seals on the clutch slave cylinder. The modification consisted of adding an insulation pad to the inside radius of the left-hand downpipe, and securing it with three clips.

The Y-pipe was changed to clear the automatic transmission when this became optional in 1982, and this later pipe was subsequently fitted to manual models. Commencing chassis numbers were AA 121296 (four-door automatic), AA 121865 (two-door automatic), AA 125310 (four-door manual) and AA 125322 (two-door manual).

The main silencer box is bolted directly to the flange at the rear of the Y-pipe. Engines with Suffixes A to E have a silencer with a single exit (intermediate) pipe, and these were double-skinned from February 1980, at the same time as double-skinned downpipes were introduced. Dual intermediate pipes and a silencer with dual exhaust were fitted from engine Suffix F. Range Rovers for Switzerland had a special silencer box. The construction of the silencer was also improved from chassis number BA 155500, because the baffles had tended to become loose on earlier examples. A heat shield is mounted directly above the silencer, bolted to the body floor and to the chassis cross-member; the shield

The earlier type of exhaust has a single tailpipe, but engines from Suffix F onwards have twin tailpipes.

used with the twin-pipe silencer differs from the earlier one for the single-pipe type.

The final section of the exhaust consists of a long pipe section in unit with a rear silencer and tailpipe. On single-pipe systems, the rear silencer has a single tailpipe, with its end cut away at an angle to direct the exhaust gases downwards. On twin-pipe systems, the rear silencer has twin tailpipes, which are cut away at an angle to direct the gases towards the left of the vehicle. The pipes in this rear section of the exhaust were modified slightly when the automatic transmission option was introduced, and the revised version was introduced at the chassis numbers noted above for the modified Y-pipe. On Range Rovers sold in Germany, bright finishers with rolled-over edges were fitted to the twin tailpipes in order to meet safety regulations.

This view of the exhaust system on YVB 151H shows how the two downpipes meet at a Y-junction just ahead of the main silencer.

Chapter 8

Transmission

All Range Rovers have permanent four-wheel drive, with the front and rear pairs of wheels being driven by propshafts running from a transfer gearbox. This transfer gearbox also provides two ratios – one for road use and a crawler ratio for off-road work – which gear down the output from the main gearbox. The transfer gearbox also contains the centre differential, which allows for variations in speed between the axles. This differential is lockable to give maximum traction in difficult off-road conditions.

Four basic types of main gearbox were used on the carburettor models. From the beginning of production until July 1982, all vehicles had the Rover-built LT95 four-speed all-synchromesh manual gearbox. In August 1982, a three-speed automatic alternative was made available; this gearbox was made by Chrysler in the USA and was known as the A 727. Then in July 1983, the LT95 manual gearbox was replaced by the Rover-built LT77 five-speed type. Finally, the three-speed automatic was replaced in October 1985 by a four-speed type made by ZF in Germany and known as the 4 HP 22.

Four-speed manual LT95

The LT95 gearboxes built for use with low-compression Range Rover engines (8.13:1, 8.25:1 or 8.5:1) are identified by serial numbers beginning with 355 and ending in suffix A, B or C. A new numbering sequence with a 12C prefix was introduced in 1981 for gearboxes intended for use with the high-compression (9.35:1) engines; these serial numbers also had suffix letters. It is worth noting that a version of the LT95 was also used in the military 101-inch One Tonne Forward Control Land Rover during the 1970s, and that a later derivative called the LT95A was used in some Australian-built Land Rovers during the 1980s and 1990s.

The LT95 gearboxes are mounted to the chassis by means of rubber bobbin-type bushes sandwiched between brackets. These gearboxes have an oil pump mounted in the front cover of the main casing. The main casing also incorporates the transfer gears (these are described in the

section below on the transfer gearbox).

During its 13 years of production for Range Rovers, the LT95 gearbox went through numerous detail modifications. The more obvious external changes are explained here, and the full list is given in the accompanying panel.

Early examples of the LT95 have a filler plug in the top cover, held in place by a sprung steel finger. At gearbox number 355-07192A, a screw-type filler plug which doubled as an oil level indicator was fitted to the left-hand side of the gearbox casing, but the top filler remained until gearbox number 355-15847B. Early gearboxes had their own dipstick with an O-ring to seal the dip tube, and by mid-1972 there was an integral rubber ferrule instead of the O-ring. However, the dipstick was deleted altogether in October 1976, leaving the side-mounted filler plug to act as an oil level indicator.

A valve-type breather was screwed into the top cover on all early gearboxes, but from the mid-1970s this was replaced by a plastic tube breather.

Basic layout of the four-speed LT95 gearbox is clear in this view of the driveable demonstration chassis in the Heritage Collection. Also visible are the transfer gearbox (with long selector lever) and centre differential lock control (with associated tubing). The drum of the transmission brake and the front propshaft have been painted blue and white for demonstration purposes, instead of black. This is a left-hand-drive chassis, with the hand-brake on the left of the transmission tunnel.

LT95 GEARBOX MODIFICATIONS
By gearbox number unless otherwise stated

355-00474A Modified selector fork and associated outer member for 1st, 2nd and reverse gear.
355-01147A Ferrobestos front cover oil pick-up ring replaced bronze type.
355-01475A Bolt replaced spring pin to retain reverse gear idler shaft.
355-03062A Reverse idler gear modified; straight shaft replaced offset type.
355-03377A Wider grooves in 1st/2nd speed selector shaft.
355-03444A Angled needle rollers in reverse idler gear bearings.
355-03605A Brass oil filler plug for transfer box, to reduce noise transmission.
355-03639A Differential lock control moved from gearbox to tunnel, to prevent heat and vibration blowing the indicator bulb; gearbox top cover modified to suit.
355-03803A Modified female cones in synchromesh units.
355-04037A Wider grooves in 3rd/4th speed selector shaft.
355-04079A Spacing washer added as over-travel stop for 3rd gear; stop lug removed from 3rd gear selector fork.
355-04081A Sealing gasket and backing plate interposed between clutch slave cylinder and bell housing.
355-05070A Strengthened reverse stop hinge assembly.
355-05244A Modified synchromesh inner members; locating pads for outer members now machined to closer tolerance.
355-05247A Felt and rubber seal added to prevent oil leakage from rear output shaft splines.
355-05926A Modified reverse selector shaft and selector finger.
Jul 1972 (approx) New detent springs to reduce gearchange load.
355-06067A Transfer box selector finger modified.
355-07192A Side oil lever/filler plug added.
355-08626A to 355-08677A Two riveted rings added to transfer box intermediate gear to reduce noise level.
355-09638A Two riveted rings now permanently added to transfer box intermediate gear (see 355-08626A).
355-12006B Angle of synchromesh dog teeth gears altered from 4 to 6 degrees.
355-14053B Intermediate shaft journal bearings changed from steel-caged type to INA nylon-caged type.
355-15342B Mainshaft gear journal bearings changed from steel-caged type to INA nylon-caged type.

355-15848B (Mar 1974) Oil filler deleted from top cover.
355-20820B (Jul 1974) New mainshaft and spacer.
355-21653B (Sep 1974) Improved waterproof switches for differential lock selector and reversing light.
355-27419B (Apr 1975) New mainshaft and synchromesh gear; new selector forks with separate pads, to reduce gearbox noise.
355-38474B (Mar 1976) New 3rd and 4th speed synchromesh assemblies, and new 3rd and 4th selector fork and stop, to cure jumping out of gear.
Oct 1976 Dipstick deleted; casing modified to suit.
355-45841C (Feb 1977) New reverse idler shaft and gearbox casing; idler shaft bush now deleted to prevent it from working loose.
355-56664C Stronger detent spring with wider location hole on reverse, to cure sticking in reverse gear after lever returns to neutral.
355-65494C (Mar 1979) Bigger oil feed holes on intermediate shaft, and reduced thickness of plating on thrust washers, to improve life of intermediate thrust washers.
355-75524C (Nov 1979) New main gear lever, selector jaws and selector fork to give shorter travel of lever across gate.
Jan 1980 New oil baffle plate, thrust washers and intermediate shaft, to increase durability of thrust washers; also introduction of new bearing housing, bearing outer race and spring pin to give positive location of bearing.
355-81800C (Mar 1980) Stronger one-piece spring on reverse stop replaces two-piece spring with swivel hook, to obviate adjustment after assembly.
355-83618C (May 1980) Modified front cover oil seal, to ease assembly.
355-84391C (Jun 1980) Both ends of reverse selector rail chamfered to ease assembly.
355-87220C (Aug 1980) Build tolerances tightened and new machinery and checking equipment in use to reduce noise.
355-87662C (Oct 1980) Hylomar sealant added to various places to tighten up leak control.
355-89590C (Dec 1980) New reverse selector shaft, reverse jaw and hinge stop; also longer roll pin with larger diameter, to improve security of reverse jaw on selector shaft.
Chassis AA 111700 (Mar 1981) Modifications to improve gear selection.
355-99382C (Jan 1983) Mainshaft output gear and sleeve now assembled using Loctite 275.
12C-11398A (Jan 1983) Mainshaft output gear and sleeve now assembled using Loctite 275.
12C-16554A, 356-01420C (1985) Late type of centre differential assembly fitted (Service exchange units only).

There were also changes to the gear selector lever itself, which started out as a single forging but soon changed to a two-piece shaft with a sleeved join near the bottom. A third type of shaft was fitted with effect from gearbox number 355-75524C in November 1979.

Three types of bellhousing were associated with this gearbox. The first was fitted with engines up to 355-06011A, and had a pressed steel bottom cover plate. The second was fitted from gearbox number 355-05973A in approximately August 1972 up to gearbox number 355-67045C in 1979, and had a machined cast aluminium bottom cover. The third, introduced in September 1979, was fitted with all subsequent LT95 gearboxes and had a slightly different cast bottom cover.

The LT95 four-speed gearbox has a transfer gearbox which is integral with the main casing. This transfer gearbox always had a vacuum lockable centre differential, supplemented on vehicles built before December 1970 by a limited-slip feature; this was deleted because it chattered during operation. Parts for this limited-slip element have been unavailable since the early 1970s, and the Rover Service recommendation was always to replace unserviceable examples with the later standard differential.

On all suffix A gearboxes, the centre differential is of Salisbury manufacture. On subsequent gearboxes, from approximately July 1973, the differential is a Rover-built four-star type.

The vacuum servo for the lockable differential is mounted to the selector housing on the front of the transfer box and connected to it and to the control switch inside the car by plastic tubing. The control is a push-pull switch, which was attached to the gearbox itself on early vehicles but to the tunnel inspection cover from gearbox number 355-03639A. On vehicles with Suffix A and Suffix B chassis, the switch has an integral warning lamp with a clear lens and a 2.2-watt bulb. However, from Suffix C chassis, the switch operated a separate warning lamp on the dashboard. In June 1971 approximately, a balancing ring was added to the centre differential assembly in cases of need. This ring was marked with the serial number of the differential unit, and fitted between the high-ratio gear and the differential casing. Further minor modifications to the centre differential came at gearbox number 12C-16554A.

Early transfer boxes have a three-piece selector lever, but later types have a single-piece lever. The date of this change is not clear, but it had occurred by mid-1972. A valve-type breather was used on the top cover until the mid-1970s, when a tube-type breather replaced it.

Exhaust pipe run and vacuum system for the centre differential lock can be seen here. Also visible are the bolts securing the removable gearbox cross-member to the chassis side rails.

LT95 Transfer Gearing Specifications

Gearbox no	Date	High ratio	Low ratio
Suffix A and Suffix B	Jun 1970	1.174:1	3.32:1
Suffix C to 355-94059C	Oct 1976	1.113:1 with 19° 10' helix	3.32:1
355-94060C on	Sep 1981	1.227:1 with 22° helix	3.32:1
12C-00001A to 01060A	Feb 1981	1:1 with 19° 10' helix	3.32:1
12C-01061A on	Sep 1981	0.9962:1 with 22° helix	3.32:1

LT77 Gearbox Modifications
By gearbox number unless otherwise stated

52A-0086544D Approximately 100 gearboxes fitted with adjustable reverse plunger assembly.
52A-0104663D Improved assembly procedures to prevent mainshaft spigot bearing failures.
Jan 1985 Molybdenum-coated contact face on 3rd gear synchromesh baulk ring, to improve synchromesh.
Chassis BA 157412 (Feb 1985) Loctite 270 added to bolt securing gear lever yoke to selector rail, to cure looseness; Service modification for earlier gearboxes includes use of lockwire.
Chassis BA 159962 (Feb 1985) Solid pins replaced roll pins in lower gear lever.
Chassis CA 165500 (Nov 1985) Molybdenum-sprayed synchromesh baulk rings on all gears.
Chassis CA 263958 (1986) Fifth gear interlock spool welded rather than brazed to increase its strength.
Chassis CA 265383 Modifications to cure gearbox whine.
53A-0173665D Modified reverse gear train.
53A-178851E Improved material specification of the two plastic bushes in the direct-change mechanism; new bushes colour-coded off-white to distinguish from earlier black bushes.
Chassis DA 288562 (late 1987) New selector forks (first gearbox number probably 53A-0200581E).

This change took place at the same time as the breather changed on the main gearbox.

Five-speed manual LT77

The serial numbers of five-speed gearboxes used on 1983 and 1984 model-year Range Rovers begin with 52A. On 1985 and 1986 models, the serial numbers have a 53A prefix, which indicates that the later type of direct gearchange (usually known as the 'short-stick' type) is fitted. Both LT230R and LT230T transfer gearboxes were used with the LT77 primary gearbox.

The flywheel assembly and clutch cover associated with the LT77 gearbox are the same as those used with the four-speed LT95. However, the clutch plate differs. The clutch pivot is also different and a release bearing guide is added. In the release assembly, the sleeve is the nylon/glass-fibre type with associated bearing, as used with the final four-speed gearboxes. The bell housing differs from the four-speed type, but uses the same bottom cover as the last four-speed models.

Clutch

The clutch is a 10.5in type made by Borg and Beck, and both plate and clutch cover remained the same with all versions of the LT95 gearbox. However, the ring gear on the flywheel was strengthened at an early stage, when the original 0.380in thick type was replaced by one that was 0.442in thick.

Minor changes affected the clutch release mechanism. A steel sleeve was used on gearboxes up to 355-06638A, but from 355-06639A this was replaced by a ferrobestos sleeve and the bearing was changed to suit. The release lever pivot changed at the same time. The steel sleeve was unavailable by February 1975, and the ferrobestos type was recommended as a Service replacement, together with its associated bearing and pivot. Later still, a nylon/glass-fibre sleeve was specified.

The clutch lining changed in approximately June 1971 from a light material with straight-woven zinc to a dark material with interwoven brass. Lockheed Raybestos 148805 facing material was introduced in January 1981 at engine numbers 355-41353 and 341-39729.

From gearbox number 355-04081A, a gasket

and packing plate are fitted between the clutch slave cylinder and the bell housing. From February 1977, however, these were deleted and replaced by Hylomar sealing compound.

The clutch master cylinder is mounted to the bulkhead, directly behind the pedal box. Two types are used, the later one introduced in November 1978 having different internal seals and being identifiable from the outside by a groove machined into the body just ahead of the mounting flange. Pipework remained unchanged until AA 112529 (RHD) and AA 112612 (LHD) in 1981, when the section connected directly into the master cylinder was modified.

Three-speed automatic

The three-speed automatic gearbox was introduced in August 1982 on four-door models only. UK dealers were advised in December 1982 that orders could then be accepted for two-door models, and the first two-door automatics were probably made early in 1983. However, two-doors were rarely ordered with automatic transmission.

The Chrysler transmission does not have integral transfer gears, but drives through a separate transfer gearbox manufactured by Land Rover. The transfer gearbox is bolted to the back of the main gearbox via an adapter housing, and carries the transmission brake on its rear output shaft. Most Chrysler automatics have the LT230R transfer gearbox, but the LT230T type was introduced shortly before the ZF automatic replaced the Chrysler type in 1986.

Engines used with the Chrysler automatic gearbox have a drive plate and starter ring gear in place of the flywheel and clutch on those used with manual gearboxes. There is an adapter plate which uses the same bottom cover as the bell-housing on contemporary manual models, and the transmission mountings include a strut and tie plate. The gear selector quadrant has an integral indicator marked PRND21, and the selector knob is a square black plastic type.

Four-speed automatic

The four-speed automatic gearbox introduced in October 1985 was built by Zahnfabrik Freidrichshafen (ZF) in Germany. It was a well-proven unit which had seen service in BMW saloons during the early 1980s, and brought the key advantage of an overdrive top gear. When the transmission was in top gear and the vehicle speed exceeded 43mph (69kph), a clutch locked the torque converter. This prevented the slip which is wasteful of engine power and so improved both fuel economy and top-gear responsiveness.

All ZF automatic gearboxes have a rear

extension housing which allows them to be mated to the LT230T transfer gearbox.

A small number of modifications were introduced on the ZF gearboxes during the production of carburettor Range Rovers. At chassis number CA 264978, the A clutch was modified to prevent circlip failure which could lead to loss of drive. In February 1986, detail improvements were made to reduce driveline shunt on engagement of gear. Then at DA 298104, the selector cable was secured to the gearbox casing by a P-clip.

A single-row oil cooler is fitted with the ZF four-speed transmission. It is bolted to right-angled brackets and is mounted ahead of the radiator on the front panel. Oil flows to it through pipes from the gearbox, entering on the left-hand side and returning from the right-hand side.

Separate transfer gearbox

As already noted, the transfer gears for the LT95 four-speed manual gearbox are integral with the main gearbox casing. However, carburettor Range Rovers fitted with the LT77 five-speed manual, the Chrysler A727 three-speed automatic and the ZF 4 HP 22 four-speed automatic primary gearboxes all have separate transfer gearboxes. These transfer gearboxes are bolted to the casing of the main gearbox in every case. The extension casing between LT77 main gearbox and transfer gearbox contains an oil pump.

There are two basic types of transfer gearbox. The LT230R is used on both manual and automatic models up to May 1985. Thereafter it is replaced by the LT230T (the T denotes taper roller bearings on the intermediate gears). The first Range Rovers with this later type of transfer gearbox were BA 155993 (automatic) and BA 156163 (manual). The LT230T is fitted to every automatic Range Rover with the ZF gearbox, and to the final examples with the Chrysler three-speed as well.

Some very early automatic Range Rovers were built with pre-production LT230R transfer gearboxes. These gearboxes are not numbered in the standard 14D production sequence, but have a unit number stamped on the left-hand side of the casing with a date stamped below it. Unit numbers start at PP1, and the build date takes numerical form, eg 26.5.82.

In January 1985, at gearbox number 14D-023074 (chassis number AA 146244), slight dimensional changes were made to the teeth on the transfer gear pairs of the LT230R. This modification reduced backlash in the transfer gears.

When the suffix C LT230T transfer gearboxes were introduced in January 1987, they brought with them modified gear teeth profiles to reduce the characteristic whine of the Range Rover's

The propshafts were offset to the right of the vehicle. This is the rear one, seen on YVB 151H.

YVB 151H again, this time showing the rubber gaiter on the front propshaft sliding joint. Also visible are the steering damper, ball swivels and right-hand front brake.

transfer box. At the same time, slightly lower high-ratio gearing was specified to improve acceleration. Some of the suffix C transfer boxes have a non-adjustable bolt-type detent plug: those affected are numbered 28D-008925C and 28D-009677C to 28D-017442C.

Propeller shafts

Range Rovers have open propeller shafts front and rear, with a diameter of 2in (51mm). Both propshafts have a 1310-type universal joint at each end, one of those on the front shaft being a wide-angle type. There is also a splined sliding joint on each propshaft, the one on the front shaft being protected by a concertina-type rubber boot attached with Jubilee clips.

Vehicles with manual gearboxes all have the same front propshaft. However, there is a second type for the three-speed automatic gearbox, and some very early vehicles with the ZF automatic gearbox have a third type.

TRANSFER GEARING SPECIFICATIONS

LT230R

Gearbox no	Main gearbox	High ratio	Low ratio
14D series	Automatic	1.003:1	3.32:1
15D series	Manual	1.192:1	3.32:1

LT230T

Gearbox no	Main gearbox	High ratio	Low ratio
27D series, suffix A and B	Manual	1.192:1	3.32:1
27D series, suffix C on	Manual	1.222:1	3.32:1
28D series	Automatic	1.003:1	3.32:1

Chapter 9

Electrical Equipment

The Range Rover started life with a very simple electrical system, and that system changed in only small details over the first decade of production. However, in the early 1980s the top models began to acquire more and more luxury and convenience equipment, most of which was electrical. As a result, battery capacity and alternator output were both increased.

In the beginning, the main wiring harness was conventionally bound with black PVC tape, and the engine harness was sheathed in Hypalon. Bullet-type connectors were used throughout, and relays were Lucas 6RA types. From June 1984, with the introduction of the BA-series chassis, a completely new type of wiring harness was fitted. This has the individual cables grouped together in a flat transparent plastic sheath, with shaped multi-connector plugs. Relays used with this later harness are uprated 28RA types.

There were several different configurations for the main harness, and several sub-harnesses for major components or optional equipment. The details of these can best be determined from the appropriate handbook for the vehicle. However, it is worth noting that from BA 147552 in 1985, a seven-pin male connector to suit trailer wiring was fitted as standard between the left-hand rear corner panel and the wing. The harness supplied with the optional towing kit could be plugged directly into this.

Battery

The battery is mounted on a platform behind the right-hand headlamp, and should be secured by a clamp. This clamp has a rectangular steel top section, sheathed in black plastic. This is held in place by two J-rods whose hooked ends are inserted into the metalwork of the inner wing valance; brass wing nuts on their threaded upper ends hold the top section in place. The battery on early Range Rovers is a 57 amp-hour type; later models have a 60 amp-hour battery. From the introduction of CA-series vehicles in October 1985, a nine-plate low-maintenance battery was the standard fit, and a 13-plate heavy-duty type was an optional extra.

From the start of Suffix C production in November 1973, a Lucas CP 13/11 heavy-duty battery was optional for cold territories. This larger battery had different fixing arrangements, with a simple clamp bracket along its front edge only; this was held in place by two J-rods running diagonally down the sides of the battery and locating in the metalwork. Nuts and washers, rather than wing nuts, were used at the threaded ends. A vertical support bracket was pop-riveted to the rear of the battery platform, with a rubber buffer pad between the bracket and the battery.

An auxiliary battery, charged from the existing alternator, was an optional extra. It was located behind the left-hand headlamp and clamped into position. For further details of the split-charge system, see Chapter 12, on options and accessories.

Fuse box

On all models up to the end of the AA-series, the fuse box is mounted on the engine side of the bulkhead, next to the windscreen washer bottle. It has a black plastic clip-fit cover, and contains three working 35-amp glass fuses and two spares.

Range Rovers sold in Italy up to AA 100782 in 1979 have their headlamps fused separately. There are two additional fuse boxes, one for each lamp, and each one contains two fuses. The boxes have black plastic covers, with a central screw-type fixing. Additional wiring runs from the main wiring harness to each fuse box, and then on to the associated headlamp.

From the start of the BA-series chassis in June

OPTIONAL FUSE POSITIONS (BA-SERIES ONWARDS)

Number	Rating	Function
10	3 amps	Electric mirror heaters
15	20 amps	Air conditioning (1)
16	20 amps	Air conditioning (2)
17	5 amps	Air conditioning compressor clutch
18	20 amps	Air conditioning blower motor
19	7.5/10 amps[1]	Central locking
20	25 amps	Electric window lifts

[1] Changed from 7.5 to 10 amps in August 1984.

1984, the fuse box is fitted in the lower centre facia panel, on the passenger's side. It is a much bigger item, with provision for 20 Autofuse pin-type fuses. A plastic fuse extractor tool is clipped to the lid of the fuse box. When a radio is fitted, its power input lead incorporates a separate holder with an in-line 7-amp fuse.

Up to seven fuse positions may be unoccupied. These are reserved for the special equipment which was optional on some models and standard on top-of-the-range four-doors. The optional fuse positions are given in the accompanying table.

Starter

The starter on early Range Rovers is a Lucas M45 pre-engaged type, operated from the ignition keylock by means of a relay and a solenoid. From the start of Suffix C production in November 1973, this was replaced by a Lucas 3M 100 metricated type with a sealed casing. From the start of the DA-series chassis in November 1986, a Lucas M78R type is fitted.

Alternator

The battery is charged by an alternator mounted at the top left of the engine and driven by a vee belt from the crankshaft pulley. On vehicles equipped with air conditioning, a cogged belt is used to reduce slippage. On early engines, the adjustable alternator bracket is secured to the engine by a bolt which passes through the water pump cover. When this was slackened to allow adjustment of the belt tension, it tended to cause leaks from the pump. So from engine number 355-04822A in approximately May 1972, the bolt was replaced by a stud with locknuts to allow the bracket to be moved without disturbing the water pump fixings.

The first Range Rovers had a Lucas 16 ACR (30-amp) battery-sensed alternator. A machine-sensed 16 ACR replaced it in August 1971 approximately, at engine number 355-00788A and chassis numbers 355-0649A and 358-00097A. The machine-sensed type lasted until engine number 355-15552B. Both types have metal shields around the fan and pulley, painted in back enamel, and both types have the same add-on radio interference suppresser.

As more and more electrical equipment became standard on the Range Rover, so higher-output alternators were fitted. A battery-sensed 40-amp 18 ACR type replaced the 16 ACR in January 1973, when the heated rear window and rear wash-wipe were standardised. From the start of Suffix C production in November 1973, a surge protection device was added to this alternator. From September 1979, the standard alternator

was a Lucas 25 ACR with a 60-amp rating; this had integral suppression, and so did not have an external suppresser attached.

From February 1981 (engines numbered 355-41501F, 341-39776F and at some point in the Suffix F 398 series), the 25 ACR was replaced in turn by a 65-amp Lucas A133 alternator. The original pulley on this had a diameter of 66mm, but from November 1983 a 60mm pulley was substituted to improve battery charging. The final carburettor Range Rovers, from approximately the start of the DA-series chassis, have a 65-amp Lucas A127 alternator, which has an additional supporting strut.

Uprated alternators were available from early on, either for heavy-duty use or for the optional split-charging system. Details are given in Chapter 12. By 1980, the 36-amp 17 ACR machine-sensed alternator was being supplied as a Service replacement for the machine-sensed 16 ACR used on some vehicles in the early 1970s.

Different mounting brackets are used on models with air conditioning and on Australian-market vehicles with F-suffix engines in the 398-series; on the latter, the air pump is attached to the same bracket.

Distributor, coil & HT leads

All Range Rover engines built before summer 1981 have distributors with conventional contact-breakers. Early engines have a Lucas 35D8-G distributor with an off-set pivot, but this was replaced from engine number 355-05695 (approximately April 1972) by a modified version with a base-plate which rotates concentrically around the driven shaft. This type of distributor uses a different type of contact-breaker set with a Zytel heel. A thicker washer was used on the distributor drive gear from January 1981, and engines numbered 355-41354F, 341-39734F and 398-02801F. Between summer 1981 and May 1984, engines have a distributor with sliding contacts.

From June 1984 and the start of the BA-series chassis, an electronic ignition system is fitted. The change to electronic ignition coincides with the change to B-suffix engines. Service literature noted that it was possible to convert an early engine to electronic ignition, by replacing the distributor, amplifier, coil and associated leads.

The different distributors fitted to carburettor Range Rover engines are itemised in the accompanying panel. The HT leads were always black. On very early engines, they have shiny black PVC cap covers, but these were found to work loose. So from August 1970, matt black Hypalon covers were moulded to the leads.

On Range Rovers with contact-breaker ignition, the coil is mounted on a bracket and rests at

Coil is mounted on the left-hand inner wing on early models. Later coils, both with and without a separate ignition amplifier, are mounted on the horizontal surface of the inner wing.

DISTRIBUTORS

Engine codes	Rover or Unipart no	Lucas type	Lucas part no	Remarks
355, suffixes A to E (early)	611390	35D8-G	41385	Contact breaker
355, suffixes A to E (late)	614179	35D8-G	41487	Contact breaker, with Zytel heel on points
355-02933A to 355-030082A	611080	–	–	Contact breaker, used during supply shortage; minor installation differences
341, 355, 356, 357 & 359, suffixes B to E	614003	35D8	41382D	Contact breaker; detoxed engines only
341, 359 & 398, suffix F	ERC 3341	–	–	Contact breaker; 8.13:1 compression engines
355 suffix F, 13D & 18D	ERC 3342	–	–	Contact breaker; non-detoxed engines
11D, 15D, 16D, 17D & 19D, all suffix A	ERC 7131	35 D 8	–	Contact breaker; 9.35:1 compression engines
15D, 16D, 17D & 19D, all suffix B	ETC 4715	35 DM 8	–	Electronic; 9.35:1 compression engines
13D & 18D, both suffix B; 28D to 28D-00138C; 29D to 29D-00033C	ETC 4717	35 DM 8	–	Electronic; 8.13:1 compression engines
20D, 21D & 30D to 30D-00015C	ETC 5090	35 DM 8	–	Electronic; Saudi Arabia only; for use with amplified ignition coil
26D to 26D-01513C; 27D to 27D-00291C	ETC 6122	35 DM 8	–	Electronic; for use with amplified ignition coil
26D from 26D-01514C; 27D from 27D-00292C	ETC 6952	35 DLM 8	–	Electronic; amplifer on distributor body
28D from 28D-00139C; 29D from 29D-00034C; 30D from 30D-00016C	ETC 6976	35 DLM 8	–	Electronic; amplifer on distributor body

The early washer bottle (right) is a single-outlet Trico. The later bottle (below right) has dual outlets, for the front jets and the rear washer system.

a slight tilt from the vertical on the left-hand inner wing, just ahead of the suspension tower. On 1985 and 1986 models with electronic ignition, the coil is mounted on top of its amplifier box, and the assembly is bolted flat on top of the left-hand inner wheelarch. The 1987 and 1988 models (from engine numbers given in the distributors table) have a conventional coil once again, because the ignition amplifier module is mounted on the distributor. All coils are fitted with an external radio suppresser.

Windscreen wipers

All carburettor Range Rovers have a two-speed Lucas permanent magnet wiper motor. Various types were fitted over the years, with minor dif-

ferences. The early wiper motor had part number 607914; by 1980 it was GEU 712, and this then changed to RTC 3870. From chassis numbers AA 139409 (four-door) and BA 147027 (two-door) in 1984, the motor had part number AEU 4127, and was attached by a clamp bracket. Finally, at EA 327675 in 1988, a new motor which incorporated a driven link was introduced. This had part numbers PRC 7096 (RHD) or PRC 7097 (LHD).

The wiper drive is by links attached to a bracket which is bolted behind the scuttle panel, and there are different brackets to suit the different wiper positions on LHD and RHD vehicles. The wiper arms push-fit over splined drive hubs and are handed to suit LHD or RHD. Early wiper arms had an aluminium finish and have been unavailable for some time. Black wiper arms were introduced at chassis numbers 358-42959F, 356-42965F and 355-43073F in 1978. All wiper blade assemblies are a push-fit onto the ends of the arms; early ones had support frames with an aluminium finish, while the later ones are black.

From June 1981 and the start of four-door production, a programmed wash-wipe system is fitted. This gives two speeds as before, plus an intermittent-wipe setting (initially set at one sweep every 4-6sec) and a linked wash-wipe cycle (the wipers operate automatically after the washer button is released for around five sweeps). The delay unit for the intermittent wipe is located under the facia on the driver's side.

Windscreen washers

On Suffix A Range Rovers only, the windscreen washer assembly is a Trico type with a translucent plastic bottle and a grey plastic screw-fit lid with the pump mounted vertically in the centre. The bottle is held to the passenger side of the bulkhead in the engine compartment by a cradle-type metal bracket. It is probable that very early examples of this washer bottle had the motor attached to the lid by four rivets, instead of the two used later.

From Suffix B until the end of the CA-series,

the washer bottle is a much larger type with two necks, each covered by a black-painted metal screw cap. One neck supplies the windscreen washers, and the other supplies the rear washer jet. This bottle is again made of translucent plastic, and is held to the bulkhead on the passenger's side by a larger cradle-type metal bracket. This bracket was modified at chassis number CA 268593, to reduce stress on the bottle and consequent cracking. The washer tubing passes through holes in the caps directly into the bottle, where it is finished by filters incorporating non-return valves. Two separately-mounted pump motors are used, each in its own metal bracket attached to the inner wing; one serves the windscreen, and the other the rear window.

A third type of washer bottle is fitted from the start of the DA-series in 1986. This has a single filler cap made of the same translucent plastic as the bottle itself, and the two motors are mounted to its rear. The bottle is held to the inner wing assembly by three bolts.

From around 1975, vehicles for Sweden had a headlamp wash-wipe system as standard. The standard washer bottle was used, but the cap serving the windscreen had two plastic connectors on it. The second fed washer tubing which was clipped to the inner wing and ran to the right-hand headlamp washer jet, and further tubing tee'd into this fed the jet on the left-hand headlamp. The headlamp washers were fed by a third Trico washer pump, mounted in a bracket on the right-hand inner wing. Unlike caps for other markets, the one feeding the rear washer jet on Swedish-market vehicles had an angled plastic connector for the washer tubing.

The washer tubing was always a green-tinted flexible plastic type, with white translucent plastic connectors. Black metal spring clips hold the washer tubing to the folded-under edge of the bonnet. These clips could sometimes crush the tubing, so modified clips and stiffer tubing were fitted from CA 264072. DA-series and EA-series vehicles have a pancake-type non-return valve in the tubing next to each pump.

The washer jets in the bonnet were initially chromed metal types with a single outlet which could be adjusted by means of a screw-type slot on its outer end. However, from chassis number AA 114957 in 1981, twin-jet plastic types with a D-shaped base were fitted. These were always fitted to the factory-built four-door models covered by this book, but most Monteverdi four-doors probably had the chromed type.

Rear wash-wipe

There was no rear wiper or washer on the Suffix A Range Rovers, although a bolt-on accessory kit was made available in April 1972 (see Chapter 12, about options and accessories). From January 1973, with the introduction of Suffix B chassis, a rear wash-wipe was standard equipment for most markets. However, the rear wash-wipe was not standardised for all vehicles until the start of the BA-series in 1984.

From chassis Suffix B, the rear washer is fed from the washer bottle in the engine bay, and the tubing runs behind the trim up the left-hand windscreen pillar, along the cantrail under the headlining, and finally to the washer jet above the tailgate window. With this arrangement, the wiper arm is to the right of the jet on RHD models but to the left of it for LHD. The jet distance piece was changed at AA 106593 in 1980 to allow the washer fluid to strike the glass higher up, for improved coverage.

Wiper arms are handed to suit, and have an aluminium finish until 1978. Black arms are fitted from chassis numbers 358-42959F, 356-42965F and 355-43073F. The wiper motor is a different type, mounted to the body under the headlining above the tailgate on the left-hand side. It drives the wiper wheelbox through a short rack, encased in protective tubing. The switch for the rear wash-wipe is a large rocker type, mounted on the dashboard just above the radio mounting pocket, outboard of the driver.

With the introduction of the DA-series chassis came a new wiper motor. This does not have a separate rack and wheelbox, but has a directly-driven spindle protruding from its body. The motor is handed to suit LHD or RHD, and is attached to the tailgate frame by a bracket which differs from the earlier type. The wiper arms differ from the earlier type, and are again handed to suit LHD or RHD. The wiper blade assembly, however, is unchanged from the earlier type.

Headlamps

All British-assembled Range Rovers were fitted with 7in circular headlamps. The lamps were fitted to apertures in the front panel: a rim was screwed to the front panel, the light unit was held to this by a bright metal retainer ring, and there was a rubber seal between this and the black front finisher panel.

Early vehicles have sealed-beam units with tungsten-filament bulbs. These are Butlers 1697/4DE types giving 75 watts on main beam and 50 watts on dipped beam. The French market required yellow bulbs, and so lamp units with replaceable Duplo bulbs were specified. When supply difficulties of the sealed-beam lamps used on LHD Range Rovers arose in December 1977, these switched to the French type of headlamp but with clear glass bulbs. As already noted, early

The early type of sealed-beam headlamp is seen on a 1973 model.

This is the correct type of front sidelight and indicator unit, seen on a 1979 vehicle.

Indicator repeater lamps were standardised on 1980 models.

The early type of rear light cluster (above) has a full-width lens for the reversing light. The later type (below) has a smaller reversing light segment, a repositioned indicator portion, and also incorporates a fog guard lamp.

Range Rovers built for the Italian market have separately-fused headlamps.

In mid-1979, at chassis serial number 59271G, quartz halogen headlamps were introduced. These are fitted to all vehicles except those with a headlamp wash-wipe system (see below). The lens units differ between LHD and RHD vehicles, and the original bulbs were Lucas SP 472 types with clear glass, 60 watts on main beam and 55 watts on dipped beam. French-market vehicles are once again equipped with yellow bulbs, which were originally Phillips SP 467 types with the same ratings. Italian-market vehicles no longer have separately-fused headlamps.

A further change was made with the introduction of the DA-series chassis in 1986. The lamp bodies were no longer mounted to the surround panels but rather to a plastic bowl screwed to the inner wing assembly. The same 60/55-watt quartz-halogen bulbs are used as on earlier models, with yellow bulbs for France. Note that UK-market vehicles, and certain others, also have a dim-dip system. This prevents the vehicle from being driven on sidelights only, by providing a reduced current to the headlamps when the 'sidelights' switch position is selected and the engine is running. When the engine is switched off, the sidelights can be selected in the normal way. The voltage transformer for the dim-dip system is mounted at the top end of the steering column support bracket.

From 1974 approximately, a headlamp wash-wipe system was fitted as standard on Range Rovers destined for Sweden. In the later 1970s, the system was also fitted to Range Rovers exported to Finland. In both cases, it was probably discontinued when the bumper-mounted washers became available in 1984. The wash-wipe system was suitable for use only with the tungsten-filament bulb headlamps. The wiper system consists of a revolving blade suspended over the face of each headlamp and driven by a cable from a motor mounted in the front of the engine bay. Additional cables and relays are part of the system, which is wired to operate only when both the windscreen wipers and the headlamps are on.

Sidelights & front indicators

The handed front indicator and sidelights clusters wrap around the corners of the vehicle. On all models up to the end of the CA-series they have alloy bodies, but on DA-series and EA-series Range Rovers they have black plastic bodies. The lamp bodies in each case are held to the vehicle body by drive-screws, and Philips-head set-screws attach the plastic lenses in turn to the lamp bodies. There is a waterproofing gasket between lens unit and lamp body.

The lenses consist of two segments bonded together. The upper segments are amber for the indicators, the lower segments clear for the sidelights. Early Italian-market vehicles had clear lenses for the indicators as well. Indicator bulbs are Lucas 382 21-watt types; sidelight bulbs on lamp units with alloy bodies are Lucas 233 4-watt types, and those for the plastic-bodied types are 5-watt. On all models up to the end of the AA-series in 1984, wiring connections are bullet connectors. Lamp units intended for the BA-series and later models have circular plug connectors.

Side repeater lights

Range Rovers for Denmark, Italy and Norway always had an indicator repeater light on each front wing, just below the bonnet shut-line and ahead of the wheelarch. These lights became standard for all markets in 1979 at chassis number AA 100783. They took on plug connectors in place of the original bullet connectors in June 1984, to suit the new wiring harness. The lights have a plastic body, a plastic lens with a gasket between them, and a Lucas 989 6-watt bulb.

With the introduction of the DA-series chassis in November 1986, these side repeater lights were relocated to the lower front of the wing, just above the bumper end cap. This light unit differs from the earlier type, is retained to the wing by two pegs and friction bushes, and has a 4-watt bulb.

Rear light clusters

Like the front light units, the rears are handed and wrap around the corners of the vehicle. They have alloy bodies and plastic lenses, with a sealing gasket between them. The alloy bodies are held to spring nuts pushed onto the body metal by drive-screws, and the lenses are held to the light bodies by Philips-head set-screws. The rear and side sections of the lens are separate units.

There are four different types of rear light cluster. The first type, used up to August 1979 and AA 100782, has a full-width reversing light section. The second type, made by Magnatex, was used from AA 100783 and incorporates a fog guard light so that the reversing light sector covers only half the width of the lens. The third type is similar, but has a single plug connector for the wiring instead of individual bullet-type connectors, and suits the revised harness introduced in June 1984 at the start of AA-series production. In these three types, the bulb for the stop and tail lights is a twin-filament Lucas 380 with a 6/21-watt rating.

All other bulbs – for indicator, reversing light, and fog guard light – are Lucas 382 single-filament types with a 21-watt rating.

The fourth type of rear lamp cluster was introduced on DA-series models in November 1986 and was designed to give better lighting performance. The lenses have an oval Land Rover logo. The twin-filament bulb for the stop and tail lights has a 5/21-watt rating, but all others are once again 21-watt.

On Range Rovers for the German market up to VIN 100782 in 1979, the red reflector segment of the rear lamp is covered by an alloy badge with 'V8' printed on it. The badge has two prongs on its reverse which are pushed through holes drilled in the lens. To suit regulations of the time, a red reflector is fitted to each bumper over-rider.

Rear number plate lights

On all Range Rovers built up to the end of the CA-series, the rear number plate is illuminated by two lights attached to the hinged number plate bracket. The lamps have black metal casings with glass lens inserts. Early vehicles used 6-watt Lucas 989 bulbs, but by May 1975 the owner's handbook was recommending 4-watt Lucas 233 bulbs.

The hinged number plate bracket was not fitted on DA-series and later vehicles, which consequently had different number plate illumination. These later Range Rovers have two rectangular black plastic lights with plastic lenses, screwed to the overhanging top section of the lower tailgate, directly above the number plate.

Horns

All Range Rovers have twin horns, one sounding a high note and the other a low note. Suffix A and B models have circular metal horns, mounted to brackets on either side of the radiator opening by two bolts each. 'Mixo' horns with trumpet mouths are fitted from the start of Suffix C production in November 1973 until the end of the AA-series in summer 1984. These horns, which give better sound penetration, were introduced to comply with EEC requirements. They are mounted to triangular brackets by a single bolt each.

From the start of the BA-series, circular metal horns are fitted again, although this time they have an integral bracket which is attached to a second bracket by one bolt. From CA 172590, the horns are mounted with a 50° angle of tilt, to prevent water ingress and aid drainage.

Service literature refers to the introduction of improved Lucas horns in October 1983 at AA 130715, but it is not clear what these were.

Interior lights

All Range Rovers from Suffix A to Suffix D have a single interior light, controlled either by a switch on the steering column or by door-operated switches. From Suffix E onwards, two interior lights are fitted.

Two-door models have two door switches, and four-door models have four. These switches have a plated finish on all models up to the end of the CA-series, and are made of stainless steel on DA-series and EA-series vehicles. From June 1981, and the introduction of the factory-built four-door model, an interior light delay unit is fitted. This allows the lights to remain on for a few seconds after the doors have been closed. With the introduction of the BA-series in 1984, an additional switch allowed the upper tailgate to operate the interior lights as well.

The interior lights are all of basically the same circular design, with a clear plastic lens ribbed on the inside and a metal body which is screwed to the roof cross-members. There is a plastic gasket between lens and body, and the lens has lugs which screw into the body. However, a number of minor changes were made over the years.

It appears that alternative types of interior light were fitted indiscriminately on Suffix A to Suffix D models. Some had a single 18-watt festoon bulb, and others two 10-watt bulbs (later, the recommended replacement for the single-bulb type was a 21-watt festoon bulb, Unipart number GLB 273). From Suffix E and the introduction of twin interior lights, however, all lights have a single 10-watt festoon bulb; the recommended type was Unipart GLB 265.

Some problems were encountered with shorting between the light casing and feed wire, so at AA 105378, in May 1980, the bulb contact was lengthened and bent at 90° over a rolled cable terminal to prevent this.

A further minor change was made in 1982 at AA 125166 (two-door) and AA 125477 (four-door). During 1986, at chassis number CA 269000, a modified seal between lens and body was introduced to cure looseness.

Heated rear window

A heated rear window was standardised for most markets when the Suffix B models were introduced in January 1973. The intention was to standardise it on UK-market Range Rovers at the same time, but the plan was cancelled in order to keep showroom prices down. It therefore became standard on UK-market models with the Suffix C models in November 1973.

The heated rear window was made by Triplex and carries horizontal yellow elements across the upper two-thirds of the glass. For details of the optional heated rear window available for early Range Rovers, see the information in Chapter 12 about options and accessories.

The first optional radio was a Smith's Radiomobile set (top), with Long Wave and Medium Wave reception. By the early 1980s, the optional radio/cassette unit was a push-button type with six station pre-sets (above), made specially for the Range Rover.

Central locking

Central locking was introduced in July 1983 for four-door models only. It was fitted to all five-speed manual models from the beginning of production, but was not available on Range Rovers with automatic transmission until late August or early September 1983. Vehicles with central locking are identifiable by keylocks incorporated in the door handles, rather than lower down on the door panel.

On early vehicles, the central locking operates from the keylock on both front doors. However, from BA 150235 in approximately March 1985, it operates from the driver's door only. Why this retrogressive change was made is not clear.

Early central locking systems were not wholly reliable, and at CA 269837 in 1986 a number of improvements were made to cure intermittent operation. These changes mostly affected the actuators and the linkages.

Radio systems

A radio became an optional extra in May 1971 and remained optional until the start of the DA-series vehicles, although one was fitted as standard to the limited-edition In Vogue models and to the 1985 BA-series Vogue. A radio aerial, front door speakers and associated wiring were fitted as standard to all models except Fleet Line types from July 1981.

Early radios have mono reproduction; later examples are stereo and the final types incorporate a cassette tape player as well. The location of the radio also changed. On all models up to the end of the BA-series, it is outboard of the driver. On CA-series and later models, it is mounted low down on the transmission tunnel, ahead of the transmission controls.

The radio was always a dealer-fitted option until the end of CA-series production, except on In Vogue special editions and the 1985 Vogue models, when it was fitted on the assembly lines. It was also factory-fitted on DA-series and EA-series Range Rovers. There were recommended types in the early days, but from about 1973 the choice of radio was left more or less to the customer. Unipart branded types were often fitted during the later 1970s and early 1980s.

On early UK-market Range Rovers, the most commonly fitted set was a Radiomobile with medium-wave and long-wave reception; this had part number 589080 and was introduced in May 1971. Between April and September 1972, two other Radiomobile sets were offered, but these were withdrawn (presumably because of poor sales), and the original medium-wave and long-wave type became the only option again. The

additional sets were a medium-wave only type (part number 589081) and a medium-wave and short-wave type (589082).

From summer 1981 and the introduction of the four-door Range Rover, the recommended set was a radio-cassette with part number PRC 3815. From the start of BA-series production in 1984, a Clarion radio-cassette unit was fitted. The first few vehicles were fitted with one type, which has Land Rover part number PRC 4375, but from BA 147037 a different type with part number PRC 4500 was used. This later type has medium-wave, long-wave and FM reception, 18 station pre-sets, and an auto-reverse cassette deck with noise reduction circuitry. It has silver-finish buttons on a dark face-plate, one large and two small knobs on the left, and a digital LED read-out.

Special installations were used on the In Vogue limited-edition models. The 1981 In Vogue two-door Range Rover came with a Radiomobile Model 421 stereo radio-cassette player, and the 1983 In Vogue Automatic limited edition model had a Philips AC 807 stereo radio-cassette. The 1984 In Vogue limited edition had a Clarion radio-cassette with part number PRC 4500, the same as that standardised shortly after the start of BA-series (1985-model) production.

Early Range Rovers have a single radio speaker in the centre of the facia top, underneath a removable cover panel. Two speakers are fitted to the 1981 In Vogue limited edition, all four-door models from the start of four-door production in summer 1981, and all two-doors from August 1982. On two-door models they are in the leading edge of each lower door trim pad, and they are similarly located in the single-piece door trims of four-door models. All four-doors to the end of the AA-series in 1984, and two-doors to the end of the CA-series in 1986, have speakers with part number RKC 5518. These have a black plastic face-plate with perforations and a centre panel carrying a silver speaker symbol.

From the start of the BA-series the front speakers on four-door models are concealed behind the door trims, and from the start of the DA-series uprated speakers are fitted in all four positions. Two-doors from the start of the DA-series continue to have exposed speakers, now with part number RKC 5518 L (probably the same speaker as RKC 5518 but with a new part number) if leathercloth door trim pads are fitted. Other two-doors have a different speaker, listed as RTC 6325.

Four speakers are fitted to the 1983 In Vogue Automatic limited edition and to all 1984 and later Range Rovers. The additional two are in the headlining above the tailgate. The speakers used in all four positions on the In Vogue Automatic are PRC 3816, with a square surround in bright metal and a circular black grille.

Chapter 10

Range Rover Monteverdi

The Range Rover Monteverdi was a short-lived four-door luxury conversion, approved by the factory and sold through a small number of Land Rover dealers. It is generally considered to be the first four-door Range Rover, although this is not strictly correct. In fact, Solihull built its own four-door prototype as early as March 1972 (with Engineering chassis number 100-41 and registration number YXC 905K) but did not put the design into production. Then from 1974, Land Rover Approval was granted to a four-door conversion by FLM Panelcraft of London.

The Panelcraft conversion was sold almost exclusively in the Middle East and may have been made in greater numbers than the better-known Monteverdi. Its shortcomings were edge-pull exterior door handles like the production two-door model, and sliding windows in the rear doors. The great attraction of the Monteverdi conversion was that it eliminated these two shortcomings, providing flush-fitting car-type exterior door handles and proper drop-glasses for the rear doors. In addition, much of the door furniture was sourced from the Austin-Morris car range, which

simplified the provision of spare parts.

Automobiles Monteverdi was an established maker of expensive hand-built luxury cars, based in Basle, Switzerland. In late 1978 Peter Monteverdi designed and built a four-door Range Rover, which he showed to Land Rover early the following year. An agreement to convert two-door vehicles was reached, and work got under way in about October 1979, continuing until March 1982. Line-produced two-door Range Rovers in Arctic White were shipped from Solihull to Italy, where the conversion work was carried out by Carrozzeria Fissore in Savigliano, a bodyshop in which Monteverdi had a 50% stake.

The exact number of Monteverdi Range Rovers built has not yet been established, and estimates run as high as 300. However, records so far discovered suggest that Peter Monteverdi put his name to a total of just 129. Of these, 128 were conversions of two-door models and one was a design study based on Land Rover's own four-door body.

The two earliest known examples are thought to be prototypes. The first was built on a LHD chassis (358-54552F) which left Solihull for

Profile view of Peter Kenworthy's superbly restored Monteverdi shows the main features of the model: the angled shut line for the rear door and the full-size quarter-light in the front door.

Four-door Monteverdi
Range Rover has
special badging on grille
and tailgate.

France in November 1978 and was first registered in France in March 1979. The second was on a RHD export chassis (356-59870G), which left Solihull in August 1979 for British Leyland's Dutch importer. This vehicle was first registered LKV 242V on 1 May 1980.

The Range Rover Monteverdi was announced at the Geneva Show in March 1980 and was in theory available immediately, but only five examples were built before the end of that model year. It was also shown at the Birmingham Motorfair in October 1980, but did not become available in the UK until autumn 1981 – by which time the Solihull-built four-door model had also gone on sale. Current information suggests that most of the LHD vehicles were sold in the Gulf states and most of the RHD examples in Britain.

The Range Rover despatch records held by the British Motor Industry Heritage Trust show that the first production vehicles built in 1980 all had LHD, and that the first RHD models were not built until the end of that year. The conversion of LHD vehicles ceased before that of RHD types, although one final LHD Range Rover left Solihull for the Fissore works – along with the final batch of RHD models – in March 1982. UK dealer information of the period reveals that the final vehicles returned to Solihull after conversion in approximately November 1982. Records show that most LHD vehicles were despatched direct from the Fissore works to their final destination, but that RHD examples were returned to Solihull before despatch to dealers.

The chassis, engine and transmission of the Range Rover Monteverdi are unchanged from the standard two-door model of the time. However, every external panel below roof level between the A-pillars and E-pillars is unique to the Monteverdi, and most of the interior trim too.

Body sides

The basis of the Monteverdi conversion is quite straightforward, and is best understood by a description of the build process.

The doors, rear wing outer panels and upper body side glass of the two-door Range Rover were removed, leaving the sides of the vehicle open. The B-pillars were removed, and then the rear inner wings were cut short to just forward of the rear wheelarch centre. A new rear quarter outer wheelarch was welded to each original inner wheelarch and to the trailing edge of the sill. This wheelarch panel is quite different from its equivalent on the factory-built four-door bodies and, like many of the other unique Monteverdi components, has been unavailable for many years. Its lower edge remains exposed when the door is closed (which makes it prone to rust), and the whole panel should be painted in the body colour.

The D-pillar is completed by three further panels. An inner panel is welded to the shortened inner rear wing, and a door lock striker plate panel is welded to this at right angles. The third panel is a tapered top-hat section, which is welded to the other two to form the top of the D-pillar, the visible boundary between the rear side window and the door aperture.

The rest of the body-side structure is completed by the insertion of a modified two-door B-pillar between the sills and cantrail on each side. Each pillar is modified by the addition of an extended sill plate at the foot, and by a pair of hinges for the rear door welded to its rear face. The original pillar fixing point on the sill, which is further rearwards, is concealed by the extended foot plate. The exposed upper section of this B/C-pillar is angled towards the rear of the vehicle, as on the two-door Range Rover, whereas the B/C-pillar on factory four-door bodies is straight. The exposed upper section of the B/C-pillar and D-pillar should be finished in satin black, and the hidden lower part in the body colour. However, the exposed upper A-pillar (windscreen pillar) remains painted in the body colour, as on the contemporary two-door Range Rover.

All four door apertures are fitted with handed rubber seals unique to the Monteverdi conversion. The kick-plates are also unique, being one-piece pressed aluminium items. Sill finishers are the standard two-door items modified at the rear with a steel angle plate which aids the fixing of finisher to sill and closes the gap between the two.

Floor

The original heelboard was also removed during conversion, and the front edge of the load space floor shortened by 3½in. The side frame floor panel was also shortened and angled back towards the wheelarches. A new angled and tapered heelboard was welded in place, and this allowed better access and more foot room for rear seat passengers.

Front doors

The front doors are unique to the Monteverdi. They are in fact shortened two-door types, with modified trailing edges to accept car-type catches. They retain the standard swivelling quarter-light and fittings of the two-door model. This quarter-light is larger than the one used on the early factory four-door bodies, and is another characteristic of the Monteverdi conversion.

The basic construction of the door is the same as that of the standard factory item, with a steel inner and a Birmabright alloy skin which is clinched in place. The window frame, which is shortened and finished in satin black, is inserted into the door in the same way as on the standard vehicle. The drop-glass was specially made by Saint Gobain and tinted green to match the standard Triplex Sundym items retained for the windscreen, front quarter-lights and heated rear window. The waist sealing rubbers, both inside and outside, are unique to the model.

The join between wing and lower D-post (right) reveals the detail of the Monteverdi's construction. Door handle with textured finish is from the Morris Marina, while childproof lock on rear door (far right) is another Austin-Morris component.

The front quarter-light retains its original Triplex glass, but the drop-glass is made by Saint Gobain.

Features unique to the Monteverdi conversion are the leading edge of the rear wheelarch (right) and the door latch pin.

Crude, but effective: the sill panels were secured at the rear by screws through an angled plate.

The doors have letter-box style outer handles of the type used on contemporary Austin Allegro and Morris Marina cars. These handles incorporate keylocks and have textured metal pull-plates, unlike the smooth finish of the car type. The door locks, catches and associated internal linkages are also Austin-Morris parts, and are not found on other Range Rovers. However, the window regulator mechanisms come from the two-door model.

Rear doors

The rear doors are also unique to the Monteverdi. They are reworked and shortened doors from the two-door model, and have a distinctive angled trailing edge which is not present on their equivalents for the factory four-door body. They have the same construction as the front doors, although there is a fixed rear quarter-light. Both this and the drop-glass are smaller than their equivalents on the factory four-door Range Rover, and both have glass specially manufactured by Saint Gobain. As on the front doors, the waist seals are unique to the Monteverdi.

The doors have letter-box outer handles to match those on the front doors, although these do not have keylocks. Once again, these handles, the door locks and catches, and the associated internal linkages are Austin-Morris parts. The childproof lock is another Austin-Morris item, with a push-pull action and a plastic knob which protrudes horizontally from the rear face of the door. The window regulator mechanisms are modified production two-door Range Rover items. The doors operate courtesy light switches in the B/C-pillar, exactly like those for the front doors.

Rear wings

The Monteverdi has unique rear wing panels, with a tapered leading edge. These are riveted to the D-pillar, but bolted to the inner wing at their top edges and to the rear tail light panel in the same way as on the contemporary two-door Range Rover. The right-hand wing incorporates the standard fuel filler box and filler cap.

The upper section of the rear body side is completed by a fixed window, slightly smaller than the factory four-door equivalent. Again, this glass is manufactured by Saint Gobain and is green-tinted. The glass is housed in a separate frame which is peg-located in the wing top and bolted to the cantrail. Each frame has a rubber seal on three sides, and separate waist seals. All these seals are unique to the Monteverdi.

The upper E-pillar remains unchanged, and should carry a standard outer panel, trimmed in grained black vinyl and incorporating a plastic air outlet vent.

Door mirrors

The Monteverdi is fitted as standard with a black-bodied mirror on each front door. These mirrors are not the same as those fitted to the contemporary factory-built Range Rover, or to any subsequent Land Rover product. The mirrors are handed, from an unknown Italian source.

Badges

The badges are unique, although they appear to have changed during the production run. The earliest vehicles had a large alloy plate badge in an L-shape, with '4-door, Monteverdi Design' stamped in and painted black. Vehicles converted before October 1980 carried four of these badges: one on the grille, one on each side of the scuttle, and one on the lower tailgate.

These badges were in use as early as the RHD prototype built in 1979, but the first Swiss sales brochure shows an early LHD vehicle with different badges. They are rectangular alloy plates, stamped with the inscription 'Monteverdi Design', which is painted black; the word 'Design' is italicised. The vehicle has four badges, in the same positions as noted above.

Later vehicles, built from October 1980 on, had a more discreet rectangular alloy plate badge which carries the Monteverdi name with a stylised crown above the central E and V, and the word

The special rear window channel is visible here. This vehicle's owner has etched the chassis number into the glass for security.

The mirrors are handed, and are Tornado types manufactured by Vitaloni in Italy.

'Design' in small print under the last three letters. As on earlier badges, the words were stamped into the plate and painted black. Only two badges were fitted, one on the grille and the other on the lower tailgate. This type of badge was fitted until production ceased in 1982. One 1981 vehicle (AA 117316) was used for styling development by Land Rover and carries decal Monteverdi badges.

Dashboard & cubby box

The in-dash ARA air conditioning system was fitted to all Monteverdi Range Rovers. Otherwise, the dashboard was completely standard except for the addition of a neat plastic cover over the instrument binnacle, which helped it to blend into the

Cubby box between the front seats was another feature unique to the Monteverdi.

Monteverdi conversion included a special instrument panel surround. Note also the switch alongside the eyeball vent, which on this example is for the electrically-operated driver's door window.

Pleated door trims, combined armrest and handle, and chrome-framed release are all seen here (right). Neat rear quarter-light design was a revelation, and contrasted sharply with the crude sliding glass of the earlier FLM Panelcraft four-door conversion (far right), shown for comparison.

Two of the three different Monteverdi badges used on these vehicles.

dashboard. This binnacle cover was made of glass-fibre and painted grey to match the dashboard. It was peg-located to the dash at the rear and held in place by two covered screws at the front. A high-quality ICE system appears to have been standard, but the type of head unit fitted probably depended on the country of sale.

A special centre cubby box was bolted to the transmission tunnel behind the transfer box lever. The box was always trimmed in black grained vinyl, but its hinged lid was trimmed to match the upholstery colour. The ashtray normally mounted on the transmission tunnel was moved to the top rear of this cubby box, where it could be shared by the rear seat passengers: for front-seat passengers, however, it was not best placed.

Door trims

Both front and rear doors have unique trim pads with aluminium backing panels. The trim is in Beige, Black or Tan leather to match the upholstery. The lower section of each trim is carpeted, the middle has vertical padded panelling, and the upper section has additional padding. Combined grab handles and armrests are fitted, with chromed plastic finisher inserts. These handles are always trimmed in black, regardless of the main interior colour.

The black plastic window winder handles are standard two-door Range Rover items. The door release catches are also of black plastic, and fit flush to the doors with square frame-type pulls.

There are also black plastic sill locking buttons. At the leading edge of the carpeted section on each front door trim is a radio speaker with a square black face-plate.

Pillar & footwell trims

The inside surfaces of the B/C-pillars and D-pillars are trimmed in vinyl to match the upholstery. The upper A-pillars retain their standard moulded plastic coverings. The outer footwell trim panels and the E-pillar upper trim panels are replaced by black ABS plastic mouldings.

Seats

The seats could be trimmed in velvet cloth, which was available in Beige or Black. The more sumptuous alternative was leather upholstery, available in the same two colours and in Tan.

The seats themselves are the standard two-door Range Rover type, completely retrimmed and with some extra padding. The upholstery is pleated and buttoned, and the front seat head restraints with their detachable cushions are trimmed to match. There are ruched map pockets on the backs of the front seats, and the metal underpan of the rear seat is painted to match the upholstery colour. Black ABS plastic seat side finishers replaced the standard Palomino Beige type when black upholstery was specified, and were possibly also used with the Monteverdi Beige and Tan colours.

The rear seat is located 3½in further back than its equivalent on two-door models, to give additional legroom and ease access to the rear passenger compartment. The seat squab and underpan were modified to enable the seat to be moved back and to clear the rear wheelarches. The rear seat pan was also painted to match upholstery colour.

Carpets

The Monteverdi has high-quality bound carpeting throughout the passenger compartment, on the rear wheelarches and on the load floor and lower tailgate. There is a carpeted tool curtain on the right of the load area, and the spare wheel is encased in a carpeted cover, with a circular cutout which allows access to the wheel securing screw. Carpets are coloured to match the upholstery. The gear lever gaiter is made of leather and also matches the upholstery colour.

Paint finishes

On its announcement in March 1980, the Range Rover Monteverdi was available in just four colours. A fifth became available later, probably some time around the summer of 1980 for the

The rear seat (below) has no central armrest. Note the black board panels on the leading edges of the wheelarches. Optional leather upholstery, special seat finishes and unique carpets can all be seen in this view (above right).

Front seat head restraints were the standard Range Rover items with detachable cushions, re-covered in leather when this option was specified.

The back of the rear seat was painted to match the colour of the upholstery. Note also the carpeting in the load area.

MONTEVERDI PAINT COLOURS

1980 MODEL YEAR (BL COLOURS)

Colour	BL paint code
Silver Grey (metallic) 'no. 60'	RTC 7361
Light Green (metallic) 'no. 50'	RTC 7362
Light Blue (metallic) 'no. 40'	RTC 7363
White 'no.10'	RTC 7365

1981 MODEL YEAR (BL COLOURS)

Colour	BL paint code
Silver Grey (metallic) 'no. 60'	RTC 7361
Light Green (metallic) 'no. 50'	RTC 7362
Light Blue (metallic) 'no. 40'	RTC 7363
White 'no. 10'	RTC 7365
Anthracite 'no. 30'	RTC 7364

1982 MODEL YEAR (BMW COLOURS)

Colour	BMW paint name	BMW paint code
Blue	Stratos Blue	150
Brick Red	Chestnut Brown	157
Brown	Brazilia Brown	154
Dark Green	Cypress Green	152
Gold	Kashmir	143
Pale Green	Reseda Green	075

With the three British Leyland metallic finishes, a Clear Varnish (RTC 7393) was used. All six BMW colours were metallic finishes by Glasurit Beck, and all were used with a clear Glassodur twin-pack polyurethane lacquer top coat.

MONTEVERDI PRODUCTION FIGURES

Chassis number(s)	Steering	Build date	Total
358-54552F	LHD	Nov 1978	1
356-59870G	RHD	Aug 1979	1
100015	LHD	Oct 1979	1
104446 to 104447	LHD	Mar 1980	2
104455 to 104456	LHD	Mar 1980	2
110062, '066, '070, '074 & '078	RHD	Dec 1980	5
110082, '086, '090, '094 & '098	RHD	Nov 1980	5
111721 to 111735	LHD	Mar 1981	15
112040[1]	LHD	Apr 1981	1
114863 to 114872	RHD	Jun 1981	10
115832 to 115844	LHD	Aug 1981	13
115880 to 115883	RHD	Aug 1981	4
115884 to 115891	LHD	Aug 1981	8
115985 to 115992	RHD	Sep 1981	8
116450	RHD?	N/A	1
117314 to 117318	RHD	Oct 1981	5
117521 to 117525	RHD	Oct 1981	5
118117 to 118119	RHD	Jan 1982	3
118864 to 118866	RHD	Dec 1981	3
119555 to 119560	LHD	Dec 1981	6
119592	RHD	Jan 1982	1
121146 to 121151	RHD	Mar 1982	6
121152 to 121159	LHD	Feb 1982	8
121170	RHD	Feb 1982	1
121967	LHD	Mar 1982	1
121968 to 121979	RHD	Mar 1982	12

[1] Four-door design study vehicle.

1981 model year. The 1982 model-year vehicles, which started with VIN 114863 in June 1981, were offered with a different range of six colours, all drawn from the 1981 BMW colour palette.

There are two known exceptions to the standard colours listed in the accompanying table. The first production vehicle, on chassis number 100015, had burgundy paint when it was found in Saudi Arabia, but this colour may not have been

original. The original paint scheme on vehicle number 115881 was two-tone Brown over Gold.

Wheels

The Rostyle wheels on early models were normally painted to match the body colour, although the June 1980 sales catalogue shows an early LHD Light Green vehicle with gold-painted wheels. From October 1980, the wheels had the standard aluminium alloy finish. Records suggest that unpainted three-spoke alloy wheels became optional on the Monteverdi at the start of the 1982 model year, as they did on other Range Rovers from chassis number AA 115578.

Identification

Monteverdi conversions normally carry an R identifier in the VIN prefix. Thus the prefix (to which SAL was added from October 1980) is LHARV1AA for RHD or LHARV2AA for LHD. However, two vehicles assumed to be prototypes were converted from 1978 358-series and 1979 356-series Range Rovers built before the introduction of VINs. In addition, the earliest known production vehicle still carried its original two-door chassis number (LHABV2AA100015) when it was found in a scrapyard in Saudi Arabia in 1994. The special design study converted from a four-door vehicle carries its original chassis number of SALLHAMV2AA112040.

A mystery attaches to one vehicle, which was a RHD Monteverdi conversion when discovered in 1996. However, it had left the factory for Belgium as a LHD four-door in March 1982, and still carried its original chassis number of SALLHAMV2AA121170. The body from another Monteverdi may have been transplanted onto the chassis during a later conversion to RHD.

Of the 129 Monteverdi conversions so far traced in BMIHT records, 43 vehicles were built with LHD and 85 with RHD; the steering configuration of one is unclear. The 1979 specimen assumed to be a prototype was built on a RHD chassis, but no production RHD Monteverdis were built before December 1980.

Chassis serial numbers of the known Monteverdi conversions are given in the accompanying table, together with their build dates at Solihull. Completed vehicles returned to Solihull for despatch to dealers anywhere between four and nine months later.

Monteverdi displayed a turbocharged edition at the Geneva Show in March 1981. The identity of this vehicle is not known, but it was probably one of the first five production examples, as none of the 1981 models would have been completed in time for the show.

Chapter 11

Special Editions

Schuler Automatic (1980)

The Schuler Automatic Range Rover was not a line-built model but a small-volume conversion carried out on behalf of Land Rover and sold through Land Rover dealers. Just 25 examples were built in 1980, and probably all were originally supplied to customers who had special links with Land Rover. They were probably used as part of Land Rover's own development programme for the automatic Range Rover which would be introduced in 1982. Customer feedback was also doubtless an important factor in establishing the final specification of the line-built automatic Range Rover. None of these vehicles is known to survive.

By 1980, Schuler had established itself as the front runner in high-performance Range Rover conversions. The company, based at Sunningdale in Berkshire, had also developed an automatic-transmission conversion and a silent-running, chain-driven transfer box. This was linked to an anti-skid braking system which used Ferguson Formula principles and had been developed by Schuler in conjunction with FF Developments.

The 25 vehicles built for Land Rover all had the full Schuler transmission conversion, with a Chrysler Torqueflite A727 three-speed automatic gearbox, the Schuler-Voith chain-driven transfer box and the Ferguson Formula anti-skid braking system. Externally, they were standard two-door models, but inside there were several special features. These were a T-handle automatic transmission selector behind the transfer box lever, a special instruction plate below the heater controls (bearing both Rover and Schuler logos), and a neatly-trimmed carpet cover for the transmission tunnel, complete with bound edges.

In Vogue (1981)

The first widely-available special edition Range Rover was the In Vogue model, introduced for the UK market in February 1981. Its manufacture had been made possible by the increased production line flexibility available in the new North Works at Solihull which opened for business on 16 March that year. There is some confusion about

The Schuler Automatic has a special instruction plate below the heater control panel, and there is special carpeting to go with its automatic selector lever.

the numbers built: a press release dated 26 February 1981 claims that 1000 were planned, but dealer literature of the time puts the figure at 400. The lower figure is the more likely one. One way or another, all examples were probably built during February, and sales began during March.

The name of In Vogue came from a promotional tie-up with the fashion magazine *Vogue*, which was lent the prototype for a trip to Biarritz in the south of France to photograph the 1981 collections by Jaeger (clothes) and Lancôme (cosmetics). The results appeared in an eight-page advertising feature in the magazine's March 1981 edition, published on 26 February. A linked promotional activity was the hand-over of the first production vehicle to film star Julie Andrews and her husband, film director Blake Edwards.

The In Vogue model was based on the contemporary production two-door Range Rover, with a number of special features designed in

Elaine Cannon's In Vogue two-door is entirely original except for the addition of a tow hitch on the front bumper.

conjunction with coachbuilders (and leading Range Rover custom-builders) Wood & Pickett of London. The vehicles were finished in a new colour called Vogue Blue Metallic, and carried a broad decal coachline in two shades of grey. They had Rostyle steel wheels on the latest universal hubs, and these wheels had plain black plastic centre caps.

Home market models were the first Range Rovers to be fitted with the 11D-series 9.35:1 compression engine and 12C-series high-ratio gearbox; however, some of those delivered outside Europe had the standard 8.13:1 compression engine. It appears that all these engines had polished rocker covers and carburettor elbows. The high-compression engines met the latest ECE 1503 emissions regulations, and so the vehicles carried a certification sticker (part number MRC 8322) on the bonnet lock platform. This carried the E11 code in a circle, followed by 15-03727.

The in-dash air conditioning system optional on other Range Rovers was part of the standard specification, but a blanking plate was fitted over the driver's side vent to allow a combined radio/stereo cassette player to be fitted. On UK-market vehicles, this was a Model 421 MW/LW with five pre-set push-buttons for the radio. Mounted behind the standard ashtray between the front seats was a lockable cubby box trimmed in beige, and this had a second, pull-out ashtray in its rear face. The tops of the doors were capped with polished walnut, and there were ruched map pockets on the backs of the front seats.

The remaining special features were all in the load area, which had carpeting on the floor and on the lower tailgate, carpet over the wheelarches, a carpet curtain over the tools and a carpet cover for the spare wheel. The tailgate capping was in stainless steel – a feature never seen on any other Range Rover – and there was a sturdy picnic hamper trimmed in beige cloth behind the right-hand wheelarch, where it was secured by two vertical straps. The hamper contained place settings for six people. Many In Vogue models lost this hamper when they were sold on to new owners,

Two-tone side stripe and light metallic blue paint were unique features of the In Vogue two-door.

Upholstery of the In Vogue two-door was the standard contemporary type, but there was wooden trim alongside the rear seat as well as on the door cappings.

and it is consequently a prized possession today.

It is worth noting that the light blue metallic paint was first seen on a Range Rover supplied to Captain Mark Phillips under Land Rover's sponsorship of the Range Rover Team in equine events. The colour was, admitted dealer literature of the time, "not dissimilar to the Austin-Morris 'Denim'." The twin coachline was used in conjunction with Denim paint on some special editions of cars like the Austin Metro and Austin Allegro, although it is not clear whether the paint and the decals are an exact match for the Range Rover In Vogue versions.

In addition, the prototype used by *Vogue* magazine, registered HAC 414W, had differences from the production models. These included a different cubby box between the front seats, twin

Load area of the In Vogue was fully carpeted, for the first time on a production Range Rover. On the right of the load area is the picnic hamper, with contents on display in the second photograph.

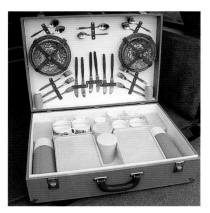

Special interior features include air conditioning (note the control panel under the eyeball vent) and a lockable cubby box.

Rocker covers and carburettor elbows of the In Vogue two-door model were polished to give a good under-bonnet effect. These were the first high-compression Range Rover engines – note the sticker on the air cleaner – and had Pulsair air injection.

narrow black coachlines higher up the body, and three-spoke alloy wheels of the type that became available in summer 1981. The plan had originally been to fit all In Vogue models with these wheels, but supply problems meant that every production example left the factory with the standard Rostyles. Early examples of the Owner's Manual Supplement referred to the alloy wheels as standard, and dealers were instructed to withdraw these and replace them by an amended version. Whether any escaped destruction is not clear.

In Vogue Automatic (1982)

The second In Vogue special edition was announced in August 1982 and was a four-door model with the new automatic transmission. There were 500 In Vogue Automatics built for the UK, and in theory they were the first 500 UK-specification automatics to come off the assembly lines. The model was a big success and the majority had been sold by November.

The In Vogue Automatic was available in two colours only – Sierra Silver and Nevada Gold. Both types were distinguished by broad two-band coachlines similar to those used on the 1981 two-door In Vogue. With Sierra Silver the coachlines were metallic grey, and with Nevada Gold they were metallic brown. All models had three-spoke alloy wheels, uniquely finished with grey enamelled spokes which contrasted with the unpainted

alloy of the rims. These wheels had black plastic centre caps with the Range Rover name moulded in relief and picked out in white.

The interior featured adjustable front and rear armrests on the seats, plus rear head restraints with removable cushion pads. The doors had special cappings of American walnut veneer with lighter wood inlays, and each capping was held in place by two black japanned Philips-head screws. A four-speaker ICE system was fitted, the two front speakers being in the doors and the rear pair mounted in the headlining above the tailgate. The head unit was a Phillips AC 807 stereo radio-cassette, with an output of 4x6 watts. The redundant speaker grille in the centre of the dash top was replaced by a coin tray with a rubber anti-slip mat insert. In-dash air conditioning was an option.

The load area had the expected levels of carpeting, and came with a colour-matched removable cool box which stood on the right, behind the wheelarch. The tailgate capping on these models was black.

In Vogue four-door (1983)

The third limited edition Range Rover to bear the In Vogue name was announced to the public on 25 August 1983. Promotional activities included an eight-page advertisement feature in the September 1983 issue of *Vogue* magazine, where the vehicle was linked to the DAKS autumn fashion

The 1983 In Vogue was the third special edition to bear that name. This beautifully-kept example is owned by Tony Megginson.

Enamelled three-spoke alloy wheels were initially confined to the 1982 and 1983 In Vogue models; this is a 1983 example.

collection and to one of the collection's stockists, the prestigious Simpson's of Piccadilly, in London.

There were 325 examples of the 1983 In Vogue, all four-door models painted in Derwent Blue Metallic and carrying grey coachlines with a broad band above a narrow band of the same colour. Some had the new five-speed manual gearbox and others the established three-speed automatic, and a small number of each were built with air conditioning. They had three-spoke alloy wheels with the enamelled spokes, unpainted rims

and centre caps with white relief lettering of the 1982 In Vogue Automatic.

Interior features were polished walnut door cappings with lighter wood inlays, adjustable front and rear armrests, rear head restraints, rear seat belts and a digital radio-cassette with four speakers. The tailgate capping was black, and the load area contained both a picnic hamper (the same as that supplied with the 1981 In Vogue two-door) and a beige plastic cool box, which had the Range Rover name in relief on its lid.

Wood trim was again added to the interior to create the special ambience of the 1983 In Vogue. Cubby box now has a sloping front edge and a trinket tray for rear seat passengers, while the front seats have adjustable armrests. Rear seats (right) have three folding armrests – the outboard one is just visible beside the seat belt – and head restraints with detachable cushions.

Wood trim has a satin finish and twin inlays in lighter wood. Note the visible screw head.

Carpet in the load area even extended to the lower section of the rear seat back. Picnic hamper and cool box were retained by longer versions of the straps used for the hamper on the 1981 model. Picnic hamper and cool box are seen here (below) with an original sales brochure for the 1983 In Vogue. There are minor differences between the contents of this hamper and those of the 1981 model.

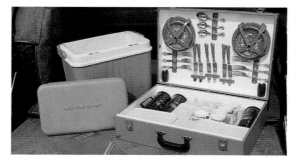

Chapter 12
Options & Accessories

Air conditioning

An add-on air conditioning system made by Frigiking was made available from some time in 1973 or 1974. The underbonnet hardware was fitted by Rover, but the vehicles were then passed to Spencer Abbott in Birmingham to have the roof-mounted unit fitted. This rather ungainly system was superseded in 1978 by the in-dash ARA system (see Chapter 6).

Alternators

Uprated alternators were available from October 1971, when an 18 ACR type was available to special order in place of the standard 16 ACR type. The 18 ACR type was standardised in January 1973, and there was then no uprated alternative until November 1973, when a 20 ACR type became available. A 25 ACR alternator was made available in October 1976, and this was in turn standardised in September 1979.

Auxiliary lamps

Fog lamps and long-range driving lamps were listed from May 1971. They were normally fitted in pairs, either as two fog lamps or as a fog lamp on the passenger's side and a long-range lamp on the driver's side.

The lamps are Lucas Square 8 types, as offered on Rover saloons of the time. Both types have chromed bodies and black plastic lens covers, the latter attached by a plastic strip which fits round the back of the lamp. They are suspended from brackets bolted to the front panel, so that they hang below the bumper. They do not really suit the Range Rover and were never very popular.

Badge bar

A chromed badge bar was introduced in September 1972. This was attached to the rear edge of the front bumper by screw clamps. Despite similarities, it was not the same as the type available as an optional extra for the contemporary Rover P6 saloons. It was not listed after October 1985.

The compressor for the optional air conditioning, seen here (on the driveable demonstration chassis in the Heritage Collection) with some pipework disconnected. The position of the compressor meant that the alternator had to be relocated on the other side of the engine.

Optional Lucas 'Square 8' lamps came with these moulded black covers.

Brake vacuum loss indicator

This was standard for early Australian-market Range Rovers. It was available to special order for other markets, although its use was normally confined to vehicles used for heavy-duty towing and to some special conversions.

Centre PTO: mechanical

From November 1972, a mechanical centre power take-off was available. Made by Fairey Winches, it bolted directly to the rear of the gearbox and was driven through a dog-clutch which engaged with the mainshaft transfer gear. The PTO drive was engaged by an operating rod with a black control knob located inside the vehicle.

Lamp guards became a popular accessory. This rear guard is seen on a Wood & Pickett 'Harrods' Range Rover, one of a limited number made specially for sale through the famous London department store. Also visible is the side rubbing strip which became available through Land Rover Parts and Equipment.

OPTION PACKS

OPTION PACK
Oct 1975 to Sep 1979
Brushed nylon upholstery
Front seat head restraints
Inertia-reel front seat belts
Sundym tinted glass
Power-assisted steering

OPTION PACK
Jul 1981 to Jun 1983
(four-door only)
Metallic paint
Electric windows
Rosewood door cappings
Loadspace carpet
Three-spoke alloy wheels

OPTION PACK A
Jul 1983 to Jun 1984
(four-door only)
Front and rear armrests
Rear head restraints
Wood veneer door cappings
Loadspace carpet
Lower tailgate carpet
Alloy wheels
Metallic paint
Air conditioning

OPTION PACK B
Jul 1983 to Jun 1984
(four-door only)
As Option Pack A, less
Air conditioning

OPTION PACK C
Jul 1983 to Jun 1984
(four-door only)
As Option Pack B, less
Alloy wheels
Metallic paint

The PTO allowed various pieces of special equipment to be driven by the engine while the vehicle was stationary. It was most commonly found on special-purpose conversions, such as fire tenders. After October 1985, it was listed as available for Finland only.

Centre PTO: hydraulic

A hydraulic centre power take-off was available by the end of 1979. This was bolted to the transfer gearbox and could be used to drive various types of special equipment while the vehicle was stationary. It was normally found only on special-purpose conversions, and was not listed after October 1985.

Cigarette lighter

This was an optional extra on Suffix A models only. Thereafter, it was part of the Range Rover's standard equipment.

Dog guard

A dog guard which fitted behind the rear seats was made available in September 1972. It consisted of a tubular alloy grille with six adjustable telescopic pressure pads. Two butted up to the roof, two to the floor, and one to each side of the body. The tubes were unpainted.

By 1985, however, a new type of framed guard was on offer. This was finished in black and had two rubber feet on screw adjusters to allow it to be fitted tightly in place. Later, it became possible to buy two rows of gun clips which hung on the framework of the dog guard.

A third type of dog guard was specified for 1987 and 1988 models. This has horizontal bars and channel-type fixings. The gun clips for the earlier type of dog guard can also be fitted to this one.

Door mirrors

Door mirrors were listed as an optional extra from 1973. They had stainless steel bodies on chromed metal bases, and were screwed to the doors. These mirrors were made standard equipment for some markets, including the UK, in October 1977. Black door mirrors became standard equipment in 1979, and these were supplied for Range Rovers of all years when stocks of the bright metal mirrors were exhausted.

Emissions-controlled engine

The emissions-controlled or 'detoxed' engine was always available to special order in countries where a non-detoxed engine was standard.

Fire extinguisher

By 1980, a fire extinguisher was listed. This was held in a wire bracket screwed to the leading edge of the driver's seat base. It remained available through the rest of the production period of carburettor Range Rovers.

Floor mats

By 1973, the accessories list included a set of rubber link floor mats. This consisted of two front footwell sections, a rear passenger floor section, and a load floor section. These mats were no longer listed after October 1985.

Heated rear window

A heated rear window was optional on Suffix A models, but was standardised for most markets at Suffix B. On Suffix B and subsequent vehicles normally fitted with a plain glass window, the heated type was always available to special order. The optional heated rear window was identical to the type which was later standardised.

Instruments

On Suffix A Range Rovers, an oil temperature gauge, oil pressure gauge and ammeter were all optional extras. The ammeter had a 50-0-50 calibration, but the later 80-0-80 type was used if a vehicle was fitted retrospectively with the later 20 ACR alternator. The 80-0-80 ammeter also replaced the standard type on Suffix B and later vehicles fitted with the 20 ACR alternator.

Option packs

Between 1975 and 1984, some of the most popular options and accessories were combined into Option Packs which offered savings over the cost of the items ordered individually. Option Packs available in Britain are listed in the table.

Overdrive

An overdrive was made optional for the Range Rover from October 1978, some four years after the same unit had been introduced as an option for Land Rovers. It had a 0.782:1 ratio, and was made by Fairey Winches, incorporating geartrain elements from the Rover 2200 saloon gearbox. It was accompanied by an additional change lever on the transmission tunnel, just behind the ashtray. The handbrake linkage was also re-routed through two relay levers. An 'overdrive' decal was made available for the lower tailgate from approximately September 1979, but was not very common. It had black and white capital letters to match those of the bonnet and tailgate badges introduced on 1980 models.

The overdrive was not recommended for use with the high (0.996:1) transfer gearbox ratio introduced in 1981 with the 9.35:1 compression engines. Land Rover also did not recommend its fitment outside the UK, and the overdrive was not covered by warranty when fitted overseas.

Rear seat belts

Rear seat belts were an optional extra from very early in production, but it is not clear when they were first made available. Static belts, in black to match the front safety belts, were available by the end of 1973. Some later models had rear seat belts as standard; for details, see Chapter 5.

Rear wash-wipe

A rear wiper and washer were made optional for Suffix A models, in April 1972. Both were standard from Suffix B, but different types were fitted.

The optional wash-wipe fitted to Suffix A Range Rovers differs considerably from the later standard type. The motor is mounted on a bracket inside the right-hand rear body pillar, and the flexible drive cable runs upwards and then under the roof above the tailgate to the wheelbox assembly. The motor is concealed by a special pillar trim panel with a large box-like bulge. The washer bottle is a tall, square-based type mounted in a bracket on the right-hand side of the tailgate frame, and the Trico pump is mounted separately on its own bracket. Washer tubing is concealed behind the pillar trim and headlining, and feeds a black washer jet next to the wiper wheelbox. The wiper arm is bright metal, and is the same on both LHD and RHD vehicles. The assembly is controlled from a switch on the heater surround panel. Between the switch and its mounting panel is trapped a circular black plastic label, with white printing reading 'Rear Wiper' and 'Press Washer'.

Removable rear parcels shelf

The 1985 Vogue models had a removable rear parcels shelf as standard, and this became available as an option for other models. It consisted of a rigid box which fitted around the spare wheel, a rigid support which replaced the tool curtain and its support on the right of the load bed, and a folding removable shelf.

Roof rack

A roof rack was listed from October 1971. This was a tubular type which clamped to the roof

gutters of the Range Rover. At the end of the 1970s, a matching extension section was made available. Neither was listed after October 1985.

Split-charge systems

A split-charging system, allowing the alternator to charge a second battery on the vehicle, became available in October 1971. The second battery was carried behind the left-hand headlamp, and secured in the same way as the main vehicle battery. A system of cables and relays was used for the electrical connections. Second batteries were often favoured by caravanners, who needed additional electrical power for camping equipment.

The system came with its own wiring harness. The original diode unit in the split-charge system was made by Wipac, but this was replaced by a Lucas type from March 1979.

The split-charging system was often fitted with an optional uprated alternator, and was available for carburettor models throughout their production run. There were six different systems. The first was used with the 16 ACR and 18 ACR alternators up to suffix D; it also suited the 17 ACR service replacement alternator. The second was used for 18 ACR alternators from Suffix E onwards. Two more types were used for the 20 ACR alternator, one up to Suffix D and another from Suffix E onwards. There was a fifth type for the 25 ACR alternator, and a sixth for the A-series

Armrests, rear head restraints and wood door trim were all part of the Option Packs available on the 1984 models.

Optional rear wash-wipe installation for Suffix A models was quite different from later types.

Bumper-mounted headlamp wash system was an option on most models in the second half of the 1980s, but standard on top models.

In theory, the optional overdrive could not be fitted with a cubby box. However, it was achieved successfully enough on this 1979 model!

alternators. The wiring harness for this final type of split-charge system was changed at DA 279129.

Sunroof

During the 1970s, it appears that Land Rover Approval was granted to an after-market folding fabric sunroof. This was probably made by Tudor Webasto, whose products were approved for Rover saloon cars of the time.

From February 1983, Land Rover approved a sliding steel sunroof called the Skyrange, which was manufactured by Idex (UK) Ltd of Stoke Mandeville, near Aylesbury, Buckinghamshire. This was an Anglo-Swiss company with offices in Geneva, Paris, Lyon and Gex (France). The sunroof itself was available in steel or in toughened glass, and was an electrically-operated slide-and-tilt type. When the glass type was fitted, it was provided with a sliding blind to match the headlining. Range Rovers fitted with the Idex sunroof also carried a black embossed GRP panel which was attached to the roof panel and concealed its corrugations. This was designed to give the impression of a vinyl roof covering, and to match the black vinyl on the rear body pillars.

Towing equipment

A towbar was first listed for the Range Rover in May 1971 – rather late for a vehicle which its manufacturers expected to be popular for towing! The basic towbar consisted of two long pieces of angle-iron which bolted to the chassis at one end and to a drop-plate at the other. Two further bolts located the drop-plate to the rear cross-member.

A trailer electrics kit was made available at the same time. This consisted of a heavy-duty flasher unit, a seven-pin trailer socket, a mounting plate for the socket, and appropriate additional wiring. When side repeater indicators became available

This is the adjustable drop-plate of an early Range Rover towbar. The tow ball is fitted with the much later type of cover, which incorporated a red reflector.

for export, a different version of the kit was made available with an uprated heavy-duty flasher unit. This flasher unit was used for all markets from September 1979, when the repeater indicators were standardised. Rear fog guard lights were standardised at the same time, and the wiring supplied with the trailer electrics kit was modified to suit. For BA-series and later vehicles, the wiring was modified again to include a plastic connector which plugged straight into a socket on the vehicle's wiring harness.

Several different types of towing attachments were offered, and all of them were bolted to the drop-plate. The most common was the 50mm tow ball. By 1973, there were two different types of towing jaw, one for standard and the other for heavy-duty applications. In both cases, the pin was chained to prevent its loss. Fixed or rotating towing hooks could also be bought. All these items remained available until the end of carburettor Range Rover production.

Underside protection

For Range Rovers used in rough terrain, a fuel tank guard plate and a steering protection bar were available. The tank guard plate was available as early as 1973, and the protection bar (which service literature called a chassis or under-ride protection bar) was available by 1980. Both remained available until the end of carburettor Range Rover production.

Front mudflaps were available from October 1972, and were standard on Range Rovers sold in Sweden. These are moulded in black rubber, with a raised outer edge on their rear faces. They bolt to retaining plates which in turn are bolted to the underside of the body.

Viscous fan drive

A viscous fan drive was available to special order on engines that lacked it as standard.

Winch

Early Range Rovers could be equipped with a front-mounted capstan winch, but this was rare. A Warn electric winch was on offer by the end of the 1970s, and this was often concealed behind the radiator grille. The grille remained bolted to the bonnet lock platform at its top edge, but the bottom edge was not bolted in place and was moved forwards, resulting in an angled effect. The grille, of course, had to be removed before the winch could be used. When the winch was likely to be in regular use, the grille was normally cut to fit around it. The Warn winch remained available throughout production of carburettor models.

Chapter 13

Special Range Rovers

Fleet Line

The price of the Range Rover increased when its equipment and trim levels were upgraded in September 1979. This had an immediate impact on fleet sales to UK Police Forces, and on sales to the conversion specialists who catered for the commercial and utility markets. Neither needed the new features, and neither was willing to pay for them. So Land Rover responded in February 1980 with a stripped-out Range Rover at a more attractive price. This was known as the Range Rover Fleet Line, and remained available until the

cessation of AA-series production in 1984.

Fleet Line specification varied over the years, and was defined mainly in terms of deletions from the standard specification. As introduced in February 1980, the Fleet Line had Ambla upholstery, and its spare wheel cover and tool curtain were made of black leathercloth. No carpets or head restraints were fitted, the steering wheel did not have a leather rim, and the steering was manual instead of power-assisted. There were no options, and if a customer wanted special features (such as power-assisted steering), these had to be fitted by the supplying dealer. From November 1982, the

The Greater Manchester Police was one of the largest users of Range Rovers, often having as many as 40 on the fleet at once.

None of the original Range Rovers run by Greater Manchester Police survives unmodified, but a former communications vehicle has been mocked-up as a Motorway Patrol vehicle of the late 1970s. Actually a 1981 model, it is nevertheless a convincing replica which the force uses for displays. Different forces had different livery and equipment, and many changes occurred over the years.

UK POLICE SPECIFICATION

From 4/2/80
Ambla trim
No head restraints
Manual steering
Two heavy-duty batteries with split charge system and 25 ACR alternator
12-function switch panel, two warning lights, fuse box
Auxiliary wiring harness for six roof-mounted functions
Calibrated speedometer on dash centre (standard speedo inoperative)
Battery condition meter
Observer's rear-view mirror
Observer's map-reading light
Heavy-duty rear springs
Detoxed engine

From 31/3/82
Bronze velour trim
Rubber floor mats

Vinyl spare wheel cover and tool curtain
Calibrated speedometer on dash centre
Auxiliary switch and warning light panel with wiring
Battery condition meter with battery changeover switch
Observer's rear-view mirror
Observer's map-reading light
A -post reinforcement for door hinges
Two heavy-duty batteries with split charge system and 25 ACR alternator
Heavy-duty rear springs
Michelin X M&S tyres
Rear brake splash shields
Monsanto Clear Pass mud flaps front and rear
Optional: Head restraints
Fiam horns
Blue flashing beacon
Power-assisted steering

Calibrated speedometer of Police vehicles was always located in the middle of the dashboard, and the observer usually had a map-reading lamp of the sort shown here. A blanking plate covers the location normally occupied by the extra switch panel on Police vehicles.

original stitch pattern used with the Ambla trim was changed to the type used with the contemporary Bronze velour trim.

Changes came with the introduction of the BA-series models in summer 1984. As announced in May that year, the Fleet Line versions were to be available in Arctic White or Venetian Red only. They had no passenger floor carpets or head restraints, and no leather on the steering wheel rim. The cubby box and rear heater ducting were deleted, and a unique plastic moulding at the rear of the transmission tunnel compensated for their absence. Radio speakers and radio aerial were

The Wadham Stringer ambulance body for the 110-inch wheelbase chassis was prototyped on YVB 158H, chassis number 355-00010A.

Ambulance proudly displays its coachbuilder's plate.

deleted, the spare wheel had no cover at all, and there were no mudflaps or underbonnet lamps.

Police Range Rovers

The first Police Range Rovers were delivered in 1971, and the vehicle remained very popular as a motorway patrol vehicle throughout its production. Four-door models replaced two-door types as the Police favourite in the early 1980s. Both two-door and four-door models were normally delivered with a basic specification (Fleet Line when that was available), but individual Police forces demanded different additional features. As early as March 1972, a Service Information bulletin complained that electrical wiring for additional equipment was sometimes being installed by Police Authority sub-contractors, and that as a result some installations did not comply with Rover standards.

Nevertheless, Solihull did attempt to bring some order to the potential chaos by standardising certain items. A UK Police specification was

released on 4 February 1980, followed by a 'rationalised' specification from 31 March 1982. These specifications were known as S2471 (two-door models) and S2493 (four-door models). Both were painted Arctic White and normally had manual steering instead of power assistance. The full specifications are itemised in the accompanying panel.

Ambulances

An ambulance conversion was developed during the early part of 1971 by the Special Projects Department at Solihull. The development vehicles were built on the chassis of pre-production prototypes, in each case with a 10-inch section added ahead of the rear axle. The first to be converted was number 10 (YVB 158H), bodied by Wadham Stringer of Waterlooville, Hampshire, and the second was number 25 (YVB 168H), bodied by Spencer Abbott in Birmingham. The Spencer Abbott body design did not prove popular, and was withdrawn after an abortive attempt to market it as a 10-seater shooting brake.

Blue light is neatly recessed behind a modified radiator grille.

This folding step was incorporated into the rear lower panel.

This Wadham Stringer ambulance was used for many years by the Worcester Red Cross, and is now preserved by Chris Elliott. Tail-light units on this vehicle differ from later production types.

The windscreen washer bottle was relocated to make room for additional fuses on the bulkhead. Note the interesting two-tone colour scheme: YVB 158H was built as a green Range Rover, and only the visible areas were sprayed white when it was converted to an ambulance!

Nevertheless, the company was awarded the contract for all the 10-inch chassis conversions.

The Wadham Stringer ambulance body was the first to go on sale, but Special Projects also gave their approval to similar designs by other leading ambulance makers. These were Herbert Lomas of Congleton in Cheshire, and Pilcher-Greene of Burgess Hill in Sussex; both types were on the market by the end of 1972. The Wadham Stringer and Pilcher-Greene bodies remained available right through the period of the carburettor Range Rovers; Herbert Lomas, however, closed during the 1980s and its successors, MMB International of Macclesfield, did not build any Range Rover ambulances.

From 1976, an even larger ambulance was available, with a chassis extended (again by Spencer Abbott) to give a 135-inch wheelbase. Bodies were commonly by Wadham Stringer. These rather unwieldy vehicles were always much less common than the 110-inch types.

The Range Rovers were supplied to Spencer Abbott in chassis-cab form with heavy-duty front and rear springs, and the extra 10in (or 35in) section was inserted into their chassis at that company's Birmingham premises. Two-door models were always used as the basis of these conversions. The chassis-cab supplied normally came with the lowest level of equipment then available, which between 1979 and 1984 meant it was to Fleet Line specification. The final specification of each Range Rover ambulance depended on the requirements of the customer, and there were many individual differences. However, it is possible to give a flavour of the ambulances with a cross-section of basic specifications.

Wadham Stringer 110-inch

The standard Wadham Stringer body on the 110-inch wheelbase is built on an alloy underframe insulated from the chassis with rubberised mountings. The floor is constructed of 15mm exterior grade tropicalised wood and covered with vinyl, while the wheelboxes are moulded from GRP. The ambulance body is constructed of light metal sections with GRP panels, while the interior is lined with plastic-faced panels and the panel cavities filled with thermal insulant.

Each body side has a large two-pane window, with a sliding quarter window at the top of the forward pane. A sliding quarter window is sometimes found in the rear pane as well. There are double rear doors, each with its own window, and a centre stepwell with folding step. All the main glass sections are glazed with safety glass and are dark tinted.

The ambulance may be configured as a two-stretcher type or a single-stretcher type with the stretcher on the left and either an inward-facing bench seat for three or two forward-facing high-back seats with armrests on the right. The two-stretcher design has a full-height partition between the driving compartment and the ambulance body, with a half sliding window. A rearward-facing attendant's seat is mounted to the partition between the two stretchers. No partition is fitted with the single-stretcher layout, although there is a half-height bulkhead in front of the stretcher.

Both versions of the design have a storage locker above the driving compartment, and the stretchers are always of Wadham Stringer's Reasac trolley design.

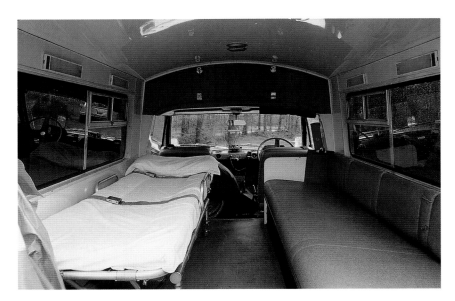

Interior configuration of this ambulance provided a stretcher trolley on the left and three seats on the right, all seated patients having their own fold-down armrests.

Pilcher-Greene 110-inch

The Pilcher-Greene ambulances on the 110-inch wheelbase are most easily recognisable by the pronounced gutter mouldings along the sides of their high roofs, and by the three-pane side windows with sliding sections at the top of the centre pane. Although a single basic design was used, it was built with either aluminium alloy body panels as the Type SA or with GRP panels as the Type CS. The Type SA roofline was slightly flatter, and the Type CS had a pronounced peak over the rear doors. In each case, the body framework was made of aluminium alloy and the floor of 10swg Duralumin with mild steel wheelboxes, while the interior was lined with 3mm plastic laminate. The bodies have twin hinged rear doors with a folding rear step, a translucent roof panel and two storage lockers over the cab.

Interiors were built to the client's specification, but there were two standard types. One carried two stretchers, and had a full-height bulkhead between ambulance body and driving compartment. This bulkhead carried a folding attendant's seat. The other standard type carried a single stretcher and had a bench seat for four seated patients on the right-hand side, with backrests and folding armrests. There was no partition between ambulance body and driving compartment with this design. Cot stretchers, in each case, were Ferno Washington 'Warwick' types.

Lomas 135-inch

The Lomas 135-inch ambulance body is made of GRP with metal framing bonded between the inner and outer skins. It is mounted on a reinforced mild steel subframe which incorporates a hinged rear step. The body sides have one-piece sliding window units in toughened glass, and ahead of these is an additional door with its own

Spare wheel on this ambulance was re-located behind the front passenger seat, which bears the familiar 'tram-lines' from close contact with the door-pull.

A two-way radio is mounted on the facia. This vehicle also retains certain pre-production features, such as the smooth facia top panel. The choke knob is not the original.

window. The lower two-thirds of the glass are darkened or opaque, while the upper third, which incorporates a full-width sliding section in every case, is of clear glass. There is normally a single-piece tailgate which hinges upwards and incorporates a fixed window, although some vehicles had a sideways-opening centre rear door. The spare wheel was normally stowed in the driving compartment behind the passenger's seat, but in some cases it was carried in a side compartment in place of one of the doors, with external access only.

Several interior configurations were available, in each case featuring one or more of the Lomas patented stretcher or trolley designs.

A useful locker was built into the roof above the cab.

Typical of the Carmichael six-wheel fire tender is this 1973 example delivered to Somerset Fire Brigade. Like many – perhaps all – of these Carmichael conversions, this one is on an export-specification chassis, in this case 356-00645A.

As on the ambulance conversions, the spare wheel had to be re-located.

Fire tenders

The Range Rovers commonly described as fire tenders were known to their manufacturers as Rapid Intervention Vehicles, and were designed primarily as high-speed first-response airport crash tenders. They were designed by Solihull's Special Projects Department in conjunction with Carmichael of Worcester, who carried out all the chassis conversions.

As with ambulance conversions, fire tenders were normally supplied to Carmichael as low-specification chassis-cabs. The chassis was extended by 40in behind the rear axle, the additional length supported by an undriven third axle.

A new body with GRP panelling on an aluminium alloy frame was constructed behind the B-pillars, containing equipment racks at the side and pumping equipment at the rear. There were ladder-racks on the roof and a first-aid foam tank was fitted amidships for even weight distribution. These early vehicles normally had roller shutters on each side of the rear body, to give access to equipment racks. They were marketed by Carmichael as the Commando, and often carried a Commando badge on the sides of the scuttle in place of the Range Rover badge. Some carried

The third axle (left) was undriven, but had the same A-frame, self-levelling strut, and trailing arms as the powered second axle. An additional mounting (below left) was welded to the chassis to take extra trailing arms.

The fire pump was mounted at the front and protected by an extended bumper. Those chequer-plate sections are hinged and conceal stowage compartments. Note also the Carmichael decal on the bonnet; several different types were used over the years, and some vehicles were supplied without one.

Many Carmichael fire tenders carried this spot lamp, which is attached to the windscreen pillar on the passenger's side.

Carmichael plate badges on the bonnet as well.

However, not every body was constructed by Carmichael. As early as 1974, at least one chassis was supplied to Hess AG of Bellach, Solothurn in Switzerland, who built an emergency rescue tender body on it for Swiss Railways. Later in the decade, the Royal Air Force sought tenders for a contract to build 6x4 Rapid Intervention Vehicles with four-door cabs. The contract was won by Gloster Saro, who put their own design of body on the Carmichael chassis. This body is easy to distinguish because of the high-mounted external handles on its rear doors. There is a single roller shutter at the rear, and moulded recesses on each side carry pipes for the large foam tank which is mounted above the twin rear axles. Later vehicles were bodied to the same design by HCB-Angus, who applied their own plate badges.

When the four-door Range Rover arrived in the early 1980s, so four-door fire tenders became available. These used the standard doors and were bodied by Carmichael and Gloster Saro. Later Carmichael vehicles have decal badges, and there were also some variations on the body design, to suit the differing requirements of buyers.

It is impossible here to give full details of every fire tender produced, as there were so many minor variations. However, it is worth noting that Gloster Saro vehicles not specially painted (as some of the RAF types were) had Signal Red (BS 381 no. 537) as the exterior colour, and Light Grey (BS 381 no. 627) for the interior. Variations to the running specification seem to have been mostly unrecorded, although a Service Bulletin does note that the oil cooler adapter originally fitted by Carmichael caused premature wear of the camshaft and distributor drive gears. So with effect from chassis serial number 50290F, the Land Rover V8 type was fitted instead.

Many Carmichael 6x4 Range Rovers were supplied to the Royal Air Force as airfield crash tenders. This example shows a later style of maker's plate.

Chapter 14

Identification, Dating & Production Figures

Chassis numbers

The chassis number of all Range Rovers is stamped into the manufacturer's plate attached to the right-hand side of the bonnet lock platform (left-hand side when standing looking at the engine). Two types of plate were used. On all vehicles with a Rover-type chassis number, the plate is made of alloy and printed black with the lettering showing through in the silver colour of the alloy. It is screwed to the bonnet lock platform. Later VIN (Vehicle Identification Number) plates are slightly larger, have black printing on an alloy background, and are attached by pop rivets.

From October 1979, the VIN is also stamped into the top of the right-hand chassis rail, just behind the front axle. Either an asterisk or the BL Cars logo was used to obliterate mistakes made in stamping this number during production.

In the 'Chassis Number Sequences' table, the year indicated is the calendar year of manufacture and not the model year, except where indicated for the 1986-88 period. First and last serial numbers are necessarily approximate because Range Rovers did not come down the assembly lines in exact chassis number order. The figures for the 1972-73 changeover – vital in the UK, where vehicles built before 1 January 1973 are exempt from road tax – are typical: the last home market Range Rover built in 1972 was 355-05718, while the first built in 1973 had the much lower chassis number of 355-05309.

1970-75

Range Rovers built before February 1975 (approximately) have a nine-digit chassis number. The first three digits are the type code; the next five are the serial number; and the suffix letter denotes design modifications that are of importance in servicing the vehicle. The type codes are 355 (RHD, home market), 356 (RHD, export), 357 (RHD, CKD), 358 (LHD, export) and 359 (LHD, CKD). Each type code had its own serial number sequence starting with 00001. A typical chassis number from this period would be 3557301B (in this book a dash is used, for clarity, to separate identifier from serial number, eg 355-7301B).

CHASSIS NUMBER SEQUENCES (BY CALENDAR YEAR)

1970-75 (separate sequences by vehicle type)

Year	355-series (RHD, home)	356-series (RHD, export)	358-series (LHD, export)
1969	00001 to 00003	None built	None built
1970	00004 to 00312	00001 to 00005	00001 to 00006
1971	00313 to 03157	00006 to 00068	00007 to 00745
1972	03158 to 05718	00069 to 00820	00746 to 03227
1973	05719 to 08659	00821 to 01857	03228 to 05837
1974	08660 to 10572	01858 to 03156	05838 to 09850
1975	10573 to 11062	03157 to 03292	09851 to 10556

A total of 2772 Range Rovers were shipped CKD (Completely Knocked Down) in kit form for overseas assembly during this period. Unfortunately, there are no detailed records to confirm how many were shipped each year, or where overseas assembly took place (other in Costa Rica and Venezuela). The final chassis numbers of these vehicles were 357-00432 (RHD) and 359-02340 (LHD).

1975-79 (one sequence for all vehicle types)

Year	All types
1975	12024 to 21662
1976	21663 to 31094
1977	31095 to 40479
1978	40480 to 55741
1979	55742 to 61821

1979 onwards (VIN system)

Year	All types
1979	100001 to 102163
1980	102164 to 110584
1981	110585 to 119702
1982	119703 to 131429
1983	131430 to 143040
1984	143041 to 154589
1985	154590 to 167941
1986[1]	167942 to 173008 (Apr 1986)
	261902 to 273922 (Oct 1986)
1987[1]	272923 to xxxxxx (DA-series)
1988[1]	xxxxxx to 351846 (EA-series)

[1] Indicates model year, not calendar year.

1975-79

The numbering system changed in January 1975, and this second system continued until October 1979. Instead of separate serial number sequences for each vehicle type, a single sequence was used. According to a Service Information bulletin dated July 1975, this sequence started at 12000. However, the despatch records held by BMIHT have no details for any vehicles before 12024. The same three-figure identifying prefixes as before were used (ie, 355, 356, 357, 358 and 359).

1979 onwards

On 1 November 1979, VIN codes were introduced to conform to new international standards. The first Range Rovers built with these were the final 1979 models in October 1979; all 1980 and subsequent models had the new style of numbers.

The new VINs have 14 characters on 1979 and

The earliest Range Rovers had this type of chassis plate. Note that this Suffix A chassis is a RHD export model with a 356 prefix code.

By Suffix D chassis, manufacturer's plate had changed to read 'Rover-British Leyland UK'.

Earliest vehicles with a VIN-type chassis number had a plate identifying the manufacturer as BL Cars Ltd.

By the time of this 1983 model, chassis number plate also carried the Land Rover logo. Both this and the earlier VIN plate carry the same part number (NRC 4201) in bottom left-hand corner.

The engine number is most commonly found on this cast pad on the left-hand cylinder bank. Above it is the compression ratio, in this case 9.35:1.

1980 model Range Rovers. They consist of an eight-character prefix code which indicates the basic specification of the vehicle, followed by a six-digit serial number in a sequence beginning at 100001. This sequence was used only for Range Rovers, and the numbers continued without interruption when an SAL code prefix was added on 1 October 1980, to give a total of 17 characters. Note that the French-market 'utilitaire' vans built in this period carry a prefix of RR200 above the VIN on the chassis number plate.

This system remained in use until April 1986, when the number sequence stopped at 173008. Prefix codes remained unchanged, but the serial numbers started again in May at 261902. This was the next number in the sequence previously used for Land Rovers, and from now on both types of vehicle were numbered within the same sequence.

A typical VIN is SALLHAMV7BA147005. The 11 letters and numbers which make up the prefix code break down as follows.

SAL Land Rover Ltd (manufacturer's identity code)

LH Range Rover (model code)

A Additional model code letter to allow for variants (none in practice)

M Body type (A = van; B = two-door; M = four-door; R = Monteverdi)

V Engine type (V is used for all variants of the carburettor V8)

7 Steering and transmission (1 = RHD four-speed manual; 2 = LHD four-speed manual; 3 = RHD three-speed automatic; 4 = LHD three-speed automatic; 7 = RHD five-speed manual; 8 = LHD five-speed manual)

B Major model change code (A = until June 1984; B = 1985 model year; C = 1986 model year; D = 1987 model year; E = 1988 model year)

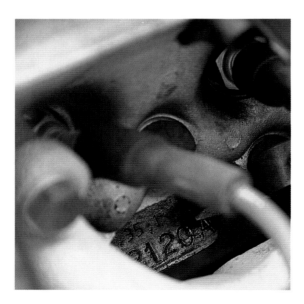

IMPORTANT CHASSIS NUMBERS

Series	Number	Remarks
Suffix A	–	Used from first chassis
Suffix B	–	Used from Jan 1973
Suffix C	–	Used from Nov 1973
Suffix D	355-10200D[1]	Used from Oct 1974
	356-02850D[1]	Used from Oct 1974
	358-08620D[1]	Used from Oct 1974
Suffix E	–	Used from Oct 1975
Suffix F	355-39600F[1]	Used from May 1977 approx
Suffix G	355-60000G[1]	Used from Sep 1978 approx
	358-61821G	Final Suffix G chassis
AA series	100001	Still to 1979 specification
	100783	First 1980-specification vehicle
	103441	First 1981-specification vehicle
	111527	First 1982-specification four-door
	114957	First 1982-specification two-door
	123568[1]	First 1983-specification vehicle
	130854[1]	First 1984-specification vehicle
BA series	147005	First 1985-specification four-door manual
	147009	First 1985-specification four-door auto
	147027	First 1985-specification two-door
CA series	162497	First 1986-specification vehicle
	173008	Final number in unique sequence
	261902	First number in shared sequence
DA series	273923	First 1987-specification four-door
	274121	First 1987-specification two-door
EA series	Not known	First 1988-specification vehicle
	351846	Final 1988-specification vehicle

[1] Approximate numbers

A Manufacturing plant (A = Solihull; F = CKD)

Engine numbers

On early Range Rover engines, the serial number is stamped into a ledge at the rear of the left-hand cylinder bank. This number was partially obscured by the bodywork, so in October 1972 (approximately) the number was relocated to comply with European regulations and Police requests. On these later engines, the serial number is stamped into a ledge beside the dipstick on the left-hand cylinder bank. The BL flying wheel logo is stamped at either end of it, to make illegal alteration difficult. Note that replcement engines supplied by Rover carry a Service engine number, but that 'short' engines were supplied without numbers; the dealer or distributor who fitted such an engine was obliged to stamp the new cylinder block with the number of the original engine.

The engine prefix numbering system changed in 1980, shortly after the change from old-style Rover chassis numbers to the VIN system. A typical early number would be 355-012345D, the 355 being the prefix, the 012345 the actual serial number, and the D a suffix indicating design changes of importance for the servicing of the engine. A typical later number would be 16D-012345A, the 16D being the prefix and the other characters having the same significance as before. Note that the hyphens used here for clarity are not found on the actual engine numbers.

ENGINE TYPES

Dates	Home (and high-compression for export, from 1981)	Export
1970-71	355/A	–
1971-75	355/B to 355/D	341/C to 341/D Germany, Norway & Sweden 359 other European
1975-77	355/E	341/E Germany, Norway & Sweden 398/E Australia
1977-80	355/F	341/F Germany, Norway & Sweden 398/F Australia 355/F others
1981-82	11D	341/F Germany, Norway & Sweden 398/F Australia 355/F others
1982-83	11D manual 15D/A automatic	341/F Germany, Norway & Sweden, manual 398/F Australia, manual 355/F others, manual 13D/A automatic 16D/A Australia, automatic
1983-84	17D/A manual 15D/A automatic	18D/A manual 19D/A Australia, manual 20D/A Saudi Arabia, manual 13D/A automatic 16D/A Australia, automatic
1984-86	17D/B manual 15D/B automatic	18D/B manual 19D/B Australia, manual 20D/B Saudi Arabia, manual 13D/B automatic 16D/B Australia, automatic 21D Saudi Arabia, automatic
1986-88	26D manual 27D automatic	28D manual 29D automatic 30D Saudi Arabia, manual

From 1981, all export engines except those for Australia were low-compression types. Note that '/A' etc indicates a suffix letter (in this case, A). Number sequences not included are 342 (Service exchange engines for 359 series), 344 (supposedly for CKD build in Pakistan), 357 (Service exchange engines for 355 series) and 399 (Service exchange engines for 398 series).

By the time of the 1985 models, the chassis number plate had been re-designed yet again.

PRODUCTION FIGURES, 1970-88

In 1998, Land Rover Ltd quoted the following production figures for Range Rovers.

1970 financial year	1567
1971 financial year	3590
1972 financial year	5965
1973 financial year	7107
1974 financial year	8779
1975 financial year	10585
1976 financial year	9552
1977	9696
1978	11217
1979	10989
1980	9684
1981	10441
1982	13235
1983	12181
1984	11897
1985	14212
1986	14486
1987	20778
1988	24021

The financial year ran from 1 September to 31 August until 1974. The 1975 financial year was a few days longer, running to 26 September, and the 1976 financial year covered the 15 months from 27 September 1975 to 31 December 1976. Thereafter, the financial year and calendar year coincided. The 1985, 1986, 1987 and 1988 figures include turbodiesel and fuel-injected Range Rovers in addition to the carburettor types.

The accompanying table is a concordance of the main engine types and dates. Fuller details of the individual types are found in Chapter 7.

Gearbox numbers

Early four-speed manual gearboxes carry their serial numbers on the bearing plate just ahead of the gear lever. This number is not visible when the gearbox is installed unless the floor cover plates are removed. In April 1974, at gearbox number 355-18800B, the number was relocated more visibly on the machined face next to the rear of the transfer bottom cover plate; this applied to Service-rebuilt gearboxes from 355-01263B.

On five-speed gearboxes, the number is stamped high up on the right-hand side, near the front. Automatic gearboxes have their serial numbers on a plate attached to the casing.

Identifying prefix codes are 355 (four-speed LT95 up to 1981), 12C (four-speed LT95 from 1981), 52A (1984 model year five-speed LT77 with remote change), 53A (1985 and later LT77 with direct change), PK (Chrysler A727 three-speed automatic), and 4HP22 (ZF four-speed automatic). Suffixes indicating detail differences are explained in Chapter 8.

Transfer gearbox numbers

Transfer boxes are integral with the main gearbox on four-speed manual Range Rovers. On automatic and five-speed models, however, the transfer box is a separate component. Its serial number is stamped on the casing, near the filler plug. The identifying prefix codes are 14D (LT230R, for three-speed automatic), 15D (LT230R, for five-speed manual), 26D (LT230T, for three-speed automatic), 27D (LT230T, for five-speed manual) and 28D (LT230T, for four-speed automatic).

Axle numbers

Axles also bear an identifying number, stamped on the left-hand side of the casing, looking forward with the axle on the vehicle. On front axles, it is on the leading face of the casing, and on rear axles it is on the rear face. The three-figure prefix numbers are 355 on all rear axles and on RHD front axles, and 358 on LHD front axles. The suffix letters are explained in Chapter 8.

Body numbers

The monocoque bodyshells introduced during 1985 have an identification number just below the VIN plate on the bonnet locking platform. An example is M46 25085.

Index